FIGHTING OVER FIDEL

FIGHTING OVER FIDEL

The New York Intellectuals and the Cuban Revolution

★

RAFAEL ROJAS

Translated by Carl Good

PRINCETON UNIVERSITY PRESS
PRINCETON AND OXFORD

Published by Princeton University Press, 41 William Street,
Princeton, New Jersey 08540
In the United Kingdom: Princeton University Press,
6 Oxford Street, Woodstock, Oxfordshire OX20 1TW
press.princeton.edu

Jacket image: Photograph of Fidel Castro, taken during his visit to Princeton University on April 20, 1959. Photograph by Richard A. Miller, from cover of *Princeton Alumni Weekly*, Volume LX, October 16, 1959, No. 5.

ISBN 978-0-691-16951-4
Library of Congress Control Number: 2015951261
British Library Cataloging-in-Publication Data is available
This book has been composed in Sabon LT Std
Printed on acid-free paper ∞
Printed in the United States of America
1 3 5 7 9 10 8 6 4 2

To my father, Fernando Rojas Ávalos (1935–2009),
a Cuban doctor who joined the Revolution

And to my professor Arcadio Díaz Quiñones,
who lived what is narrated here

CONTENTS

FIGHTING
OVER
FIDEL

INTRODUCTION

In April 1959, during his first trip to the United States after the triumph of the Cuban Revolution, Fidel Castro spent several days at Princeton University. His visit was organized by the American Whig-Cliosophic Society and the Woodrow Wilson School's Special Program in American Civilization. These groups had learned of Castro's trip to Washington, which had been sponsored by the American Society of Newspaper Editors, and with the encouragement of Roland T. Ely, a scholar of the Cuban sugar industry, they invited Castro to deliver a keynote address on April 20 for a seminar entitled, "The United States and the Revolutionary Spirit."[1] Another celebrated speaker during the seminar was Princeton professor Hannah Arendt, who was doubtless also in attendance for Castro's address that evening.[2]

Castro, who at the time held the post of Cuban prime minister, began his speech by clarifying that he was neither a theorist nor a historian of revolutions. As he reminded his audience, his knowledge of revolutions came rather from his engagement with a revolution that had taken place in a small Caribbean nation close to the United States. In his view, the Cuban Revolution had debunked several myths propagated by the Latin American Right: that a revolution was impossible if the people were hungry, and that a revolution could never defeat a professional army equipped with modern weapons. In keeping with the seminar's predominant perspective, Castro described himself as a product more of the 1776 American Revolution than of either the 1789 French Revolution or the 1917 Russian Revolution, insofar as the last two upheavals had been driven by "force" and "terror" wielded by minorities.[3] As he put it, the groups that took power in France and Russia "used force and terror to form a new terror."

During his address, Castro situated his ideology well within the scope of a democratic American humanism shared by the United States and Latin America. The two regions, despite their cultural specificities, did not constitute "different people," he assured his audience.[4] He also declared that elections would soon be held in Cuba and that political parties would also be formed, although first it was necessary to implement a social transformation in order to eradicate unemployment and illiteracy and to construct schools and hospitals. The United States could assist in this social development of Cuba by implementing friendly policies and by rejecting any fear of communism, since an authentic social revolution on the island would make democracy a "real" process and ward off the communist danger: "I advise you not to worry about Communism in Cuba. When our goals are won, Communism will be dead."[5] At the conclusion of his remarks, Castro invited his young American audience to visit Cuba, and—implicitly—to become involved in the revolutionary spirit that was propelling social change on an island that the United States had first intervened in, and had then neocolonized and modernized, during the first half of the twentieth century.

Castro's message was received enthusiastically by his audience of university students, members of a generation that was becoming aware both of the imperial role played by their country during the Cold War, particularly in the Third World, and of the civil rights disparities that cut through American society itself. However, as easily as the Cuban Revolution entered the social imaginary of this young, pacifist, libertarian, anticolonial, and antiprejudice generation, that revolution also generated fierce ideological and geopolitical disputes between 1959 and 1971.

This book explores these debates over the Cuban Revolution during the 1960s, particularly those centered on the New York public sphere and intellectual field. That decade and this city constituted a microcosm of activity whose resonance was felt around the globe. New York in the 1960s was the moment and the place for progressive movements of all kinds: artistic vanguards, women's liberation, sexual liberation, civil rights, and opposition to the Vietnam War. But these movements and struggles were also privileged scenarios for the emergence and circulation of debates over the ideological identity of Cuban socialism—its truths and its errors, its coincidences and divergences from the Soviet model, its lessons for the Western Left—as well as for the articulation of critiques of US government policy toward Cuba.

The energy of the New York debates over the Cuban Revolution can be explained in part by the close economic, political, and cultural ties that came to be established between the Cuban island and the United States during the first half of the twentieth century. One result of that historical process, as Louis A. Pérez Jr. and other historians have demonstrated, is that when the revolution broke out, most prominent New York media organizations, such as the *New York Times* and NBC, already had bureaus and correspondents in Havana whose reporting had made the island a central topic of these organizations' Latin American coverage.[6] In New York, with its strong liberal and socialist traditions, the Cuban Revolution was discussed as nowhere else, just as the Mexican Revolution and the Spanish Civil War had energized the city's public discourse decades before.

This book examines the practices of New York intellectuals who took public positions in the Cuba debate and wrote books or essays on the Cuban experience, including Waldo Frank, Carleton Beals, C. Wright Mills, Allen Ginsberg, Amiri Baraka, Susan Sontag, Norman Mailer, Irving Howe, Paul Sweezy, Leo Huberman, Paul Baran, Eldridge Cleaver, Stokely Carmichael, José Yglesias, and Elizabeth Sutherland Martínez. It also reexamines publications such as the *Monthly Review*, *Kulchur*, and *Pa'Lante*, as well as cultural and political movements such as the Beat Generation and the Black Panthers. By means of this review of diverse social and political actors, ideologies, and aesthetics, the study seeks to map the ways in which Cuba was represented by the New York Left.

Plurality had long been a distinctive trait of New York's intellectual map. In the debate over the Cuban Revolution, this plurality was not merely ideological or political but was also characterized and sustained by the dissimilar identities of the subjects who participated in the debate: beat writers, hippies, Jews, blacks, Hispanics, academics, writers, and activists.[7] Veterans of the Rooseveltian Left, such as Frank and Beals, did not see the revolution as it was perceived by young liberals like Mills or Mailer, or by young socialists like Sweezy and Baran. Even within the same currents of sympathy and solidarity with the Cuban project, different inflections and priorities can be detected, whether in the Hispanic Left of Martínez and Yglesias or the Afro-American Left of Cleaver and Carmichael.

In few cities on the planet was such a plurality of discourses on Cuban socialism generated. Echoes of the polemic were heard in Havana. For example, *Pensamiento Crítico*, the Cuban journal most clearly identified with critical Marxism and opposition to Marxist-Leninist hegemony of Soviet inspiration, devoted a special issue to intellectuals associated with the Black Panthers. New York's critical debates on the Cuban Revolution naturally had few effects, or only adverse effects, on Washington's policies toward the Caribbean and Latin America. In fact, for all their intellectual and moral richness, the debates in question were viewed with disfavor by all the powers involved in the Cuban conflict. During the 1960s, New York once again functioned like an island in the middle of the Atlantic currents, this time those of the Cold War.

The topic of this book is one that has been previously treated from a number of perspectives. Many of the protagonists of this period of New York intellectual history wrote memoirs and testimonies of their involvement in the debates over Cuba, and many intellectuals and academics have sought to provide a general reconstruction of that archive. The polarization generated by the revolutionary event itself, in the context of the Cold War, has often been transferred to their analyses. Two emblematic examples of this ideological polarization are the chapter devoted to Cuba in

Paul Hollander's classic *Political Pilgrims* (1981) and Kepa Artaraz's more recent study, *Cuba and Western Intellectuals since 1959* (2009). Whereas Hollander portrays the intellectuals of the New York Left as "pilgrims" enchanted by their faith in an exotic revolution, Artaraz, from the other ideological extreme, mostly stresses the political consonance between Cuban socialism and the Western New Left.[8]

Classic studies of the Marxist Left in the United States, such as Paul Buhle's *Marxism in the United States* (1987), have attributed little importance to the debates over the Cuban Revolution during the 1960s, even when these studies acknowledge—following Fredric Jameson—that one of the New Left's principal intuitions was its conviction that capitalism threatened to absorb two fields, or dimensions, that had hitherto remained beyond its scope: the unconscious and the Third World.[9] The importance that Buhle attributes to the African American Left in the history of US Marxism would be difficult to ascertain without citing the support that many US black leaders expressed for the Cuban Revolution as a landmark moment of Third World decolonization.[10] Although more recent analyses such as Razmig Keucheyan's *The Left Hemisphere* (2013) attribute a more central role to the debates over Cuban socialism, they tend to inscribe those debates in a broader, transnational contextualization of the New Left's relation to the Third World, which includes decolonizing processes in North Africa, Vietnam, Egypt, India, and, of course, Latin American guerrilla movements.[11]

Without dismissing the contributions of such studies, this book seeks to explore the interplay of tensions and sympathies that were generated in the relation between the New Left and the Cuban Revolution. It is clear that New York intellectuals participated in the widespread enthusiasm generated in New York public opinion immediately following Castro's January 1959 triumph, but not all of these intellectuals supported the socialist radicalization of Cuban society that was subsequently introduced over the course of the 1960s. In fact, many intellectuals who defended the socialist transition earlier in the decade later distanced themselves from it when they perceived the effects on Cuba's economy, politics, and culture of the regime's alliance with the Soviet Union and the island's reproduction of the institutions and styles of Eastern European socialism.

TRANSLATION AND UTOPIA, BOUNDARIES AND EMPIRE

The study of the debate over the Cuban Revolution in New York during the 1960s must consider the politics of the translation of Latin American experience that emerged from the public sphere of this Western cultural metropolis. Since the sixteenth century, translation has served as a constitutive cultural practice for Atlantic intellectual history. Historians, anthropologists, and literary scholars—working particularly from postcolonial perspectives—such as Mary Louise Pratt, Laura Lomas, Douglas Robinson, Robert Stam, and Ella Shohat, have situated translation at the very center of the historical confrontations and contacts among the cultures of Europe, United States, and Latin America, and have highlighted the importance to the process of modernity of this intercrossing of mutual representations between different languages and cultures.[12]

In the case of the Cuban Revolution, what was subject to translation was not just a culture but also a political project that unfolded in the midst of Cold War ideological tensions. Just as the Mexican Revolution earlier in the century had impacted the US-Mexican border culturally and politically—as Claudio Lomnitz and other scholars have demonstrated—Cuban socialism likewise challenged the US public sphere as an American domestic dilemma, particularly due to the Soviet presence that accompanied the revolution over the course of the 1960s.[13] It was imperative for New York intellectuals and politicians to take a public stance on Cuban communism at the time, insofar as the very identity of the United States in a bipolar world was at stake.

Like Mexico, the Caribbean islands have always comprised a border zone delineated by Atlantic imperial dynamics. Since the 1898 consolidation of US hemispheric hegemony, the Hispanic Caribbean was fully integrated within the new world power's southern border. In the Cuban intellectual tradition itself, the nation's borderland status generated prominent reflections in the work of José Martí, Enrique José Varona, Fernando Ortiz, and, especially, Jorge Mañach, who devoted an entire study to the topic: *Teoría de la frontera* (1961).[14]

The Cuban Revolution and its accelerated communist radicalization only served to reinforce the island's emplacement within a US border region. However, the translation of the Cuban revolutionary experience in the work of New York intellectuals in fact downplayed Cuba's status as a border community. Both those who defended and those who rejected communism in the Caribbean treated the revolution as a US domestic drama, a fact all the more striking given that the drama in question constituted the very definition of an international and transnational event, as a crucial episode of the global transformation symbolized by the construction of the Berlin Wall. The clash between defenders and critics of Cuban communism in New York reflected the struggle between two notions of universalism: on the one hand, that of democracy and the philosophy of human rights, as articulated by Lynn Hunt and Samuel Moyn, and on the other, that of communism and "proletarian internationalism," as characterized by David Priestland and Archie Brown.[15]

New York intellectuals' portrayal of Cuba as a utopia, along with the stereotypes inherent to such a representation, was generated both by those who celebrated the revolution's turn toward communism and by those who called for the construction of a model democracy in the Caribbean. On the left, this American translation of utopia did not merely seek to express support for the concrete policies of the Cuban experiment or for the Latin American and Caribbean movements that it inspired; rather, and more fundamentally, it also sought to reinforce reformist or antisystem currents among young New York intellectuals themselves. For these leftist currents, the Cuban Revolution symbolized something quite different from the Soviet Union or any of the communisms of Eastern Europe.

Some of the movements studied in this book, such as the Black Panthers or the League of Militant Poets, appropriated the Cuban example as a genuine referent for the revolution that the African American and Hispanic Left sought to promote within the United

States. However, these appropriations, just like the extensive critiques of Cuban communism articulated by New York Marxists, social democrats, and liberals, were not lacking in a strong factor of ideological distanciation that highlighted the significant contextual differences between the United States and Cuba. Within the New York Left's discourse of solidarity with the revolution, an imperial, even colonial, perspective frequently emerged, one that viewed radicalism and violence as components of Caribbean culture.

Although the New York debates over the Cuban Revolution reflected Cold War ideological polarization, these debates were far from constituting a simple binarism. There were not two, but many, positions on Cuba held by the members of the New York Left. This plurality reflected not only the heterogeneity of the New York intellectual field itself, but also the changing, and at times experimental, nature of Cuban socialism during its first decade. The Cuban revolutions interpellated by the New York public sphere were multiple because multiple Cuban revolutions were taking place on the island.

Waldo Frank's humanist Cuban revolution was different from C. Wright Mills's Marxist revolution and Carleton Beals's populist revolution. The pro-Soviet, Maoist, and Guevarist socialisms debated in the *Village Voice* or *Monthly Review* were each different modalities of Cuban socialism and for Cuban socialism. The planned economy and bureaucratic, one-party regime perfectly immersed in the field of the "real socialism" of the Soviet Union and Eastern Europe, as criticized by Hannah Arendt, was not the same as the anticolonial and nationalist revolution attuned with African decolonization or Latin American anti-imperialism, as celebrated by Frantz Fanon.[16] The plurality of New York's public sphere reproduced the very diversity and experimental character of Cuban socialism itself prior to its Soviet institutionalization during the 1970s.

However, New York—and to a lesser extent other Western cultural capitals, such as Paris, Madrid, Mexico City, or Buenos Aires—supplied the theoretical debate and public clash of ideas and opinions that was often lacking in the Cuban Revolution. Although the revolution's early years were marked by openness and vibrancy in the public sphere, starting already in 1961 the island's ideological debate and intellectual field came increasingly under state control and centralization. As a transnational phenomenon, the Cuban Revolution can therefore only be fully understood by examining its resonances in other Western cultural capitals where understandings of the revolution, as well as the ideas and politics of the Cold War, were so often put into circulation. In a forthcoming work, Samuel Moyn and Andrew Sartori call for writing global intellectual histories that look beyond the "diffusion of ideas" framed by relations between cosmopolitan centers and peripheries and to instead put greater focus on networks of exchange and "intermediation," borrowing methods and models from other areas of global history such as cross-cultural trade in order to conceptualize the circulation of ideas in a similar fashion.[17] In this sense, one could say that New York served as a privileged hub of intermediation in the circulation of ideas about, and representations of, the Cuban Revolution.

INTELLECTUALS, PUBLICATIONS, MOVEMENTS, AND POLEMICS

The purpose of this book, once again, is to reconstruct the discussion about Cuba in the public sphere of New York and its surroundings. Toward that end, I have focused on personalities such as Waldo Frank, C. Wright Mills, and Carleton Beals, three rather different Americanist intellectuals: a writer, an academic, and a journalist, all of whom wrote articles and books on Cuba during the 1950s and 1960s. But I am also interested in publications during the period, such as the *New York Times*, the *Village Voice*, *Monthly Review*, *Dissent*, *Kulchur*, and *Pa'Lante*, as well as leftist movements such as the Beat Generation, the Black Panthers, and the League of Militant Poets. My reading of these public interventions on the part of very different actors, publications, and movements seeks to capture the debates and clashes of vision over the Cuban Revolution, understanding the latter as a transnational phenomenon.

Chapter 1, "Hipsters and Apparatchiks," describes the editorial evolution of the *New York Times* and the *Village Voice* vis-à-vis the Cuban experience during the sixties. Numerous correspondents and editorial writers of the *Times* were intensively involved in covering the Cuban Revolution, such as Ruby Hart Phillips, Herbert Matthews, and Tad Szulc, all of whom evolved from initially enthusiastic or romantic perceptions of the anti-Batistan epic to more critical positions toward the island's communist radicalization, a shift that reflected the anticommunist mentality of the Cold War. In contrast to the *Times*, the *Village Voice* did not demonstrate great interest in the first—democratic and liberal—phase of the revolution, but it began to express solidarity with the island in the middle of the 1960s in opposition to Washington's policies toward Cuba. The *Voice*'s identification with the figure of Ernesto "Che" Guevara is a particularly good example of the assimilation of a Latin American hero by New Left culture in New York.

Chapter 2, "Naming the Hurricane," is devoted to the writer Waldo Frank and his relation to Cuba. In 1959 Frank, together with Carleton Beals, was one of the American writers most deeply engaged with Latin America. Since the 1920s he had traveled through Mexico, Argentina, Peru, and Cuba, and had befriended important Latin American intellectual figures such as Jorge Luis Borges, the sisters Silvina and Victoria Ocampo, José Carlos Mariátegui, José Vasconcelos, Alfonso Reyes, Juan Marinello, and Jorge Mañach. When the Cuban Revolution triumphed, Frank viewed it as a confirmation of his Americanist ideas and proceeded to travel to Havana as a member of the Fair Play for Cuba Committee organized by Robert Taber. In 1959 the Cuban government contracted Frank to write a book about the revolution from his Judeo-Christian humanist viewpoint. The book, entitled *Cuba: Prophetic Island* (1961), appeared just as Marxist socialism was declared on the island. Frank opposed this shift; some of his criticisms of the radicalization of Cuba were not well received in Havana, and the book was never published on the island.

One of the groups most resolutely supportive of the Cuban Revolution's 1961 communist turn was that of the Marxists associated with *Monthly Review* magazine, which is a topic I focus on in chapter 3, "Socialists in Manhattan." Paul Sweezy, Leo Huberman, and Paul Baran placed Cuba at the center of the magazine's coverage from 1961 to 1969. These Marxists' view of the island evolved with the changing economic policies of the revolutionary government and with conflicts between different models of industrialization and agrarian development. If at the beginning of the sixties Sweezy and Huberman sympathized with the adoption of a planned economic system integrated into the socialist camp, as seen in their work *Cuba: Anatomy of a Revolution* (1961), by the end of that decade, as reflected in their second book, entitled *Socialism in Cuba* (1969), they would no longer hide their criticisms of the growing bureaucratization of Cuban socialism, which they attributed to Soviet influence.

Chapter 4, "The Cultural Apparatus of the Empire," is devoted to the figure of Columbia University sociologist C. Wright Mills. When the Cuban Revolution triumphed in January 1959, Mills was increasingly interested in two related themes: Latin America—and Third World countries in general—and the public engagement of the leftist intellectual. Both themes placed him at the center of the Cuban debate in New York during the early 1960s. Like Frank, Beals, Sweezy, and Huberman, Mills traveled to Havana and wrote a book about the island: *Listen, Yankee: The Revolution in Cuba* (1960). Like Frank's *Cuba: Prophetic Island* (1960), Mills's book was published in the midst of the revolutionary government's communist evolution, which forced the author to confront reality in the face of his insistence that the Cuban leaders were not communists. Unlike Frank and the majority of liberal intellectuals in New York, Mills defended the right of the Cuban people to adopt the socialist path.

The Cuban Revolution was also a topic and motive of cultural representation for the writers of the Beat Generation and particularly for Allen Ginsberg. Ginsberg also traveled to Havana and was interested in Castro and Guevara's visits to New York. Like other beat poets and narrators, Ginsberg opposed the US government's hostile policies toward the island and identified with the bearded Sierra Madre revolutionaries, whom he saw as similar to countercultural subjects in the United States. However, after seeing the revolution's adoption of homophobic and repressive policies toward libertarian youth during his 1965 trip to the island, he assumed a critical stance toward the Cuban regime that he would maintain for the rest of his life. Chapter 5, “Moons of the Revolution,” examines the history of this disenchantment.

Chapter 6, “Negroes with Guns,” discusses the complex relations between intellectuals of the Black Panther movement and the Cuban Revolution. I begin by focusing on an antecedent figure of this movement, Robert F. Williams, author of *Negroes with Guns* (1962), one of the first texts to assimilate the experience of Guevara’s guerrilla theory for the African American Left. I then gloss the ideas of Eldridge Cleaver, Stokely Carmichael, and other Black Panther leaders with respect to the Cuban Revolution and its socialism. Just as the Cuban Revolution’s policies against homosexuality and drugs distanced certain members of the Beat Generation from the island’s experience, Cuban socialism’s egalitarian racial strategy, with its threats to an autonomous ethical sociability, generated tensions between the Black Panthers and the Cuban regime.

Chapter 7, “The League of Militant Poets,” focuses on one of the most interesting and least well-known phenomena of the New York public sphere during the 1960s: the crystallization of a Hispanic intellectual initiative that sympathized with the revolutions and socialisms of Latin America. This ephemeral movement named itself “The League of Militant Poets,” was led by writers and poets José Yglesias and Elizabeth Sutherland Martínez, and was organized around underground publications such as *Kulchur* and *Pa’Lante*. These magazines featured translations of Cuban writers and debates over the ideology and cultural politics of the revolution during the 1960s. As reflected in these publications, Yglesias and Martínez underwent an evolution in their perceptions of the island. Like Sweezy and Huberman, they began to criticize the Sovietization of Cuban socialism between the end of the 1960s and the beginning of the 1970s.

Chapter 8, “The Skin of Socialism,” deals with the figure of veteran journalist Carleton Beals. Like Waldo Frank, Beals was a Latin Americanist traveler who had journeyed through Mexico, Guatemala, Cuba, and Peru, and since the 1920s had written books devoted to each of these countries. When the Cuban Revolution broke out in 1957, Beals began to write about the island for the *Nation*, serving as one of the journalists who covered Castro's arrival in Havana. However, Beals, who turned down the presidency of the Fair Play for Cuba Committee, early on began to publish criticisms of the revolutionary state's political organization and the leaders of its revolution. In contrast to that of other American liberals, his disappointment with Cuba was not so much a result of the island's communist turn, which he likewise disapproved of, but was due to the Cuban regime's abandonment of what he called the Latin American "revolutionary zeitgeist," an ideological lineage he identified as beginning with the Mexican Revolution.

As can be seen, each of these chapters tells a story of promise and disappointment, of enthusiasm and disenchantment, that is characteristic of the modern exercise of criticism in public life. However, I do not seek to narrate this sequence as a linear account of the displacement of identification with estrangement. Rather, I am interested in capturing the back-and-forth, even the coexistence, between these two attitudes. The Cuban Revolution, like every transnational experience, was lived by New York intellectuals as a phenomenon proper to the public sphere of New York. Those who became involved in the debate over the future of socialism in the Caribbean did so as actors and protagonists of that history without questioning the right they had to accompany or abandon it.

MICROCOSMS OF THE LEFT

As Thomas Bender has observed, the intensity of New York intellectual life since the end of the nineteenth century was the result of clear demographic and institutional factors in the city, particularly the ethnic heterogeneity of its cosmopolitan population and its concentration of universities, theaters, museums, newspapers, journals, and cultural associations of all kinds.[18] New York's formidable network of transition and mobility turned it into one of the capitals of the Western avant-garde from the 1920s onward. In addition to the city's intellectual cosmopolitanism and cultural diversity, the rise of the worker movement, which was particularly strong in New York, Boston, Philadelphia, and other cities of the North Atlantic seaboard, contributed another element of dynamism to New York intellectual life.

The New York press, which had served as the sounding board for national public opinion since the Spanish-American War, was instrumental in publicizing the socialist campaigns of Chicago railroad union leader Eugene V. Debs during the first decades of the twentieth century, and this coverage energized discussions of socialism in the city.[19] Debates broke out in New York newspapers and universities over whether the Social Democratic Party founded by Debs was appropriate in a nation like the United States. A substantial contribution to this discussion was the essay *Why Is There No Socialism in the United States?* (1906) by German economist and sociologist Werner Sombart. Initially published in a German social sciences journal, Sombart's essay was soon translated to English and subsequently generated a wide variety of reactions in the United States. Drawing on data showing the underperformance of the Socialist Party in the presidential elections of 1900 and 1904, and the gubernatorial elections for the same period in Alabama, Colorado, Massachusetts, Pennsylvania, Texas, Illinois, and New York, Sombart concluded that socialism in the United States was simply not a competitive political option.[20] American electoral support for democratic socialism in the early years of the twentieth century had not surpassed the demographic volume of German democratic socialism in the 1870s.

Following the triumph of the October Revolution in Russia and the split between the democratic socialist Left and the communist Left in the United States and other Western nations, Sombart's thesis was increasingly put into question. During the 1920s, communism in the United States expanded with the radicalization of democratic socialism, a process in which leaders such as John Reed, Charles Ruthenberg, and James P. Cannon played a fundamental role. As studied by Moshik Temkin, the massive public demonstrations in support of anarchists Nicola Sacco and Bartolomeo Vanzetti, two Italian immigrants accused of theft and murder in Boston, served as effective proof of the influence of socialism in the United States.[21]

As in most of the Western cultural capitals, the spread of socialist ideas in New York diverged into Stalinist and anti-Stalinist currents following Lenin's death. By the middle of the 1930s, the city's socialists were divided in their responses to the Moscow Trials and Stalin's consolidation of power. In a city where radical modernists, internationalist Jews, orthodox Marxists, and communist dissidents proliferated, it was inevitable that publications such as the *New Masses* and the *Partisan Review* would appear, and these organs of opinion contributed to the polarization of the ideological field of the Left.[22] Stalinist and Trotskyist associations and parties abounded in that field, with figures such as Ernest Hemingway, John Dos Passos, Eugene O'Neill, and William Carlos Williams supporting the *New Masses* and Hannah Arendt, George Orwell, T. S. Eliot, and Lionel Trilling identifying with the *Partisan Review.*

The *Partisan Review* soon established itself as the principal medium of the anti-Stalinist flank of the New York Left. As Alexander Bloom, Neil Jumonville, and Terry A. Cooney have shown, during the pre– and post–World War II period, this journal, which was founded by William Phillips, Philip Rahv, and Sender Garlin, became the central platform for a critical socialism that rapidly devolved into liberal anticommunism.[23] The evolution of intellectuals such as Sidney Hook, Dwight Macdonald, Harold Rosenberg, or Norman Podhoretz is highly indicative of the ideological shifts that were provoked by McCarthyism and the Cold War.[24]

Even as these intellectuals shifted toward liberal anticommunism—which would become an outright conservatism with the intensification of the Cold War in the 1960s—another sector of the New York Left continued to be receptive to what Cooney has referred to as the "appeal of Marxism," opening itself to the language and values of beats, hippies, and other counterculture currents.[25] This bifurcation of the New York Left during the Cold War is exemplified, on the one hand, by Irving Kristol and Norman Podhoretz, who followed the drift toward conservatism, and, on the other, by Harvey Swados and Irving Howe, two of the principal defenders of the possibility of democratic socialism in the United States.[26]

Howe and Swados serve as ideal figures for reconstructing both the radicalization of American liberalism during the Cold War and its tensions with the New Left. Howe and Swados were members of the generation that had founded the journal *Dissent* during the middle of the fifties, thereby preserving the legacy of the *Partisan Review*, and over the following decade these two figures upheld and defended *Dissent*'s socialist orientation against the anticommunist turn taken by *Commentary* (under Podhoretz's leadership) and by other New York publications. The importance of literature in both the writings of Howe, who was always interested in literary criticism, and Swados, author of various novels and collections of stories, was a clear sign of the teachings and influence of Lionel Trilling, a fundamental referent of the articulation between literature and politics espoused by the *Partisan Review*.

In key studies such as *Politics and the Novel* (1957) or *A World More Attractive: A View of Modern Literature* (1963), Howe proposed reading politics in places where it tended to be hidden: the plots and characters of great modern novels. In his view, politics was "survival" in Stendhal, "salvation" in Dostoyevsky, "order" and "anarchy" in Conrad, "doubt" in Turgenev, and "vocation" in James.[27] Already in these studies, Howe lamented the exceptionalism and isolation of the great American literary tradition represented by such figures as Hawthorne, Emerson, Whitman, and James, and called for American writers to become more involved in the ideological debates of the postwar period that were being led by European authors such as Malraux, Silone, Koestler, and Orwell.[28]

Howe and Swados both ascribed to the notion that American writers should intervene in public opinion as intellectuals and debate the dilemmas of democracy, communism, and fascism.[29] In *The Decline of the New* (1970), a collection of essays he had written for various New York publications during the 1960s, Howe characterized the New York intellectual field as a microcosm of Jews, European immigrants, Afro-Americans, and Hispanics, who debated the great themes of communism, fascism, colonization, and racism out of their predominant affinity with the critique of totalitarianism and their readings of the anti-utopian fictions of Zamiatin, Orwell, Huxley, and others.[30] Just as Trilling's example inspired his defense of the critic who reads literature while at the same time issuing opinions on politics, that of Edmund Wilson bolstered his call to preserve the Marxist and socialist referent in the discourse of opposition to totalitarianism.

Like Howe, Harvey Swados also traced the parallel paths of literature and politics. Together with his works of fiction—his novels *False Coin* (1959) and *The Will* (1963), and his perhaps greater achievement, the collection of stories *Nights in the Gardens of Brooklyn* (1960), whose title echoed Spanish composer Manuel de Falla's famous orchestral work, *Nights in the Gardens of Spain*—Swados also wrote a series of essays and articles, collected in *A Radical's America* (1963) and *A Radical at Large* (1968), in which he positioned himself as an adherent of the New Left. Without abandoning his social-democratic perspective, Swados, like Howe, reclaimed the term "radicalism" for himself, but against his friend C. Wright Mills, he openly questioned the alignment with the Soviet Union of Third World nationalist movements such as the Cuban Revolution.

During the sixties, Howe produced a number of essay collections through which he sought to condense the global and domestic view of American social democracy. The essays that he selected for *The Radical Papers* (1966), *The Radical Imagination* (1967), *A Dissenter's Guide to Foreign Policy* (1968), and *Poverty: Views from the Left* (1968), written by such authors as Michael Harrington, Daniel Bell, Michael Walzer, Harvey Swados, and Howe himself, most of which had originally appeared in *Dissent*, critically analyzed topics such as poverty in the South, the civil rights movement, the corporatization of capitalism, US interventionism during the Cold War, China under Mao, Indonesia under Sukarno, Algeria under Ben Bella, Egypt under Nasser, decolonization processes in the Third World, and, of course, the Vietnam War.[31]

Despite the intensity of the debate over Cuba in the New York public sphere of the 1960s, Cuban socialism constituted only a secondary topic in most of the essays in Howe's anthologies. One writer, Walter Laquer, referred to "Castro's type of socialism" as a political regime different from the decolonizing nationalisms of Africa and Asia; another, Richard Lowenthal, commented on

Havana's gravitation toward the Chinese model after the missile crisis; and Robert L. Heilbroner criticized the US trade embargo against the island and affirmed the social policies of the revolution while questioning the ideological difference between the Martí-inspired Castro of 1959 and the pro-Soviet Castro of 1962.[32]

Although it represented only a minor topic in these anthologies, the Cuban question was nonetheless central to the public positioning of Howe, Swados, and many of the writers they published. In *The Radical Imagination* (1967), for example, Howe and Swados's approach to this question could be seen as emblematic for the New York Left of the 1960s. The New Left that *Dissent* sought to defend—as indicated by Michael Harrington in the journal's introductory text—had been shaped during the historical cycle between McCarthyism in the 1950s and the civil rights movement and the Vietnam War protests of the 1960s. But this New Left also identified with Albert Camus's denunciation of twentieth-century totalitarianisms, both fascist and communist; with the critique of "socialist realism" as the aesthetic canon of real socialism; and with the defense of dissident writers and politicians in the Soviet Union and Eastern Europe.[33]

Howe identified the existence of diverse "styles" within the New Left. Some of these styles were closely aligned, such as opposition to the Vietnam War, the civil rights movement, and support for African and Asian decolonization—Marshall Sahlins and Joseph Buttinger covered the last eloquently in *The Radical Imagination*.[34] However, in his view, the rejection of war should not imply an acritical stance toward the adoption of totalitarian regimes in Vietnam or Cuba. Lewis Coser introduced this delicate argumentation in an essay that identified three alternatives for the newly decolonized nations of the Third World: totalitarianism, authoritarianism, and democracy—the last, of course, being the model he favored.[35]

Howe's identification of the "styles" of the New Left was even more explicit in his praise, on the one hand, for Frantz Fanon's North African nationalism (as presented in *The Wretched of the Earth* [1961]), and his questioning of the Cuban Revolution's turn toward communism, on the other.[36] Howe observed curious connections between Fanon and Trotsky, identifying the former with the heterodoxy and revisionism he admired in Polish Marxists such as Leszek Kolakowski and Yugoslavian Marxists such as Milivan Djilas.[37] US policy toward the Cuban Revolution was "unjustifiably hostile," he asserted, but the Cuban government's "suppression of democratic rights" could not be supported.[38]

INTERSECTING SOCIALISMS

Alan M. Wald has asserted that this double critique on the part of public intellectuals who ascribed to radicalism, such as Irving Howe and Harvey Swados, led to the "cul-de-sac of social democracy" in the United States.[39] Cold War polarization during the 1960s left very little room for an anti-Stalinist socialism in the United States, and a powerful current of the radical Left was unwilling to weaken its solidarity with Third World nations by criticizing their lack of freedoms or their adoption of authoritarian or totalitarian regimes. Following the Twentieth Congress of the Communist Party of the Soviet Union and the "thaw" initiated by Nikita Khrushchev from Moscow, anti-Stalinism seemed to waver even in certain liberal circles of the New York Left.

The clash between these two branches of American socialism can be traced through the relation between Harvey Swados, Irving Howe, and C. Wright Mills. The three intellectuals had been friends in New York during the 1950s and had combatted McCarthyism in their work for various publications in the city. When the divergence of what Howe had referred to as New Left "styles" took place at the beginning of the sixties, Howe, Swados, and Mills clashed over the Soviet Union and the Cuban Revolution. In the spring of 1959, Howe published a critical review in *Dissent* of Mills's book *The Causes of World War Three*, asserting that Mills's focus on Cold War bipolarism comprised an acritical acceptance of the communist organization of societies as an alternative to Western democracy.[40]

The debate between these two socialists grew bitter, adopting the binary antagonism of the Cold War itself: Mills accused Howe of defending the "socialism of Washington" and Howe responded by labeling Mills a "Stalinist."[41] The same tension resurfaced the following year with the publication of Mills's *Listen, Yankee: The Revolution in Cuba*, in which the author affirmed his solidarity with the Cuban Revolution. It was not Howe but Swados who would mark his distance from Mills in a "Personal Memoir" written for *Dissent* after Mills's death in 1963. In the piece, Swados acknowledged the value of the intellectual work of the author of *The Power Elite* but lamented his excessive enthusiasm for the Cuban regime.[42]

According to Howe and Swados, recognizing the right to independence of Vietnam, Cuba, and other Third World nations, and publically objecting to the imperial policies of the United States and the European powers, need not preclude a critique of political authoritarianism in those Third World nations. This nuance was the key factor differentiating the radicalism favored by social democracy from the radicalism that was fully espoused by the New Left and that Mills embodied. The complexity in question did not result in an "ambiguous legacy" for social democracy, as Wald argues, nor does it prevent one from reconstructing the points of ideological convergence that the two radicalisms shared despite their differences.[43]

Strictly speaking, the background of those differences had nothing to do with Vietnam or Cuba but rather with the Soviet Union and the socialist camp. Mills in the United States, like Jean Paul Sartre in France, was attempting to open a breach in liberal public opinion by insisting on recognition for the real existence of the Soviet bloc. Mills was not a Stalinist, of course—Howe himself knew this—but he differed from the democratic socialists in his defense of a Marxism and a socialism that more resolutely opposed US global hegemony. As Stanley Aronowitz has shown, this critique of Washington's global imperialism—which drew that critique toward accepting an equivalent role for the Soviet Union—came out of an apparent rejection of the social structures of power in the United States.[44]

By contrast, the American social democrats were linked to a global political network that, in tandem with or as a consequence of its demands for a parliamentary—and eventually executive—space in Western democracies, sought to position itself against the Soviet Union and real socialism. A reconstruction of the debates over Cuba that took place between 1959 and 1963 in the Socialist International, of which the Socialist Party of America and the Independent Socialist League were members (the latter was led by Max Shachtman and its adherents included Irving Howe, Michael Harrington, Dwight Macdonald, and other public intellectuals in New York), allows for a more accurate assessment of the positioning of Western social democracy vis-à-vis the Cuban question.[45]

Throughout 1959, the Socialist International was only minimally interested in Cuba, with its members more focused on China, Algeria, the Congo, or the problems of real socialism in Eastern Europe. The political identity of democratic socialism in the postwar period had been shaped at the intersection of antifascism, opposition to McCarthyism, sympathy for dissident movements in Eastern Europe, and the rejection of Soviet hegemony, which had been put to the test by the USSR's 1956 invasion of Hungary. Until early 1961, when the United States and Cuba broke off relations and the Bay of Pigs invasion took place, the Cuban Revolution was perceived by the social democrats as a nationalist movement not much different from Argentine Peronism or Mexican Cardenism.

In the *Socialist International Information* bulletin of April 29, 1961, the principal European socialist parties declared their opposition to the communist radicalization of the Cuban revolutionaries, but also repudiated Washington's hostile policies against the island, which, during that spring, did not discount the possibility of a military invasion.[46] The social democrats believed that international opposition to Cuba's transformation into a Soviet satellite was as popular in the West as disapproval of an American attack on the island. "Violence generates violence," stated the European parties, declaring that US intervention in the Caribbean, at a moment when Nasser had just nationalized the Suez Canal and a number of former colonies in Asia and Africa had declared their independence, would not favor the cause of a "free world."[47]

This perception of the Cuban problem in the spring of 1961 was shared not only by social democrats in the United States, Great

Britain, France, and Germany, but also by the Austrians, the Swiss, the Norwegians, the Italians, the Dutch, and the Finns. A communiqué issued by the National Action Committee of the US Socialist Party clearly rejected Washington's support for the Bay of Pigs invasion even while recognizing that the invasion had been an "indirect" one, backing an armed opposition that was no longer in support of the ancien régime of Fulgencio Batista's dictatorship.[48] Furthermore, the writers declared, criticism of Washington's Cuba policies was not incompatible with disapproval of the Cuban leadership's totalitarian shift:

> In saying this, we do not endorse the Castro regime. On the contrary, we have become increasingly alarmed at the anti-democratic acts of the Castro Government, particularly the repression of free speech, the political execution, and the destruction of an independent labour movement. We further note the growing evidence of greater Cuban Communist influence in the government, and we deplore it. One can no longer exclude the possibility that Cuba may become a "people's democracy," communist style.[49]

Curiously, one of the few social democratic pronouncements in favor of the Bay of Pigs invasion came from Indian socialist A. D. Gorwala. Insisting that the Cuban exiles were neither fascists nor Batistans but "revolutionary democrats," he argued that Washington's intervention was justified given the increase of Soviet Union control over the Cuban economy since the middle of 1960.[50] Gorwala, a critic of Nehru, lamented that Western democratic socialism would be so condescending toward Third World governments that they would ally themselves with the Soviet bloc.

When the Socialist International once again took up the Cuban question in the fall of 1962, the position of the Western center-left was consistent with the line it had followed since the Bay of Pigs invasion. As British Labour Party leader Hugh Gaitskell would declare in the House of Commons on October 30 of that year, the international community no longer doubted that Cuba had joined the Soviet bloc.[51] In the face of a situation like the missile crisis, social democrats applauded the negotiations between Kennedy and

Khrushchev. When those negotiations resulted in a preservation of world peace and US agreement not to invade Cuba, the democratic socialists felt that their position had won, although they did not discount the possibility that the Cuban leadership might decide to gravitate toward China out of a sense of betrayal by Moscow.[52]

A careful examination of the treatment of the Cuban topic among US socialists at the beginning of 1960 shows that the positions of democratic socialism and the Kennedy administration were not assimilable, as Mills argued during the period and as dozens of historians have repeated since that time. In contrast with Arthur M. Schlesinger Jr.'s effort to justify an invasion of Cuba in the spring of 1961 in his celebrated *White Cuban Paper*, the social democrats were consistently opposed to Washington's aggressive policies toward Havana.[53] They agreed with Mills and the Marxists of the *Monthly Review*—Paul Sweezy, Leo Huberman, J. P. Morray, and others—that cautious diplomacy would help to forestall a rigid accord between the Soviets and the Cubans, but they disagreed with the notion that public opposition to Cuban communism should form part of intellectual commitment on the left.

While recognizing that anti-Castro opposition was neither "fascist" nor "Batistan," the social democrats did not subscribe to the notion of the "revolution betrayed" that was being argued by Schlesinger and echoed by other intellectuals, including Waldo Frank and Carleton Beals, who participated in the debate over Cuba in New York. Due to their contact with Trotskyism, Shachtman and the democratic socialists were more identified with Morray's thesis of a "second revolution," which argued that the abandonment of the first "humanist" phase of the Cuban Revolution had accelerated the process of equality and social justice but at the same time had introduced totalitarian elements, such as control over the press, centralization of worker unions, the illegality of opposition, and the dependency of judicial power.[54]

The Bay of Pigs invasion, despite its scandalous failure and Havana's subsequent accelerated alignment with the Soviet Union, complicated relations with the island for US supporters of the Cuban Revolution. Many intellectuals who had defended the Cuban process as "humanistic" and not totalitarian found themselves questioning their views as reports emerged detailing the Castro government's growing economic, political, and military collaboration with the Kremlin. Even Ernest Hemingway, a writer much beloved by the Cuban leadership, found it difficult to maintain his Cuban residence in the Finca Vigía and his friendship with Castro.[55]

COUNTERCULTURE AND DECOLONIZATION

In his essay *El puño invisible* (The Invisible Fist, 2011), Colombian scholar Carlos Granés expresses surprise that the Cuban Revolution became a key point of reference for young New York liberals who combatted American conservatism during the 1960s. Granés wonders how vanguard figures like Norman Mailer and Susan Sontag, fervent defenders of sexual liberation and critics of Marxist-Leninist orthodoxy, ever came to support a political regime like Cuba's, which, from the beginning of the 1960s, exhibited notable institutional and ideological coincidences with the Soviet Union and the real socialism of Eastern Europe.[56]

Explanations for this paradox would need to be sought in Mailer's and Sontag's writings on the Cuban experience. Two texts that serve as bookends for viewpoints on Cuba in New York public opinion during the 1960s—Mailer's "Open Letter to JFK and Fidel Castro" (1961), published in the *Village Voice*, and Sontag's "Some Thoughts on the Right Way (for Us) to Love the Cuban Revolution" (1969), published in *Ramparts*—hold the keys for comprehending the complex relation between the New York New Left and Cuban socialism, a relation that over the span of a single decade oscillated between a sense of the promise Cuba represented for leftist libertarianism and the sense of disenchantment that resulted from Havana's alignment with Moscow.

That oscillation, it must be said, revealed all of its possibilities from the very start. For example, just days after the Bay of Pigs invasion, Mailer wrote his letter to Castro and Kennedy out of a conviction that the two leaders personified the arrival to power of a new generation that could and should find new rules of coexistence for the opposed ideologies of the Cold War. Both leaders, Mailer believed, heralded a "new spirit" in America, one that would leave behind both tropical dictatorships like Batista's and the "tyrannies" (Mailer's term) of public opinion such as McCarthyism.[57]

As recalled by Mailer's biographer Hillary Mills, the first version of Mailer's letter to Castro is dated November 1960, a moment when the communist radicalization of the Cuban Revolution had not yet been confirmed.[58] After the Bay of Pigs, however, Mailer still believed an understanding between Kennedy and Castro was possible, based on the generational identity he attributed to both political leaders. Mailer, the sociologist of "The White Negro," hipsters, and beatniks; the defender of homosexuality and women's liberation; and the critic of the Vietnam War and Protestant and Catholic conservatism, did not take the communism of the Cuban revolutionaries seriously.[59]

Just as Mailer's knowledge of the CIA's involvement in the military plot against the Cuban Revolution (events he would portray thirty years later in *Harlot's Ghost* [1991]) did not alter his admiration for Kennedy (as evidenced in *An American Dream* [1965]), the totalitarian elements of the Cuban regime likewise did not diminish his admiration for Castro.[60] An explanation for this behavior can perhaps be found in a passage of Mailer's account of the 1968 Democratic and Republican conventions in Chicago and Miami. Curiously, he mentions Cuba in this account, not in relation to anticommunist exile groups in Miami that were involved in Nixon's campaign but in his description of the radical and pacifist leftists who protested the National Democratic Convention in Chicago.

Mailer observed that just as the young protesters in Chicago—"modern minds," he called them—rejected "the anally compulsive oppressions of Russian communism (as much as they detested the anally retentive ideologies of the corporation)," they also paid homage to Guevara, Mao, Tito, and the leaders of the Prague Spring, who were also communists.[61] This radicalism on the left, Mailer believed, rejected the institutional paths of democratic or even socialist liberalism to instead join a more amorphous and heterogeneous current, one whose spaces of sociability would need to be located in the bohemian sectors of the student and counterculture movements. The leftist-libertarian counterculture, Mailer observed, lived out its cosmopolitan credo as much in yoga sessions as in campaigns of solidarity with Third World decolonizers.

This link between counterculture and decolonization is evident in Susan Sontag's piece for *Ramparts*, which was published in April 1969 and written after a two-week sojourn in Havana.[62] Although Sontag was not unaware of the introduction of Stalinist discourses and practices in Cuban socialism—which included the establishment of the UMAP labor camps (Unidades Militares de Ayuda a la Producción [Military Units to Aid Production]), the expulsion of Allen Ginsberg from the island, the persecution of homosexuals, and attacks on dissident writers such as poet Heberto Padilla—she firmly believed that the Cuban leaders would correct these errors. It could not be any other way, according to Sontag, because the Cuban Revolution was obliged to produce a socialism different from the Soviet model. A socialism created in an underdeveloped and colonial nation of the Caribbean, she seemed to think, could not be anything but an authentic socialism.

The liberation-seeking bohemian counterculture, whether in New York, Paris, Madrid, or San Francisco, adopted Cuba as one more icon of the aesthetic of authenticity. Freedom from sexual and moral strictures—which in Sontag's case constituted a personal epic as much as a hermeneutical premise, as evident from the diaries of her youth and her theoretical essays, such as *Against Interpretation* (1966)—was attributed to Havana unquestioningly. It mattered little to this cultural vanguard that homophobia, censorship, and other forms of cultural dogmatism in Cuba during the early 1960s were signaling the reconfiguration of a new moral code, one that would turn out to be as, or more, conservative than the Catholic or liberal codes destroyed by the revolutionary government.

In her diaries of 1960, written just as the Cuban Revolution was coming to power on the island, Sontag reflected on her readings of C. Wright Mills and Hans Gerth's anthology *From Max Weber*, speculated on the relation between totalitarianism and the imposition of the Cyrillic alphabet by Stalin and Lenin, and defended the correspondence of sexual liberation with political democracy.[63] Already in *Against Interpretation*, she would cast the search for authenticity as a rejection of interpretive "philistinism" and advocate a conception of the avant-garde as the abandonment of hermeneutics and theory in favor of an "erotics of art."[64] It is clear that this erotics was what Sontag was looking for in Cuba: an intellectual repurposing of the tourist's role that might reconcile her with the existence of an autochthonous social process.

Sontag's experience was hardly the most intense version of the experience of the Cuban Revolution on the part of the New York leftist intelligentsia. CBS correspondent Robert Taber became so involved in the revolutionary cause that he sided with the Cuban militias during the Bay of Pigs invasion; beat writer Allen Ginsberg was expelled from the island due to his support for the young leftist libertarian writers of the El Puente press; black leader Robert F. Williams, after a sojourn in Havana, went off to Mao's China in search of possible interlocutions between the US civil rights movement and the anticolonial nationalism of Asia and Africa; Hispanic activist and anthropologist Elizabeth Sutherland Martínez spent months researching the construction of a socialist utopia on the Isle of Pines off southwest Cuba; and so on. All of these figures lived an experience of countercultural radicalization that led them to a commitment with a process of socialist decolonization in the Caribbean.

Nonetheless, nearly all of these adventures that began with identification ended in disenchantment or criticism. For example, Taber, who produced the enthusiastic report *Rebels of the Sierra Maestra* for CBS, who authored an apology for the revolutionary epic *M-26: Biography of a Revolution* (1961), and who once claimed that "history would record the battles of the Zapata Swamp as the Waterloo of US imperial power," later came to question the Cuban government's support for guerrilla movements and Latin American civil wars in the 1970s and 1980s.[65]

Martínez, for her part, spent months researching the youth communities of the Isle of Pines in her project to portray Latin America's "youngest revolution." Nonetheless, her work came to pose a threat to the Western Left's acritical solidarity with Cuban socialism when she divulged such problems as racism, machismo, homophobia, the establishment of agriculture labor camps for the internment of "antisocial" elements (UMAPs), and the censorship of writers and published works such as José Lezama Lima's novel *Paradiso*.[66] Martínez was also conscious that the touristic discourse of Cuba's neocolonial past, which had been determined by dependency on the United States, was now undergoing an oppositional reconstruction with the encouragement of a new socialist and revolutionary tourism.

The critical spirit of New York's bohemian vanguard manifested itself in the limited experiences of these young intellectuals who traveled to the island with the desire to live and document utopia. The gesture of joining the Caribbean epic was a clear sign of commitment to the decolonizing project promised by the Cuban Revolution and other Third World nationalisms during the Cold War years. However, the leftist libertarianism of the bohemian counterculture and New Leftist intellectual life in general clashed with the transfer of the institutions and ideas of real Eastern European socialism to the Cuban context. Most members of the New York Left were reluctant to endorse this ideological transfer and were unwilling to support Cuba's decolonization if it involved the naturalization of Marxist-Leninist dogma on the island.

This book seeks to tell the story of this commitment and of this disencounter. Just as important as reconstructing the factors that led many intellectuals of the New York New Left to identify with the Cuban Revolution is the task of locating the moment when that identification was sundered by dissidence and criticism. Ciphered in the dialogues and tensions between the New York Left and Cuban socialism during the 1960s are the possibilities of the cultural vanguard circuit between Havana and Manhattan that sought to challenge the asphyxiating polarization of the Cold War.

1

HIPSTERS AND APPARATCHIKS

★

ARTHUR M. SCHLESINGER JR. DEVOTED MUCH OF HIS MEMOIR on the Kennedy administration, *A Thousand Days* (1965), to reconstructing the dilemma that Castro's socialist Cuba posed for Washington in 1961. Starting in the early pages of the book's chapter "The Hour of Euphoria," Schlesinger endorsed a certain historical narrative of the communist radicalization of the Cuban Revolution, one based mainly on a reading of the work of historians such as Theodore Draper and Hugh Thomas, who argued that the young Cuban leadership had rationally and deliberately chosen to reformulate its ideology, transforming the nationalist democratic ideal that had led it to power in January 1959 into a communist socialism allied with the Soviet bloc.[1]

Schlesinger incorporates into the "euphoria" unleashed by Kennedy's arrival in the White House the enthusiasm that the Cuban Revolution had awakened in national public opinion. Since 1957, when the *New York Times* began to publish Herbert L. Matthews's series on the guerrilla movement in the Sierra Maestra, Castro had come to be perceived in the United States as the young leader of a new Latin American Left, one that was nationalist and even socialist but also liberal and democratic. In Washington, this leftism was associated with Latin American political leaders who had promoted the Alliance for Progress, such as Lázaro Cárdenas in Mexico, Víctor Raúl Haya de la Torre in Peru, Rómulo Betancourt in Venezuela, and José Figueres in Costa Rica.

At the end of the 1950s, opinion in both popular and political classes in the United States had come to reject the Batista regime. As Schlesinger recalls, Kennedy himself christened Castro as a member of "Bolívar's legacy" in the President's own account of his campaign, *The Strategy of Peace* (1960).[2] Schlesinger testifies that he met Castro in person at the Harvard Faculty Club in Cambridge during the latter's triumphal visit to the United States in April 1959. Attempting to account for the bearded young revolutionary's popularity among American university students, Schlesinger observes, "They saw in him, I think, the hipster who in the era of the Organization Man had joyfully defied the system, summoned a dozen friends and overturned a government of wicked old men."[3]

As Schlesinger writes, Cuba's shift toward communism produced an adverse reaction in the United States. Within a year, Castro ceased to be exalted as a hero and instead came to be viewed as an enemy of the United States. When Kennedy authorized the plan for the Bay of Pigs invasion that had been drawn up under the Eisenhower administration, the event would become the primary stumbling block of his presidential term. In his exhaustive account of this episode, Schlesinger blames the CIA and the leaders of the Cuban exile community for the disaster and naturally exculpates his own boss, President Kennedy.[4] But he goes still further, also reproaching intellectuals and groups that had expressed solidarity with Havana in the spring of 1961, such as C. Wright Mills, Jean Paul Sartre, Norman Mailer, and the Fair Play for Cuba Committee, the last of which had organized prorevolutionary marches in San Francisco and Union Square on April 21 and 22.[5]

The present chapter of this book could in fact be read as a counterpoint between the vision of the Cuban Revolution held by Thomas Draper, to which Schlesinger subscribes, and that of Mills and Sartre, whom Schlesinger erroneously characterizes as favoring the establishment of communism in Cuba. The ideological confrontations of the period and the criticisms levied by Mills, Mailer, and others against the Kennedy administration's Cuba policies caused Schlesinger to lose sight of the fact that the New York intellectuals, from the outset, were not defenders of the Cuban Revolution's shift toward communism but objectors to Washington's Cold War policies. This misunderstanding was common to liberals and Democrats of the period, but among anticommunists of the Republican Right, it assumed the form of a rigid stereotype.

Between 1959 and 1962, public opinion in New York was a key scenario for the ideological radicalization of the Cuban Revolution and for the design of a new and audacious geopolitical strategy on the part of its young leaders. Not only was New York the headquarters of major national print, television, and radio organizations, such as the *New York Times*, the *New York Herald Tribune*, CBS, and NBC, but the United Nations headquarters in Manhattan was also the site of frequent gatherings of international heads of state, including the Cuban leaders. Castro and Guevara became central figures in the New York spectacle of world politics during the 1960s.

In the pages that follow, I will seek to reconstruct the process by which the image of the Cuban Revolution shifted in New York public opinion. Robert A. Rutland, a historian of American journalism, refers to this shift when he writes that "Cuba, under Fidel Castro, turned from friend to enemy, with shocking suddenness."[6] Rutland rigidly situates the shift in the fall of 1962, a moment when, in his view, the city's liberal press, which had earlier celebrated Castro's 1959 triumph and questioned Kennedy over the Bay of Pigs episode, began to portray the Cuban leadership as a threat to peace and US national security.

Subsequently, I will seek to account for a change within radical opinion as well, particularly in publications such as *Dissent* and the *Village Voice*, which resulted in a critique of the totalitarian elements of Cuban socialism, the anointing of Guevara as an icon of the New Left, and a double rejection of both US intervention in Vietnam and the Soviet Union's intervention in Czechoslovakia. Between 1963 and 1968, a period of discrete distancing between Cuba and the Soviet Union, the relation between American radicalism and the Cuban government was a complex one. While *Dissent* did not hesitate to qualify the Cuban regime as a dictatorship, the *Village Voice* identified with Guevarism as a current of the Latin American Left that both expanded and exceeded the ideas of the Cuban Revolution.

ROBIN HOOD IN THE CARIBBEAN

The triumph of the Cuban Revolution coincided with a restructuring of the American public sphere, as the newspapers of the postwar era were forced to adapt to the rise of large television and radio consortiums, which were heavily marked by the interests and languages of McCarthyism and anticommunism.[7] The arrival in the White House of a young Democratic leadership led by John F. Kennedy produced what Christopher B. Daly refers to as a "rocking [of] the establishment."[8] In this context, frictions grew between the formation of a "liberal arc" that supported the new administration and a powerful rightist sector that pressured the White House and threatened Democratic-leaning publications such as the *New York Times*.[9]

Cuba, its revolution, and its leaders were precipitated into the center of this conflict. The *New York Times* reported sympathetically on the insurrection against Batista's dictatorship in the Sierra Maestra and in the island's main urban centers at the end of the 1950s. Three of the paper's Cuba correspondents, Herbert L. Matthews, Tad Szulc, and Ruby Hart Phillips (the paper's Havana bureau chief and dean of the foreign correspondents on the island), wrote converging—and later diverging—articles on the Cuban Revolution between 1957 and 1962. During this five-year period the *New York Times* was indisputably the US newspaper featuring the most extensive coverage of the island's political process.

In her first book on the Cuban Revolution, Phillips provided a detailed account of the *Times*' early relationship with the new regime. After the paper printed a story from United Press correspondent Francis L. McCarthy reporting that Castro and his men had perished in combat in December 1956 after navigating by boat from Veracruz, Mexico, and landing on Cuba's eastern coast, the rebel leadership decided to refute the news through the *New York Times*. Castro and the leaders of the 26th of July Movement would henceforth choose the *Times* as their medium for transmitting messages to the world.[10]

Phillips was the widow of James Doyle Phillips, the *New York Times'* correspondent in Havana during the 1930s. Ruby had authored a book on the 1933 Revolution, *Cuban Sideshow* (1935), which argued for a repeal of the Platt Amendment and for US recognition of the revolutionary government. After her husband's death in 1937, she assumed his role as *Times* correspondent on the island. In February 1957, Phillips was contacted by Castro sympathizer Felipe Pazos, president of the National Bank of Cuba and then head of the Bacardí Company, who sought to arrange a meeting between Phillips, NBC correspondent Ted Scott, and Faustino Pérez, leader of the urban guerrilla offensive.[11] As a result of this meeting, the decision was made to send Herbert L. Matthews to the Sierra Maestra to interview Castro for the *Times*.[12]

Matthews's mountain trip produced a series of three front-page articles that were published on February 24, 25, and 26, 1957.[13] The first of these articles was accompanied by a photo of Castro, depicted from the front holding a rifle with a telescopic sight, and the second article featured a photo of mothers in Santiago, Cuba, protesting the repression that was resulting in the massacre of young anti-Batista youth. Matthews's articles served as more than mere confirmation that Castro was alive and fighting in the Sierra Maestra: they constituted the Cuban Revolution's ideological letter of presentation to US public opinion.

Matthews reported that the Cuban revolutionaries called themselves "socialists," a term the paper interpreted as a mixture of "nationalist"—in the anti-Yankee sense this adjective had acquired in Latin America—"radical," "democratic," and "anti-communist."[14] In the final section of the interview, Castro emphatically declared that the revolutionaries held no animosity toward the United States and that their struggle was against a dictatorship and in support of democracy. The *Times* highlighted these concepts when, in the third of the three articles, it defined the Fulgencio Batista regime as a "dictatorship" and referred to it as a "traditionally corrupt system."[15] The third of Matthews's articles was accompanied by a piece by Phillips that condemned the censorship the *Times* had been subjected to in Cuba since the most recent suspension of constitutional guarantees in January 1957.[16]

Over the two following years, Matthews's and Phillips's Cuba coverage was decidedly favorable to the revolutionaries, although Phillips also made some effort to save face with sectors of the Batista government. In a second visit to Cuba in June 1957, Matthews interviewed Batista and other government figures, who were already speaking of a "transfer of power," but at the same time his articles emphasized the rebels' early military triumphs, and he conversed in Santiago with insurrection leaders such as Frank País and Manuel Urrutia, a lawyer who would become the first president of the revolutionary government.[17] Thanks to Matthews's prorevolutionary sympathies, and particularly due to his description of Castro as a modern Robin Hood of the Caribbean, the *Times* correspondent came under strong attack from the anticommunist press in the United States, both before and after the socialist character of the revolution was openly declared in April 1961. Together with Assistant Secretary of State Roy Rubottom and William Wieland, the State Department's director of the Caribbean Division and Mexico, Matthews was mentioned in hearings called by the Senate's Eastland-Dodd Subcommittee at the end of August 1960, which inquired into communist penetration into the United States.[18]

In those hearings, Matthews, Wieland, and Rubottom were accused by Arthur Gardner and Earl Smith, former ambassadors to Cuba, of having encouraged communism on the island with their tolerant and friendly treatment of the Cuban Revolution.[19] This interrogation, which also investigated the *New York Times*' editorial line, was picked up again starting in April 1961, this time by the paper's own collaborators, including Ruby Hart Phillips, and by much of the anticommunist right in the United States, the latter of which perceived the *Times* as a liberal and procommunist paper.[20] Ironically, during this same period, the *New York Times* was portrayed in Cuba as a pro-imperialist enemy of the revolution, and some of the *Times*' collaborators who showed the greatest

"All the News That's Fit to Print"

The New York Times.

LATE CITY EDITION

VOL. CVIII.. No. 36,875. NEW YORK, FRIDAY, JANUARY 9, 1959 FIVE CENTS

DE GAULLE TAKES THE PRESIDENCY; DEBRE IS PREMIER

General's Entry Into Office Marks Start of Fifth French Republic

SOUSTELLE IS SELECTED

Post of Minister-Delegate Indicates He Has Second Top Spot in Cabinet

TRIUMPHANT ENTRY: Fidel Castro, Cuban revolutionary leader, waves to crowds as he rides down Havana's Malecon sea drive in a jeep at head of an armored column. Parade proceeded to Camp Columbia, Army Headquarters.

OFFICIAL AGENCY TO PLAN GROWTH OF REGION URGED

Report Asks Legal Status for Metropolitan Council as Government Adviser

G.O.P. Aims to End 'Big Business' Label

FILIBUSTER FOES FACE A SETBACK IN VOTING TODAY

Johnson Sets Up Showdown on Issue of Senate's Right to Adopt New Rules

HE ACTS TO KILL PLAN

Liberals Call Test Crucial for Success of Tighter Limitation on Debate

MIKOYAN APPEALS FOR A 'HOT PEACE'

Tells Detroit Dinner 'We're All Tired of Cold War'—President Asks Courtesy

Havana Welcomes Castro At End of Triumphal Trip

CENTRAL SPURNS PENNSY MERGER

Drops Studies to Determine Feasibility of Rail Plan—Symes 'Disappointed'

REPUBLICANS BACK MORE STATE TAXES

Leaders Predict Legislature Will Adopt Higher Levies and Withholding Plan

U.S. BARS INCREASE IN MISSILE FORCES

Rejects Air Force Request for More ICBM Groups Despite 'Gap' Warning

BREAK WITH CAIRO IS HINTED BY BONN

Nasser Is Asked to Clarify Tie With East Germany

Reds Here Suspend Touring Party Aide

De Valera to Quit as Premier And Seek Ireland's Presidency

His Government Party Seeks to Abolish the Proportional Representation System

Eamon de Valera

16 NEW CITY TAXES BEING CONSIDERED

A Big One and Several Little Ones Likely to Be Picked

The New York Times THE COMPLETE FRONT PAGES

The Cuban Revolution was on the front page of the *New York Times* throughout the first week of 1959.

sympathy toward the Cuban process, such as Matthews himself, were never publically annointed as friends in Havana.

Objectively speaking, it was hardly unusual for a journalist like Matthews and a paper like the *New York Times* to have supported a nationalist and socialist movement such as the Cuban Revolution. In March 1917, the *Times* had published an enthusiastic assessment of the onset of the Russian Revolution; Matthews himself had reported on the Spanish Civil War with evident sympathy for the Republican cause; and *Times* correspondents and reporters such as Bertram D. Hullen, Anita Brenner, and Bruce Rae had defended Mexican president Lázaro Cárdenas and his right to assert control over his country's oil industry. Matthews and other *Times* reporters had been consistently critical of US military intervention in Latin America, as had been evident just three years before during the coup against Guatemalan president Jacobo Arbenz.

A fundamental role in the dissemination of a "humanist"—noncommunist—portrayal of the Cuban Revolution in the New York press was played by a committee for the 26th of July Movement in exile, led by Mario Llerena. This young Cuban intellectual, author of the social-democratic manifesto *Nuestra Razón*, sponsored by the movement's national leadership, was responsible for the intense lobbying in support of Castro between 1957 and 1959 in the United States. Llerena responded in the *Nation* to Carleton Beals's criticisms regarding the lack of ideology and the terrorism of the rebels; contacted Oregon congressional representative Charles O. Porter and African American congressman from Harlem, Adam Clayton Powell Jr., to get their support for demanding a US arms embargo against the Batista regime and backing the Cuban revolutionaries; and organized acts of solidarity and fundraising in Palm Garden with Felipe Pazos, Raúl Chibás, Juanita Castro—Fidel's sister—and Manuel Urrutia, the future president of the revolutionary government.[21]

It was this current of opinion among its ranks that strengthened the *Times*' enthusiasm for the Cuban Revolution, particularly between 1958 and 1959. Although a few of the paper's columnists, such as Homer Bigart, supported the presidential elections that Batista called for in November 1958, as a political solution, most of the stories wired from Phillips's office in Havana reinforced the notion that Cuba had become the staging ground for a clash between two generations and two leaders, Batista and Castro, with military and moral force increasingly favoring the latter.[22] For example, after the disastrous general strike of April 9, 1958, when many American newspapers reported that the poor turnout had weakened the rebel forces, the *Times* suggested that the events, although revealing the fragmentation of rebel forces in the lowlands, had only further strengthened Castro's leadership in the rebels' mountain stronghold.[23]

Popular US enthusiasm over the Cuban Revolution climaxed during the first two weeks of January 1959. During this period, the *New York Times* devoted daily articles to the revolution—up to five in a single day—along with profiles and photos of its principal leaders. Cuban coverage by Phillips and Matthews was broadened with coverage from Washington by Peter Kihss, Dana Adams Schmidt, Gay Talese, Richard E. Mooney, and R. W. Kenworthy, all of which was highly favorable to the triumphant revolution and which, of course, included reports of the Eisenhower administration's recognition of the new revolutionary Cuban government headed by Urrutia.[24]

The *Times* featured almost daily photos of Castro as well, thereby emphasizing the notion that the rebel leader had become the new hegemonic figure on the island as Batista's replacement. This romantic personalization of the historical process was accentuated with images of the Castro family, such as one showing Fidelito Castro, the leader's son, reuniting with his father after a period of studying in a public school in Queens, or photos of the wedding of Raúl Castro and Vilma Espín.[25] The idea of the Cuban Revolution as a clash between generations and two leaders, Batista and Castro, had taken hold in the *Times* since the days of Matthews's first articles on the revolution and was confirmed by Phillips herself in her reports during the first half of 1959, which were summarized in her book *Cuba: Island of Paradox* (1959).[26]

Despite this personalized portrayal, the paper did attempt to provide a balanced perspective on the new revolutionary leadership during this period. The three biographical profiles featured in the "Man in the News" section were devoted to Castro, captioned as "Symbol of Rebellion"; President Manuel Urrutia, identified as "An Idealistic Cuban"; and Raúl Chibás, member of the first revolutionary cabinet (and brother of "orthodox" leader Eduardo Chibás, who had committed suicide), who was portrayed holding a rifle despite his civilian rather than military background.[27] Nonetheless, the editors of the *Times* would henceforth identify Urrutia and Chibás as two of the revolution's moderate and civil political figures, who were called to compensate for the Jacobinism of the young Sierra Maestra commanders.

Interestingly, the liberal and conservative press in Cuba (*El Diario de la Marina*, *El Mundo*, and *Bohemia*) represented the revolutionary leadership quite differently from the *Times*, insisting on portraying Castro merely as a "symbol" or military guarantor of the new revolution. The *Times*, while subscribing to this symbolic or epic framework, also held to the view of Castro that Matthews had introduced: as the island's political choice and new statesman. This explains both why the *Times* devoted greater coverage to Castro's January 9, 1959, arrival in Havana than to Batista's fall one week earlier and why it reported so matter-of-factly on Castro's replacement of José Miró Cardona as prime minister.

Other New York papers more attentive to the anticommunist Right, such as the *New York Herald Tribune*, clearly showed more favor to moderate leaders, such as President Urrutia and Prime Minister Miró Cardona, in detriment to Castro and the rebel commanders. The reports phoned in to the *Herald Tribune* by Frank Kelly from Havana in January 1959 were among the first to insinuate Castro's communism and to question the postponement of the elections and the legality of the executions of Batistans, such as the chief of police of Santa Clara, Cornelio Rojas.[28]

From an editorial point of view, the difference between the *Times* and the *Herald Tribune* was evident throughout 1959 and even during the escalation of the conflict between the United States and Cuba between the winter of 1960 and the spring of 1961. While the *Times* expressed the view that Cuba was experiencing a social revolution like the French, Russian, or Mexican Revolutions and needed to be understood in depth, the *Herald Tribune* maintained—as was argued by columnists such as Joel Seldin—that the Cuban Revolution was merely one more event in a long history of political violence that characterized all the Latin American nations: "Fidel Castro is a product of Cuba's continuing history of violent contention for political power, in which it is difficult to set out the revolutions from the counter-revolutions."[29]

Although as early as January 1959, Ruby Hart Phillips had delivered reports to the *Times* that were critical of the arrests and executions carried out by the new regime, particularly when these events affected American citizens, the paper's enthusiasm for the revolution did not lessen until nearly the end of that year. This enthusiasm was evident in the *Times*' coverage of Castro's first visit to the United States at the invitation of the American Society of Newspaper Editors, which took place between April 15 and April 26. The *Times* began to publicize the visit on March 4, after Castro had been prime minister for only three weeks, in an attempt to pressure the Department of State and the White House into granting official status to the visit.[30] On April 11, the newspaper announced, not without satisfaction, that Vice President Nixon and Secretary of State Christian A. Herter had met with the Cuban leader during his tour.[31]

The *Times*' Washington correspondent, E. W. Kenworthy, penned an affectionate review of Castro's meeting at the Statler-Hilton Hotel with members of the American Society of Newspaper Editors and his visit to the Capitol Building and the office of the vice president. Under the story heading, "Castro Declares Regime Is Free of Red Influence," Kenworthy reported that the Cuban leader's economic policy priorities were to develop industry and eliminate unemployment, noting that he was accompanied on the visit by an economic cabinet comprising experts with a long record on US-Cuban trade and diplomatic relations (Felipe Pazos, president of the Cuban National Bank; Regino Boti, minister of the economy; Rufo López Fresquet, minister of the treasury, Raúl Cepero Bonilla, minister of commerce; and Ernesto Betancourt, president of the Bank of Foreign Commerce).[32]

In these reports by Kenworthy and others, Castro was presented as a nationalist and "humanist" political figure. Not only was he not a communist, he was an anticommunist, interested in seeking good relations with the United States. Nor was he planning to break the treaty that had established the Guantánamo Bay Naval Base or withdraw Cuba from the Inter-American Treaty of Reciprocal Assistance (TIAR) signed in Rio de Janeiro in 1947. According to Kenworthy's report, Castro insisted he had not traveled to the United States to "beg for alms" but was seeking the ratification and signing of both old and new trade and investment agreements with Washington.[33] In another *Times* report on the trip, Dana Adams Schmidt reviewed Castro's appearance on *Meet the Press* on NBC, a network where the Cuban leader had been a familiar presence since his appearances on *The Ed Sullivan Show*. Schmidt expressed approval for Castro's assertion that elections in Cuba should be postponed for four months until the island's social rights situation had sufficiently improved, quoting his declaration, "Real democracy is not possible for hungry people; real democracy ought to be established over social justice and work for everybody."[34]

Schmidt did not hesitate to reassure his readers that in the event of a conflict between the United States and the Soviet Union, Castro would side with his American neighbor. This perception of the Cuban leader as friend of the United States despite his aggressive program of social reforms was also conveyed by Ruby Hart Phillips from Havana. For example, in the spring of 1959 she called attention to the revolutionary government's resolution of the case of the young American Alan Joseph Nye, who had been found guilty for the crime of conspiring to assassinate Castro.[35] Although Nye was initially condemned to death by the revolutionary courts, the prime minister subsequently pardoned him, a magnanimous gesture that the *Times* celebrated.[36]

When Phillips traveled to New York in the summer of 1959 to promote her book *Cuba: Island of Paradox* (1959), she did not hesitate to speak apologetically for Castro. Her book described the young, bearded revolutionary as a "phenomenon," a "magical" and "hypnotic" personality who had generated "fanatical loyalty" among his followers.[37] Despite his nationalist feelings, Fidel would always move within the framework of the 1940 Constitution, according to Phillips, because the force of his personality would prevent his manipulation by the old communists on the island, whom she considered "reactionaries."[38] In line with Matthews, Phillips called on the United States to recognize Castro as the revolution's maximum leader and privileged interlocutor for American interests on the island. She argued that the United States should keep Fidel close in order to correct a disastrous policy toward Latin America built on support for dictators such as Trujillo, Batista, and Somoza, which had done nothing but increase anti-American sentiment in the region.[39]

Over the following months, Phillips would report in depth on the denunciations of growing communist influence on the island that were being expressed by President Urrutia and commanders Pedro Luis Díaz and Huber Matos. Yet the *Times*' editorial support for the revolutionary government is evident through the middle of February 1960. Nonetheless, the accelerating sequence of events running from the end of 1959 up to that moment—that is, between the ministerial removals at the end of 1959 (which marked the exit from the government of its last remaining moderates and the installation of Marxists, such as Ernesto Guevara and Osmani Cienfuegos, in the economic cabinet) and Soviet chancellor Anastas Mikoyan's weeklong visit in mid-February 1960, which resulted in a generous trade agreement with the Soviet Union—occasioned a fracture in the *Times*' editorial line that would gradually lead the paper toward a critical, and difficult to articulate, treatment of the Cuban question.

Events during the second half of 1960 forced the *New York Times* into a position that questioned the communist radicalization of the Cuban project yet without adopting the arguments of the American anticommunist Right. "Anti-Yankee" rhetoric on the part of the Cuban leaders increased, fed by ill-proven accusations of sabotage, such as the explosion of *La Coubre* in the port of Havana, the exchange of barbs and counterbarbs over the summer in the wake of Washington's reduction of sugar import quotas, the nationalization without indemnization of dozens of American companies, and the refusal of US refineries to process Soviet crude. To achieve this critical stance, the *Times* positioned itself in favor of the Cuban Revolution but in opposition to the revolution's Castro-led shift toward communism.

The image of Castro as a Robin Hood of the Caribbean, as constructed by Matthews, Phillips, and other *Times* writers between 1957 and 1959, underwent a rapid correction starting in the summer of 1960. Reports on arrests and executions in Cuba and commentaries on Castro's declarations, in which he portrayed himself as a Marxist-Leninist or as an enemy of the United States, became constant in the *Times*. The majority of the reports sent by Phillips from the Havana office now appeared without the correspondent's byline, her presence in Cuba having become more precarious as she came under surveillance and was subject to intervention by the revolutionary government's security apparatuses.[40] In both her signed and unsigned reports, Phillips also emphasized the Cuban government's efforts to promote insurrections against anticommunist dictatorships in various Latin American countries.[41]

Nonetheless, the *Times* editorial page continued to express its resolute support for greater understanding between the United States and the Cuban Revolution. In one opinion column, journalist Arthur Krock appealed to both sides of the conflict, warning that if the Cuban government tightened its economic integration with the Soviet bloc, voices in the Department of State—including ambassador to Cuba Phillip W. Bonsal—that defended old New Deal policies supporting the sugar quota and maintaining relations with the island would lose their influence on the White House.[42] But by the end of 1960, after Castro's second visit to the United States and when the Cuban question had become an issue in the presidential race between John F. Kennedy and Richard Nixon, support for this diplomatic understanding became more difficult for the *Times*.

Castro's trip to the United Nations General Assembly in September of that year, which was covered in detail by Max Frankel in a series of articles for the *Times*, confirmed suspicions that the revolutionary government was heading resolutely toward an alignment with Moscow. In the first few days of Castro's visit, however, the Cuban leader would once again be portrayed on the front page of the *Times* in his image as a Robin Hood defender of the poor when his delegation denounced the refusals by city hotels to provide it with accommodations. When the Shelburne at Lexington and Thirty-Seventh finally offered rooms to the group, the hotel demanded a steep deposit in cash, and the delegation decided to move to the Theresa Hotel in Harlem.[43] Nonetheless, the photo on the front page of the *Times* on September 21, 1960, showing Nikita Khrushchev and Castro embracing in Harlem, marked the beginning of a progressive displacement of Castro's figure from the paper's pages.[44] In the *Times*' coverage of the UN General Assembly sessions of that year, Third World leaders such as Egypt's Gamal Abdel Nasser and Ghana's Kwane Krumah took on greater relevance due to their greater openness toward diplomatic dialogue with both the Soviet Union and the United States (both Nasser and Krumah met with Eisenhower during this time) and for their invitation to Cuba to join the Non-Aligned Movement.[45]

Fidel and Nikita's mutual praises did not go unnoticed by New York's liberal press. During the television debates between Kennedy and Nixon in September and October, the alliance of the Cubans and the Soviets was now taken for granted. Both candidates agreed that the island should be economically and politically blockaded to prevent Cuba's pro-Soviet turn, but Kennedy was the more emphatic supporter of accompanying this punitive strategy with an aggressive policy of support for social development in Latin America and multilateral military cooperation in the region.[46] His declarations prefaced the creation of the Alliance for Progress, although this initiative also took shape under the threat of plans for destabilizing the Cuban government that had been devised by the CIA at the end of the Eisenhower administration and later approved by Kennedy. The threat would be confirmed in April 1961 with the Bay of Pigs invasion.[47]

Yet in November 1960, already prior to that failed invasion, perceptions of the Cuban revolutionary government by New York's liberal press had already severely deteriorated, particularly at the *Times*. In one of its first openly critical articles, the *Times* seconded the Department of State's protests against Cuba's sentencing and execution of three young Americans (Anthony Zarba, Robert O. Fuller, and A. D. Thompson), denouncing the "Roman circus

"All the News That's Fit to Print"

The New York Times.

LATE CITY EDITION

VOL. CX..No. 37,705. NEW YORK, TUESDAY, APRIL 18, 1961. FIVE CENTS

ANTI-CASTRO UNITS LAND IN CUBA; REPORT FIGHTING AT BEACHHEAD; RUSK SAYS U. S. WON'T INTERVENE

SUPREME COURT UPHOLDS UNIONS AGAINST N. L. R. B.

It Upsets Board's Ruling That Contracts Illegally Force Membership

MAILERS' PACTS BACKED

New York Printers' Local and California Teamsters Win on Agreements

By ANTHONY LEWIS

U. S. Finds Soviet's Reply On Laos Is Unsatisfactory

Rusk Says Note Is Unclear on Timing and Verification of Cease-Fire—Calls Issue 'Very Critical'

By E. W. KENWORTHY

GIZENGA OFFICERS ACCEPT MOBUTU AS ARMY'S CHIEF

Kasavubu Agrees to Reform Troops—Signs Accord on Congo-U.N. Cooperation

By HENRY TANNER

PREMIER DEFIANT

Says His Troops Battle Heroically to Repel Attacking Force

By TAD SZULC

CARIBBEAN STRIFE: Rebel forces attacking Cuba landed in Las Villas Province in the area of Bahía de Cochinos (1, and A on the inset map). Other anti-Castro landings were said to have taken place in area of Santiago de Cuba (2) and in Pinar del Río (3).

HIGH COURT VOIDS CAFE'S NEGRO BAN

Holds Private Restaurant on State Land in Delaware Cannot Refuse Service

HAUSNER ATTACKS EICHMANN'S PLEA

Israeli Prosecutor Details His Charges After Ex-Nazi Says He Is Not Guilty

By HOMER BIGART

ROA CHARGES U.S. ARMED INVADERS

Tells U.N. That C.I.A. Aided Attacks—'Aggression' Is Denied by Stevenson

By THOMAS J. HAMILTON

Rusk Declares Sympathy Of Nation for Castro Foes

By JAMES RESTON

MOSCOW BLAMES U. S. FOR ATTACK

Izvestia Asserts 'American Hirelings' Invade Cuba—Khrushchev Confers

By SEYMOUR TOPPING

CHANTING CUBANS BACK CASTRO HERE

1,000 in Midtown March Dispersed by Police

Eisenhowers Are Welcomed Home to Pennsylvania

General and Mrs. Eisenhower in Harrisburg with Gov. David L. Lawrence of Pennsylvania

Jersey Votes Today In Primary Election

By GEORGE CABLE WRIGHT

Walker Is Relieved of Command While Army Checks Birch Ties

NEWS INDEX

The New York Times THE COMPLETE FRONT PAGES

Public opinion in New York presented the Bay of Pigs invasion as a fiasco for the Kennedy administration.

atmosphere" and "inhuman conduct" of the Cuban legal proceedings.[48] These executions and constant news of the revolutionary regime's attempts to create guerrilla movements in various Latin American nations were two of the main factors that led to an increase of critical reporting on Havana in the pages of the *Times*.

In the months prior to the Bay of Pigs invasion, the Cuban government voices being heard in New York were not those of Castro, Guevara, or other revolutionary commanders but of long-standing communists who had been promoted to high positions in the regime, such as President Osvaldo Dorticós or the head of the National Institute of Agrarian Reform, Carlos Rafael Rodríguez. Max Frankel interviewed both of these officials at the end of November 1960 and their remarks for the first time circulated the idea that a process of "socialist transition" was occurring on the island.[49] The Cuban apparatchiks—Communist Party bureaucrats—were entering the scene, obscuring or eclipsing the revolutionary hipsters, and the *Times* interpreted this as a battle between communists and liberals for the mind of Castro.

The idea of a Soviet Cuba had become sufficiently established such that by April 1961 the Bay of Pigs "disaster"—as the liberal press in New York would refer to it—did not greatly alter perceptions of the Cuban government's ideological turn toward communism. Tad Szulc, out of Miami, wrote exhaustive coverage of the invasion and its aftermath, highlighting criticisms of the CIA's planning, of President Kennedy's decision to authorize the invasion, and of the protection being provided by the US government for the Cuban defector pilots.[50] Szulc's articles, like those of Matthews before him, were balanced with dispatches from Ruby Hart Phillips and Peter Kihss, whose reporting stance was closer to that of Joseph Newman of the *New York Herald Tribune* in their defense of the leaders of the Cuban Revolutionary Council in exile (José Miró Cardona, Manuel Antonio de Varona, Justo Carrillo, Manuel Ray, Manuel Artime, and others) and the members of the 2506 Brigade invasion force.

It is interesting to note that it was precisely the latter media stance, that of greater identification with Cuban opposition and exile groups, that the Kennedy administration had privileged in its decision to proceed with the Bay of Pigs invasion. Harvard historian and Kennedy advisor Arthur M. Schlesinger Jr. drew on Newman's articles in writing *The White Paper*, a lengthy account, part political report and part historical essay, on policies toward Cuba and the invasion's prospects of success.[51] Schlesinger's document, which was later included in his book *A Thousand Days* (1965), served at the time to guide the Kennedy administration in confronting the wave of criticism unleashed by the invasion's failure.

In its editorials on the Bay of Pigs invasion, the *Times* subscribed to Schlesinger's ideas but also carefully echoed critics of the administration, such as Matthews and Szulc. For example, the April 18 editorial, "Landing in Cuba," acknowledged that the Cuban Revolution had been a "social revolution" like its French or Mexican predecessors, resulting from growing popular pressure favoring social justice in Latin America.[52] Echoing the language of Kennedy's new Alliance for Progress, the editorial admitted that the Cuban Revolution "has had repercussions all over Latin America and a widespread, popular and intellectual appeal because of its social reforms and its original ideal and aspirations."[53] The *Times*, however, covered up US and CIA involvement in the invasion, instead characterizing it as a spontaneous and autonomous operation carried out by Cuban exiles.

Once Szulc's articles had revealed both "the disaster" (as he referred to it) and the tremendous ineffectiveness of the Kennedy administration's handling of the matter, the *Times*' second editorial on the Bay of Pigs crisis, published on April 20, was limited to expressing support for the Alliance for Progress and warning of the tightening of Cuban-Soviet ties that would ensue from the failed invasion. The Cold War had now been fully established in the Caribbean, the editorial recognized, arguing that such a challenge had to be confronted with imagination by the US government.[54] The editors of the *Times* and its commentators, such as Arthur Krock, were conscious of the increased public criticism of the Kennedy administration, which followed the Cuban armed forces' deflection of the invaders, and they sought to handle the matter by stressing that the White House had at least not authorized US air and naval support for the rebel exiles.[55] This factor, which the anticommunist

Right viewed as proof of Kennedy's weakness, was seen by New York liberals as a sign of his wisdom.

The split within the *Times* between supporters and detractors of Kennedy's authorization for the Bay of Pigs invasion plan is evident from a comparison between Matthews's *The Cuban Story* (1961) and Szulc's *The Cuban Invasion: The Chronicle of a Disaster* (1962), on the one hand, and Phillips's *The Cuban Dilemma* (1962), on the other. These three books condense much of the public debate over the Cuban Revolution that took place among New York liberals at the beginning of the 1960s. Whereas Phillips backed the Kennedy administration's support for the invasion, Matthews and Szulc questioned that support.[56] Matthews's and Szulc's opposition to Washington's hostility toward Cuban socialism had its nuances, however: whereas Matthews argued persistently that it was this US hostility that had tipped Castro toward communism, Szulc ascribed some responsibility for the conflict to the Cuban leadership itself.

When the Cuban Missile Crisis broke out in October 1962 with the discovery that Soviet missiles had been set up on the island, these debate positions would be quickly replaced by a recasting of the Cuban problem within the logic of the Cold War. The final week of October 1962 marked perhaps the lowest point for Castro's image in the New York press since the triumph of the revolution. This time, articles by Juan de Onis, Paul Kennedy, Kathleen Teltsch, James Reston, Arthur Krock, and Szulc himself would be resolutely adverse to the Cuban government, which these writers presented for the first time as a threat to the real security of the United States.[57] The heroism of Kennedy in liberal public opinion now seemed inversely proportional to the villainy of Castro, who had come to be viewed as even less trustworthy than Khrushchev, since he opposed any diplomatic solution to the crisis, boycotted UN measures, and was even rejected by Latin American leftist governments such as that of João Goulart in Brazil. The distancing between Cuba and Latin America during the missile crisis was one of the recurring themes in the *New York Times* during the week in question.

Starting with the missile crisis, the figure of Castro and the very image of the Cuban Revolution lost considerable symbolic capital in New York. Rejection of Washington's hostility toward Havana did not disappear in New York public opinion, but that rejection was now accompanied by an increased leftist opposition to the revolution's shift toward communism. Curiously, this opposition, expressed from the most radical and independent sectors of New York, was reinforced starting in 1962 with the distancing between Havana and Moscow that occurred following the Kennedy-Khrushchev Pact. This would result in a paradoxical situation: as the apparatchiks monopolized the attention of the liberal press, the hipsters, especially Guevara, once again became key referents for the nascent New Left.

THE HOUR OF THE APPARATCHIKS

A smaller scandal opened within the larger scandal of the Bay of Pigs crisis when it was revealed that the *New York Times*, under pressure from the Kennedy administration, had censored a story by Tad Szulc on the CIA's training and preparation of the Cuban exile fighters—the members of Brigade 2506—in Guatemala. As Gay Talese suggests, President Kennedy himself came to regret the act of censorship, since press revelations about the invasion planned under his predecessor's administration might have helped abort the operation.[58] As recounted by press historians such as Michael Schudson and Richard F. Sheperd, the story of the suppression of Szulc's report demonstrates the Kennedy administration's ambivalence in carrying out the invasion and offers a clearer understanding of how the *Times* and other liberal media in New York came to support the effort to reinstate the notion of the "revolution betrayed" championed by the first Cuban exile group.[59]

Anger toward Washington erupted when reports of the invasion's failure began to emerge. The words "disaster," "mistake," "wrong," "blunder," "fiasco," and "debacle" resounded in nearly every publication in the United States, including *Time* magazine, *Newsweek*, the *New Yorker*, the *New Republic*, and even *Dissent*, where a young Michael Walzer, from the Left, predicted an encroachment of communist totalitarianism on the island and throughout Latin America as a result of the CIA's unfortunate intervention in support of the Cuban exile invaders.[60] Anger against the White House came from both the Right and the Left. The anticommunist Right was outraged that Kennedy had not sent US air and naval forces to support the offensive, and the liberal and socialist Left protested the administration's training and support for the 2506 Brigade.

The impact of the disaster was felt intensely by the Kennedy administration and its advisers. That impact explains the care with which the president and his team would manage the missile crisis a year and a half later, in their attempt to undo the damage from the earlier defeat. The liberal press of New York supported the Kennedy administration's management of the missile crisis in October 1962, insofar as this time the story was not about US imperial aggression against a small Caribbean island but about the threat that Soviet nuclear power posed, from its Cuban enclave, for the lives of Americans. A pair of cartoons featured in the *Times* on Sunday, October 28, 1962, effectively captures this inversion of roles. In the first frame, a coarse and paunchy Castro surveys the Caribbean with a telescope as Soviet military officers stand at his back. In the second, a handsome young Kennedy chops down a grove of coconut palms shaped like Russian missiles.[61]

Following the missile crisis, despite the erosion of Havana's image in the New York press, and the increase of negative attention that the press began to devote to the island's apparatchiks around the same time, the figure of the hipster survived in the city's radical circles. This was not so much the case in publications like *Dissent*, where Daniel M. Friedenberg and Michael Walzer had insisted that the Cuban question was more interesting as a chapter of the Cold War and as a pretext for reducing the imperialist elements of US foreign policy, but it was evident in publications such as the *Village Voice*, where, between 1963 and 1968, New Left writers and journalists publicized and exploited the rift between Moscow and Havana following the Kennedy-Khrushchev Pact.

It is useful to first describe how *Dissent* and the *Village Voice* positioned themselves with regard to the Cuban Revolution at the beginning of the 1960s in order to then account for the subsequent ideological divergence between these two groups of the New York intellectual Left. Starting in the summer of 1960, Friedenberg had warned that the political radicalization of the Cuban revolutionary government was leading to a mode of authoritarianism, although he saw this radicalization as an understandable movement forward for a Cuban leadership preparing itself to face US repudiation.[62] Friedenberg's—and *Dissent*'s—criticism of Washington's hostility toward the revolution was clear, but his characterization of Havana's ideological turn was negative:

> Xenophobia, hate campaigns, the retreat into phantasy fears, the dependence on communist support, the swollen Army, the rigid control of radio and press: all these frightening symptoms of dictatorship are devices to hold the sympathy and loyalty of the Cuban people against the tremendous pressures exerted from Washington.[63]

After the Bay of Pigs debacle, Michael Walzer would further clarify *Dissent*'s position toward Cuba. The invasion's failure had demonstrated the equivocation of US policy toward the island and Latin America in general. The invasion's error, according to Walzer, had not been that of a "technical" miscalculation on the part of the military or by CIA experts and agents. Rather, the error was a political one, committed as a consequence of the colonialist framework from which the United States had historically conducted its relations with Latin America.[64] It was the Monroist tradition, which imagined Latin America as a zone of US influence equivalent to the zone of influence that Asia and Africa had historically served for Europe, that had culminated in the fiasco of the Bay of Pigs. Furthermore, the failed invasion had demonstrated the depth of what Walzer called the crisis of "radicalism" in the United States. The era of Roosevelt and Wallace's New Deal—when the United States had refrained from punishing Mexico for Cárdenas's nationalizing of petroleum—now seemed a distant past.[65]

Walzer strongly condemned the Bay of Pigs invasion, identifying it with a pernicious line of foreign policy that had been brought to light a few years earlier with the CIA-led coup against Guatemalan president Jacobo Arbenz in 1954. The United States, he insisted, should abandon all of its CIA-orchestrated initiatives for destabilizing revolutionary governments in Latin America and reassess the effect of such initiatives in the past. In Walzer's view, deep reforms in Washington's Latin American diplomacy were necessary because by demonstrating rigorous respect for the sovereignty of the nations to the south, the United States could generate a more favorable climate for political democratization and for a rejection of authoritarian and totalitarian models such as Soviet communism.

Walzer agreed with Theodore Draper that Cuba's revolutionary leadership had chosen a totalitarian path, but he did not subscribe to the thesis of the "revolution betrayed," insofar as the question of whether Castro had been or had not been a communist in 1959 seemed irrelevant to him.[66] In his view, those who argued that Castro had been a communist, such as former US ambassador to Cuba E. T. Smith, or those who argued that he had not, such as journalist Herbert L. Matthews, were equally erroneous in their analyses. As he asserted, Cuba's path toward "dictatorship"—a term he did not hesitate to use—was associated with the need for a "romantic bourgeois" leader such as Castro (rather than a "liberal bourgeois") in order to gain the loyalty of popular rural and urban sectors that resented the Cuban political experience prior to 1959 and particularly the United States' imperial role in that experience.[67]

Walzer was not unaware that the Kennedy administration's early policies toward Cuba had been designed by the Eisenhower administration, and he had not given up hope that Kennedy would change direction. The good relations that the Democratic president had established with the leftist government of João Goulart of Brazil demonstrated a will to progress toward a climate of respect with leaders and nationalist parties in Latin America.[68] Nonetheless, Walzer's, and *Dissent*'s, concrete recommendations for the White House and the Department of State, although valid as intellectual positioning, took on an illusory or utopic cast when they called for the United States to not only abandon all hostility toward Cuban socialism but to also hold talks with revolutionary exiles and social democrats such as Manuel Ray and to request Brazil's mediation in reestablishing US diplomatic relations with Cuba. Walzer's *Dissent* piece also called for public criticism of the Cuban government's

"All the News That's Fit to Print"

The New York Times.

LATE CITY EDITION

VOL. CXII..No. 38,258. NEW YORK, TUESDAY, OCTOBER 23, 1962. FIVE CENTS

U.S. IMPOSES ARMS BLOCKADE ON CUBA ON FINDING OFFENSIVE-MISSILE SITES; KENNEDY READY FOR SOVIET SHOWDOWN

U. S. JUDGES GIVEN POWER TO REQUIRE VOTE FOR NEGROES

High Court Upholds Order Forcing the Registration of 54 in Alabama County

Chinese Open New Front; Use Tanks Against Indians

Nehru Warns of Peril to Independence —Reds Attack Near Burmese Border and Press Two Other Drives

SHIPS MUST STOP

Other Action Planned If Big Rockets Are Not Dismantled

By JAMES RESTON

ANNOUNCES HIS ACTION: President Kennedy speaking to the nation last night on radio and television. He told of moves to keep offensive equipment away from Cuba.

PRESIDENT GRAVE

Asserts Russians Lied and Put Hemisphere in Great Danger

By ANTHONY LEWIS

U.S. Bids U.N. Bar China; Denounces Attack on India

By SAM POPE BREWER

TRAFFIC DELAYED AT BERLIN BORDER

Reds Start Intensive Check of Civilian Trucks an Hour Before Kennedy Speech

By SYDNEY GRUSON

Moscow Says U.S. Holds 'Armed Fist' Over Cuba

By SEYMOUR TOPPING

BIG FORCE MASSES TO BLOCKADE CUBA

Armada Is Under Orders to Open Fire if Necessary—All Troops Are Alerted

By JACK RAYMOND

U. S. SAID TO EASE KATANGA POLICY

Reported Willing to Put Off Any Economic Sanctions —Congolese Disturbed

By LLOYD GARRISON

102 SAVED AT SEA AS PLANE DITCHES

Rescue Is Made off Alaska Minutes After Accident

Canada Asks Inspection of Cuba; Britain Supporting Quarantine

Stocks Plunge Early On Crisis, but Rally

By RICHARD RUTTER

All Military Forces Mobilized by Castro

KENNEDY CANCELS CAMPAIGN TALKS

He and Johnson Take Step to Concentrate on Crisis

By CABELL PHILLIPS

NEWS INDEX

During the Cuban Missile Crisis in October 1962, the Cuban government appeared as a threat to US security.

"suppression of liberties," such as "its attack upon trade union democracy, and its wholesale imprisonment of political opponents."[69]

Interestingly, Walzer felt that his calls for a reform of US foreign policy toward Cuba and Latin America was part of the necessary rescue of what he called "democratic radicalism" in the United States.[70] The notion of "radicalism" or "radicals" in US political culture had some connections with the proposal for a "New Left," which was being launched by C. Wright Mills during this period, but it also bore some important differences from that proposal. During this time, Walzer was living in Princeton and working on his project on the Calvinist and Puritan Reformation in seventeenth-century Great Britain and France, which he understood as the "emergence of modern political radicalism."[71] Under the guidance of his professors, Carl J. Friedrich, Louis Hartz, Barrington Moore, and Paul Sigmund, Walzer had come to reformulate a notion of "radicalism" that owed more to Max Weber than to Karl Marx.

Weber was a constant presence in Walzer's *The Revolution of the Saints* (1965), given that the topic stemmed directly from *The Protestant Ethic and the Spirit of Capitalism* (1904). Marx, on the other hand, was cited only once in Walzer's book, in a passage arguing that the Marxist interpretation of beggary or vagabondage, as negations of "necessary discipline to the salary system," was valid yet "insufficient."[72] Walzer argued for the importance of considering the role of religion—as Weber had done—in the analysis of the formation of modern society. This theoretical preference separated Walzer from Mills, who advocated a stronger synthesis of Marx and Weber. Walzer's valorization of the Reformation and the Enlightenment as cultural bridges toward the French and American Revolutions at the end of the eighteenth century, and his notion of these revolutionary movements as moments of "radicalism," placed him in an ideological and political position close to leftist liberalism.[73]

It could be argued that it was this theoretical, and at the same time ideological, difference that separated Mills's and Walzer's takes on Cuban socialism. Walzer debated with Herbert L. Matthews and Theodore Draper, but not with Mills, whose views on communism he considered acritical. In *Dissent*, however, although Walzer repudiated McCarthyism, he also questioned the Stalinist legacy and the real socialisms of Eastern Europe. The magazine's expressions of affinity with democratic socialism and social democracy between 1960 and 1980, articulated from a leftist liberal stance, would serve as proof of this critical position, which prevented Walzer from considering the totalitarian elements of the Cuban political system.

In opposition to Soviet or pro-Soviet Marxist-Leninism, Walzer sought to recuperate the early European Protestants' assault on the "traditional political world."[74] It should not be forgotten that he did so, furthermore, as a Jew and without losing sight of the persecutions and purges of religious intolerance that had marked the history of Puritanism and Judaism.[75] Throughout his book it is not hard to note the work's many parabolic or indirect allusions to the purges and persecutions suffered by dissidents in the nations of the communist bloc, and especially the Soviet Union. The cases of writers who were repressed, censored, or stigmatized by Soviet power, such as Osip Mandelstam, Boris Pasternak, Anna Akhmatova, or Aleksandr Solzhenitsyn, were central to the editorial policies of *Dissent.*

The communist transition in Cuba was also met with a critical reading by the radical bohemian community, often articulated in the *Village Voice*, a publication that also focused on dissent in Eastern Europe, particularly after the Soviet invasion of Hungary in 1956. When the Cuban Revolution triumphed in January 1959, the *Voice* was absorbed in the promotion of "beat politics," starting with its support for the socialist candidacy for Congress of intellectual David McReynolds, editor of *Liberation* magazine.[76] In a series of articles he wrote for the *Voice*, often supported with quotes from Jean Paul Sartre and Norman Mailer, McReynolds argued for a beat political movement inspired by marijuana decriminalization, free love, ecology, jazz, and Buddhism. At the end of 1959, McReynolds even proposed a "hipster general strike" to be led by US university students.

The young beats pushed for a moral transformation of politics in the United States that would involve feminism, antiracism, environmentalism, and, especially, peace and disarmament.[77] Some of the *Voice* editorial writers called themselves "socialists," as McReynolds did, and others referred to themselves as "liberals," as *Dissent* writers did, but they all joined in defending the beat and hipster youth movement against the conservative generation that had preceded it.[78] During the presidential campaign of 1960 and the early months of the new administration, the *Voice* backed Kennedy with reservations by praising historian Arthur M. Schlesinger's support for Kennedy, expressing open criticisms of Nixon, and printing ambivalent articles such as Norman Mailer's well-known "Open Poem to John Fitzgerald Kennedy."[79]

The *Voice*'s coverage of Cuba was relatively light at the end of the 1950s, with the Congo and Vietnam garnering a greater share of its international attention. The situation changed starting with the Bay of Pigs invasion, which the paper joined the rest of the New York press in condemning. The *Voice*'s Cuban coverage grew particularly during the missile crisis, an event that precipitated an interesting debate over Cuban socialism and the pacifist movement. The *Village Voice* projected itself as an alternative to the country's dominant liberal media, particularly the *New York Times*, which it viewed as undergoing a "soft decay" (Nat Hentoff's words), and the *Times*' support for Castro between 1957 and 1959 deflected whatever interest in Cuba the *Voice* would otherwise have manifested.[80]

In any event, the *Voice*'s ideological orientation, which was close to David McReynolds and Michael Harrington's "democratic socialism" and shared their opposition to "the military oriented, bureaucratic systems of Russia and United States," left little margin for applauding Cuban communism and the island's alliance with the USSR.[81] Between April 1961 and October 1962, when the debate over Cuba intensified in New York, the *Voice* wavered between supporting the position of C. Wright Mills in *Listen, Yankee* (1960) (one that McReynolds had anticipated in *Liberation*) and that of Tad Szulc in *The Cuban Invasion* (1962). In a review of various books on Cuba that had appeared in 1962, Martin Kenner drew on Sweezy and Huberman's *Cuba: Anatomy of a Revolution* (1960) in questioning Theodore Draper's liberal focus in *Castro's*

Revolution: Myths and Realities. In Kenner's view, Draper had underestimated the revolution's manifestations in the popular sector—and particularly in Cuba's rural regions, as evidenced by the agrarian reform program and literacy campaign—and had focused too much on Castro's ideological turn.[82] Kenner was more sympathetic toward Tad Szulc's book on the "debacle" of the Bay of Pigs, since the *Times* journalist had demonstrated the US government's incapacity to comprehend the Cuban Revolution.[83]

During the Cuban Missile Crisis of October 1962, the *Village Voice*'s views on Cuba became more complex. As the paper held a literary festival commemorating iconic works, such as Burroughs's *Naked Lunch* and Kerouac's *Big Sur*, the debate over the missile crisis was opening critical flanks in leftist thought. In her incisive reports from the UN headquarters in New York, Stephanie Gervis called for a diplomatic resolution to the conflict.[84] The *Voice*'s pacifism became more nuanced during this period, and even a piece so clearly opposed to US Cuban policy as Norman Mailer's celebrated "An Open Letter to JFK" (1962)—a new version of the message sent to Kennedy and Castro following the Bay of Pigs invasion in April 1961—openly objected to the Castro government's decision to "arm itself with Russia."[85]

For the pacifist movement on the radical left, the lessons of October 1962 were ambivalent. A polemical exchange between Nathan Glazer and Nat Hentoff in the *Village Voice* at the end of December of that year sought to break those lessons down. While Glazer acknowledged Kennedy's success in managing the missile crisis, Hentoff put the victory into question and warned of the precarious nature of the diplomatic accord between Washington and Moscow, and the difficulties for advancing toward a real disarmament treaty.[86] For radical bohemians in New York, one of the clearest symbolic effects of the results of October 1962 was that the Cuban topic had been reduced to one more point in the agenda "between Stevenson and Zorin" and had lost its force as a referent for mobilization and solidarity among the New Left itself.[87] The hour of the apparatchiks had arrived, and much of the debate over Cuba in New York had receded into discussions within American communist circles and the Soviet bloc's networks in the city.

Relations with the island therefore took on greater complexity, as bohemian radicals systematically rejected Soviet cultural policies, particularly the persecution of artistic vanguards in the nations of Eastern Europe.[88] The *Voice*'s support for the civil rights and Vietnam peace movements was not without kinship with these critical viewpoints. In articles treating the radical question, David McReynolds appealed to a class argument with Trotskyite resonances, which was uncomfortable to both black nationalist and Cuban integrationist perspectives; and Jack Newfield, after defining the extreme Left as a locus of confrontation between liberal and Marxist orthodoxies, pointed out that one of the most polemical attributes of black beat writer LeRoi Jones was his "support for Fidel Castro."[89]

Proof of the difficulty of a mutual accommodation between New York pacifism and Cuban socialism were the criticisms levied by some of these beat and hipster activists against the Vietcong and Vietnamese communism. For David McReynolds, for example, Vietnam was "the American Hungary," a formula that implied a critical allusion to the role of the USSR in Eastern Europe.[90] According to McReynolds, the United States urgently needed to withdraw from the Vietnamese civil war and put an end to the napalm bombings of civilian villages that were devastating the southern part of the country. However, the socialist politician did not hesitate to criticize the leaders of South Vietnam for adopting the communist model. The terms McReynolds employed in this regard—"guilt" and "innocence"—were inadmissible for the Cuban leadership:

> The Vietcong is not innocent, and let me record that here. I hold no brief for the terror used by the Vietcong or for the kind of repressive regime I think they will establish when they take over the cities. But all the terror of the Vietcong is as nothing when held against the terror the Americans have brought to South Vietnam.[91]

By the middle of the decade, as US aggression in Vietnam became ever more evident, these types of reflections lost their intensity and frequency in radical opinion. The New York perception of a Sovietized Cuba after the missile crisis did not always take note of the growing tensions between Havana and Moscow up to 1968. This loss of focus, however, resulted in great visibility for figures such as Guevara, who by this time was questioning the real socialisms of Eastern Europe and the Latin American communist parties and instead focusing his attention on the method of rural guerrilla resistance.

Guevara met with a group of columnists and editors of the *Village Voice* during his December 1964 trip to New York (the occasion of his fiery speech to the UN's Nineteenth General Assembly). As narrated three years later by Stephanie Harrington, the group included Harrington herself (then Stephanie Gervis), socialist intellectual and politician Michael Harrington (whom Stephanie would later marry), and Nat Hentoff. The *Voice* collaborators had been invited to a dinner in "Che's" honor hosted by members of Manhattan's high society in the residence of Bobo Rockefeller. Surrounded by figures from New York's liberal print, radio, and television media, such as Lisa Howard, who had traveled to the island the previous year to interview Castro for CBS; Laura Berquist of *Look* magazine, who presented Guevara to the dinner guests; and other figures, including I. F. Stone, Jack Gelber, and Lucy Jarvis, Guevara explained to his young beat and hipster audience that conditions for armed struggle against capitalism had not been created in the United States: "Guevara laughed, and gently explained that the situation here was a little different and he didn't think metropolitan America was a setting in which such tactics could succeed."[92]

The Argentine guerrilla's strange presence in a bourgeois, imperialist New York town house was only compounded by the certainty that repairing US-Cuban relations, thought possible during that winter of 1964, had once again dissipated as a possibility. In her deeply felt account, written just days after Che's death in Bolivia three years later, Harrington describes the atmosphere of the party—in which young magnates mingled with young socialists—as "unreal," an unreality that only seemed confirmed by the difficult events three years later in the Bolivian jungle.[93] It is perhaps unsurprising that Harrington concludes the account invoking the death of Emiliano Zapata and the birth of the myth of the

Mexican Revolution as portrayed by actor Marlon Brando and director Elia Kazan in the Hollywood film *Viva Zapata!* With his death in Bolivia, Che Guevara had ensured his entry into the US popular cultural imaginary.

Guevara became a regular presence in the *Village Voice* between 1967 and 1968. Marlene Nadle traveled to Bolivia to cover the trial against Régis Debray, a figure who constituted one of the doctrinal referents of the guerrilla movement for the New Left. In her coverage, published in October 1967, Nadle did not hesitate to link the Latin American revolutionary epic to hippie pacifism in the United States.[94] As she had asserted in the *Voice* several months earlier, there was no contradiction between guerrilla support for Guevara in Bolivia and the call to counter "the power of politics" with "the power of flowers" in New York or San Francisco.[95] Nadle combined the figures of Guevara and Martin Luther King Jr. in a tense articulation, reading them as part of the same "charismatic movement" in transamerican politics.[96] As seen in another *Voice* story published in the same month as Nadle's coverage of Guevara's death, the Bolivian martyrs had their equivalents in bohemian US hippies murdered in San Francisco or New York, such as James Leroy ("Groovy") Hutchinson, killed on October 12.[97]

In the wake of Guevara's death, the clash of viewpoints between the *Village Voice* and the *New York Times* once again became evident. Unlike the *Voice*, the *Times* organized its coverage of Guevara's death around the idea of the revolution's failure. The paper's placement of the Associated Press photo of Guevara's corpse on the front page on October 11, 1967; its articles by Juan de Onis and Paul Hoffman; and above all, the erroneous editorial it featured on Columbus Day, "Guevara: Man and Myth," all reinforced the view, refuted by history, that what had perished in Bolivia was a leader and an ideology.[98] Even so, the *Times* seemed to contribute to the analogy between hippies and Latin American revolutionaries by publishing stories by John Kifner from the East Village, which cast the hippies as an urban civil guerrilla movement. Racial tensions between hippies and Hispanics or between hippies and blacks could be seen as analogous to clashes between Cuban revolutionaries and guerrilla fighters in Bolivia.[99]

These heroic parallels constructed within the New Left also did not exclude notes of estrangement with Cuban socialism, such as Ginsburg, Burroughs, and Corso's open defense of the consumption of LSD in the West Village. The author of *The Other America: Poverty in the United States* (1962), Michael Harrington, condemned US military intervention in Guatemala, Cuba, and Vietnam, but his "democratic socialism" obliged him to object to totalitarian juridical order in countries like the Soviet Union and China. Just as had occurred at the beginning of the decade with JFK, these democratic socialists criticized the presidential campaign of Robert Kennedy, but they supported him in order to gain his support for the struggle for an end to the war in Vietnam, which was finally achieved in early 1968.[100]

The Cuban Revolution is a narrative plot that was often imperceptible or hidden in the great commotions of the 1960s: the assassinations of the two Kennedys, Malcolm X, and Martin Luther King Jr., and the war in Vietnam. But this plot at times broke through unexpectedly in the pages of the *Village Voice*, such as on the front page of one of the first issues of May 1967, which reported on the Worker's Day parade on Fifth Avenue. One of the main feature photos shows a black girl dressed like a Cuban militia figure with a man at her side holding a sign with Castro's portrait and bearing the following message: "I got my job through *The New York Times*. Muchas gracias, Fidel Castro."[101]

For a Left still heavily marked by its rejection of the Soviet Union's 1956 invasion of Hungary, the arrival of Soviet tanks in Prague in the summer of 1968 only accentuated opposition to the Soviet model. Castro's support for the repression of the "Czech Spring" was received with a mixture of coldness and anger in New York's liberal press and among the city's bohemian radicals. One of the reporters who covered the invasion of Prague was Tad Szulc, the New York veteran of the Cuban debate and himself a Polish immigrant. Szulc could not ignore Castro's support for the Soviets or the latter's attacks on the "revisionism" of Alexander Dubček and other Czech leaders, and he later took due note of these ideological gestures in the biography he devoted to the Cuban leader.[102]

As Tad Szulc and James Reston were writing their pieces for the *Times* about the Soviet repression of "liberal communists," and recalling the impact of the Soviet invasion of Hungary on the American Left, the *Village Voice* used the drama in Czechoslovakia to reiterate its criticism of US involvement in Vietnam. As Leticia Kent and David McReynolds argued, the occupation of Prague was just as reprehensible as the US war against the Southeast Asian nation, and it was precisely the Vietnam War critics who possessed the greatest moral authority for questioning the Kremlin's imperialism.[103] In this atmosphere of double discontentment, it was logical that news of Castro's announcement of his support for the Soviet invasion of Czechoslovakian territory, in a speech delivered on August 23, 1968, would be met with cold disapproval in New York. For a journalist like Tad Szulc, who had been involved in both the Carribean and Eastern Bloc plots, the significance of Havana's support for Moscow could not be hidden: the apparatchiks had come to stay.

2

NAMING THE HURRICANE

★

WRITING FROM A HAVANA HOTEL ROOM IN OCTOBER 1959, Waldo Frank (1889–1967) addressed a letter to Castro thanking him for the latter's gift to him of a special wooden tobacco box bearing a classic label. The American writer reported that he was using the box to hold his papers and that the cigars "would delight his friends" upon his return to New York. But above all, Frank expressed gratitude to Castro for the "generous and powerful new world" that the Cuban leader and his revolution were creating on the island and that the "old world needed to appreciate."[1]

At seventy years of age, with a long career of studying and writing about Latin America and having attained a certain position of moral authority among members of New York's intellectual Left, Frank perceived a singular role for himself in this task of helping the "old world" of the United States understand the political meaning of the "new world" represented by the Cuban Revolution. In his letter to Castro, he addressed the Cuban leader with the transparency of one conscious that his own place and time was different from that of his addressee and referred to himself as a "representative of a previous generation that had bequeathed" a "corrupt world" to Castro's generation.[2] In Frank's judgment, the corruption in question was not irreversible and might be combatted by appeals to a "loyal Americanism" or, what amounted to the same thing, by encouraging the United States to open itself to dialogue with events in Hispanic America, such as the Cuban Revolution. In Frank's view, the New World—a concept he traced from Christopher Columbus to Simón Bolívar—was facing a new semantic opportunity starting in January 1959:

> As a loyal American who has always interpreted the term "New World" seriously, always believing that the state of an authentic new world should be made into a reality in our hemisphere, I express my gratitude to you, and I sign up as a modest member of your team, for we share the same enemies and the same goal.[3]

For his part, Castro saw in Waldo Frank's support—as he did in the backing of other Western leftist intellectuals at that moment, such as Jean Paul Sartre or C. Wright Mills—yet another confirmation of the symbolic possibilities of the Cuban process: those possibilities could be realized not only in underdeveloped or colonial regions of Latin America, Africa, or Asia, but also in the public spheres of Europe and North America. In the closing lines of his letter, Frank communicated a flattering wish to Castro: "may you lead this new world for many years."[4] His tone was pitch-perfect. The revolutionary regime took Frank's letter quite seriously and subsequently offered him a Cuban project.

Frank's October 1959 visit to the island was his first—it also preceded the arrivals of Sartre and Mills—and had resulted from an invitation extended by Jorge Ricardo Masseti, director of the Agencia Prensa Latina, an important Havana media platform, as well as from Frank's personal friendship with Cuban novelist Alcides Iznaga, who had translated several of his works.[5] Frank was considered part of the favorable wing of the extensive network of journalists who followed the Cuban situation from the United States, which included Carleton Beals, Herbert L. Matthews, Ray Brennan, Ruby Hart Phillips, Jules Dubois, Warren Miller, Robert F. Smith, Robert M. Taber, Clifford Barnett, Karl E. Mayer, Tad Szulc, Robert Scheer, Haynes Johnson, Dudley Seers, J. P. Morray, Lee Lockwood, Lester D. Langley, Elizabeth Sutherland

Martínez, and James O'Conner. This network of journalists was connected, in turn, to an academic network of historians, economists, sociologists, and anthropologists who regularly analyzed the Cuban question and whose most notable representatives included Nathaniel Weyl, William Appleman Williams, Leo Huberman, Paul Sweezy (the latter two editors of the important socialist publication *Monthly Review*), Paul Baran, C. Wright Mills, Robin Blackburn, Maurice Zeitlin, Richard R. Fagen, Theodor Draper, and Wyatt MacGaffey. Over the course of just a few years, these two networks would produce more than fifty books on Cuba for American publishers and hundreds of reports and articles for the nation's most important newspapers and periodicals. [6]

Frank was a figure of distinction in these networks, not only due to his lengthy experience covering Hispanic American topics for US readers but also because, strictly speaking, he was neither a journalist nor an academic. In addition to being a New Yorker, Frank was a novelist and essayist, a writer of both fiction and nonfiction. As such, he was a singular and decisive agent for the task of constructing bases of moral and ideological authority in the public sphere and the intellectual field. The Cuban revolutionary government perceived this singularity and tailored its approach to Frank accordingly. At Castro's order, Frank was hired by Prime Minister of Education Armando Hart and Foreign Minister Raúl Roa to write a "portrait of Cuba" to be published by the Cuban government's Department of Cultural Relations.[7] Frank set his initial fee at $2,500, but over the course of the project's execution, he would request additional funds, in the end charging more than $5,000, as documented in a letter dated July 5, 1961, from Armando Hart to Cuban National Bank president Raúl Cepero Bonilla.[8]

Although Frank's Cuban interlocutors referred to the projected book as a "portrait" (*retrato*), this concept was linked from the beginning with that of biography, since what Armando Hart and Raúl Roa wanted—as Frank indicated at the beginning of the Spanish edition of his book—was "un libro sobre Cuba, digno de otras obras" (a book about Cuba, worthy of Frank's other works), such as *Virgin Spain: Scenes from the Spiritual Drama of a Great*

People (1926), *América Hispana* (1931), and *Birth of a World: Bolívar in Terms of His People* (1951).[9] These were the works that the Cuban revolutionaries had in mind in approaching and contracting the American writer.

Over the course of eighteen months, Frank conducted research, traveled to the island, and interviewed revolutionary leaders, all while complaining privately in his notebooks about how long the Cubans were taking to sign the final publication contract. The result of his efforts was *Cuba: Prophetic Island.* The English edition of the book was printed in 1961 by Marzani & Munsell, and not by Beacon Press, where it had originally been slated for publication. Frank had initially promised the book to Beacon but had failed to disclose his arrangement with the Cuban government. When Beacon learned of that arrangement, it severed its contract with Frank, at which point Carl Marzani, an old communist militant and veteran of the Spanish Civil War, came to the writer's rescue, offering to publish Frank's book at Marzani & Munsell, a publishing house that had received financing from Moscow, according to the testimony of KGB agent Oleg Kalugin.[10] However, Frank would never receive a concrete offer for the publication in Havana of the Spanish version of his book. Instead, in September of that year, the only Spanish edition of the work—translated by Luis Echávarri—was published in Buenos Aires by Losada Press, the same press that had previously produced four of Frank's books in Spanish: *América Hispana*, *Ustedes y nosotros*, *Pasión de Israel*, and *España virgen.*

Between Frank's completion of the manuscript in February 1961 and the printing of the American and Argentine editions at the end of that year, fifteen hundred Cuban exile invaders landed on the Bay of Pigs in an operation organized and planned by the CIA and authorized by President Kennedy. The invasion escalated tensions between the United States and Cuba, as the Caribbean nation drew ever closer to the Soviet Union. In response to these events, Frank decided to add a forward to both versions of his manuscript. These texts are fundamental for understanding the debate that the book provoked in New York. Although Frank writes in his clarifying text in the Losada edition that the book was written under the sponsorship of the Cuban government and had been slated for publication by the Cuban Department of Cultural Relations, he does not clarify why the book was subsequently published in Buenos Aires rather than in Havana. He does provide a clue, however, in noting

> I do not need to clarify that my obligation was to discover the truth, as I understood it, and to say it. Certain aspects of what I saw and thought may not please certain friends in Cuba. But they will agree that my only duty and obligation was to speak all the truth about what I found, and nothing less.[11]

In the pages that follow, I will explore Frank's encounters and disencounters with the Cuban Revolution as expressed in *Cuba: Prophetic Island*, as well as the debate that this book set off in the intellectual field of the New York Left during the 1960s. That debate runs parallel to and intersects with the polemic provoked by C. Wright Mills's *Listen, Yankee*, which was also published at the beginning of 1961. An advance selection of Mills's book was featured in *Harper's Magazine* in December 1960 and was responded to by seven letters to the editor published in February of the following year.[12] Although a few of these letters were favorable to Mills's (and Frank's) positions, including one signed by Charles O. Porter, a congressional Democrat from Oregon, and another by historian Ira B. Joralemon, an expert in Cuban copper, others were clearly opposed, including one written by a group of Cuban exiles, another by the important Cuban historian Herminio Portell Vilá, and yet another by Pan-American gymnastic champion Rafael A. Lecuona.

Despite the centrality of the Cuban question in debates within the New York Left during the sixties, it is striking that the majority of recent intellectual histories of this period have tended to sideline or exclude the argument over Cuban socialism in this context.[13] As we will see, that argument over Cuba not only opened the New York intellectual field to considering the role of the Caribbean and Latin America in the Cold War, but also strengthened the tendency to shift the debates of the New York Left toward topics such as African and Asian decolonization, the Vietnam War, civil rights, women's liberation, homophobia, machismo, and racism. And one of the "paradoxes" that could be added to the early intuitions of Ruby Hart Phillips in her work *Cuba: Island of Paradox* (1959) is that although Havana circulated outside of Cuba as a symbol of the New Left, on the island itself—as Waldo Frank, Jean Paul Sartre, or Allen Ginsberg make clear—the discourses and practices of the New Left were viewed negatively and even repressed.

PORTRAIT AND BIOGRAPHY

Cuba: Prophetic Island (1961) could be categorized in the tradition of "politically commissioned books." In the Latin American context, that tradition would include works such as *Brasil: País del futuro* (1942), written by Stefan Zweig for the government of Getulio Vargas; *La Catira* by Spanish Galician writer Camilo José Cela and comissioned by Venezuelan dictator Marcos Pérez Jiménez (a topic that has been explored in a study by Gustavo Guerrero); and *Biografía de una isla* (1948), written by Emil Ludwig in commemoration of what he considered Cuba's modernization under the first presidential term (and the only constitutional term) of Fulgencio Batista, which began in 1940.[14] Of course, the difference between these works and Frank's book on Cuba is that Frank's contract was never fully completed. Once again, although the writer received his payment, the book was never published in the country that commissioned it.

The comparison between Frank's book and Ludwig's *Biografía de una isla* (1948) is particularly noteworthy due to these works' shared aspiration to constitute a biography of the Cuban nation. Ludwig was a Jewish German writer and author of biographies of Bolívar, Napoleon, and Bismarck. Like Frank, he had traveled to the Soviet Union at the beginning of the 1930s and had later distanced himself from communism after the Moscow Trials. At the time of his trip to Cuba in preparation for the writing of his *Biografía*, Ludwig had become one of the most popular authors of the mid-twentieth century. He arrived in Havana in 1944, toward the end of Batista's first term of rule, invited by his friend Arístides Sosa de Quesada, Batista's minister of defense, who had previously served as mayor of Havana, head of legal services, and chief of the army's Military Culture Corps.[15]

Ludwig was impressed with the cleanness and civility of the 1944 elections, which were won by Grau San Martín. "There is true democracy in America! This has been demonstrated by the youngest republic of them all!" he exclaimed.[16] In Ludwig's perspective, the agent of this political modernization had not been the 1940 Constitution, nor the liberals or the communists (whom he viewed as engaged in a harmonious debate), nor Grau San Martín, nor Grau's opposition contender Carlos Saladrigas, but rather Fulgencio Batista himself. It was Batista—whom Ludwig compared with Mexican Benito Juárez due to his "color, factions," and humble origins—who had ensured the republican rebirth of Cuba and who was now relinquishing power and thereby setting a valuable precedent for peaceful presidential succession.[17]

Batista could in fact be read as the protagonist of Ludwig's *Biografía de una isla*, if one were to force a little the interpretation of the half-fictional, half-real character of the "indian" ("indio") or "native man [*señor nativo*] of the island," whom Ludwig encounters outside of the Presidential Palace in the company of Quesada.[18] This modern-day Hatuey, whom Ludwig invites to the Hotel Nacional, who quotes the Old Testament, Dante, Milton, and Nietzsche, and who tells him the history of Cuba, prefigures the portrait of Batista that is later drawn in the book's final pages. In short, Ludwig's vision of Cuban history was based on a Batistan cult of personality.

As noted above, the two concepts used by the Cuban revolutionary leaders in describing the book that they wanted from Frank were "biography" and "portrait." These concepts allude to the history and face of a person: what Hart, Roa, and Frank's interlocutors desired was for Frank to narrate the story of the fledgling Cuban Revolution as a recuperation of the nation's true face and deep self—a face and self that had been hidden and disfigured by three centuries of Spanish colonial subjection, half a century of American neocolonialism, and six years of unconstitutional government under Batista's second period in power. In other words, what they wanted from Frank was for him to append to Ludwig's story an auroral, pro-Castro, and anti-Batistan denouement.

That story had in fact been constructed several decades prior to Ludwig by the island's nationalist republican historiography, through the work of Rafael Martínez Ortiz, Ramiro Guerra, Emilio Roig de Leuchsenring, Fernando Portuondo, Herminio Portell Vilá, and Fernando Ortiz, all of whom were cited by Frank in his work. The historiographical account in question was also reflected in the work of numerous midcentury Cuban essayists whom Frank also read, such as liberal Jorge Mañach and communist Juan Marinello.[19] The only plot difference among the various versions of the story told by these Cuban historians and essayists prior to Ludwig and Frank was that not all of them associated the national "birth" or "rebirth" with the same government or with the same leader. But all of them had sought to give the island's biography a happy ending.

Among these historians and essayists, Fernando Ortiz is the most prominent in Frank's book. The chapter "Sugar against Tobacco" is an homage to Ortiz, manifesting Frank's sympathy for the Americanism of this Cuban anthropologist, who over the course of the first half of the twentieth century supported more than one project of intellectual and political collaboration between the United States and Cuba. Ortiz's work also helped Frank to connect the history of Caribbean slavery with slavery in the United States, to link the nineteenth-century abolitionist movements of the two contexts, and to defend Latin American racial miscegenation and civil rights equality in the United States. In a significant passage, Frank designates Ortiz's *Contrapunteo cubano del azúcar y el tabaco* (1940) as the incarnation of the Cuban national spirit:

> More than one of the American nations has produced a volume that incarnates the spirit of its people. Such is Mark Twain's *Huckleberry Finn*, the saga of a boy floating with the current of a continental river, as the immature American people has floated down with its current; such is *Os Sertaõs* of Brazil, *Martín Fierro* of Argentina—and the great playful essay of Ortiz.[20]

Following a brief review of the island's colonial history, Frank pauses to focus on José Martí, transferring to this figure the "saint of the sword" formula that Argentine writer Ricardo Rojas had applied to José de San Martín, although Frank presents Martí more as a continuation of the ideas of Simón Bolívar—or rather, of

Waldo Frank in the middle of a crowd in Havana. (University of Pennsylvania, Special Collection)

Frank's own ideas about Bolívar. [21] The narrative proceeds with a geographical and historical overview of various Cuban cities (Havana, Cienfuegos, Trinidad, Pinar del Río, Matanzas, and Santiago), which leads in turn to a summary of Cuban history in the first half of the twentieth century centered on the topic of the "betrayal" of the Martían republic by American companies and the Cuban oligarchy.[22]

Frank portrays the revolution itself as an "empowerment of Cuba by Cubans," or, what amounts to the same thing, as a recovery of lost national sovereignty.[23] Up to this point, the account coincides with what Frank's Cuban commissioners had charged him with carrying out. However, in the pages devoted to the island's present—specifically, the second and third years of the revolution and the growing conflict with the United States—*Cuba: Prophetic Island* diverges from Havana's expectations. In addition to committing several factual errors, or fantasies, such as claiming that Che Guevara was a psychiatrist who practiced psychoanalysis in

Buenos Aires or that Raúl Castro was a tall man, Frank makes certain critical observations—regarding the "methods" of the revolutionaries, Castro's leadership, and Cuban culture in general—which would certainly have displeased his patrons.[24]

Like Sartre had done in *Huracán sobre el azucar* (1960), Frank focuses on Castro's charismatic bond with both the island's population and the international community. His book starts out, in fact, with Castro's four-and-a-half-hour speech to the United Nations General Assembly on September 26, 1960, in an account that emphasizes the magnetism and "heat," the high temperature and speed, of the words—likened to gusts of wind—that the Cuban leader projected into the traditional calm sobriety of the UN forum.[25] The metaphor of the revolution as a natural phenomenon, like a hurricane or cyclone—equivalent to the Mexican Revolution's frequent depiction as an earthquake or seismic shift—was common in New York writings on Cuba in the 1960s.

But Frank did not see only virtues and advantages in Castro's personal magnetism; he also saw threats. For example, he observed in the members of the Cuban UN delegation "a sign of man's indifference for the dictatorships of Latin America, Europe, and Asia—soldiers captive to the values of the army, men in power, enchained by power" and referred to the delegation as the "little group that listens to its boss in the Assembly."[26] In Frank's view (in contrast to Sartre's), although Castro seemed to "be" the revolution when he was onstage, the Cuban leader and the revolution were not identical: he refers to Castro's identification with the massive social phenomenon that had unleashed the fall of Batista and the possibility of reconstructing the republic in Cuba as a "false simplification."[27] Furthermore, Frank considers Castro's charismatic bond with the masses "an event that has its danger" and warns that "the intimate and immediate embrace could become a necessity for Fidel, could corrupt him."[28]

Along the way, Frank makes other observations about Cuban culture that would have greatly displeased the revolutionary leadership. He comments frequently on the Cuban people's "lack of sophistication," "immaturity," and "innocence," as reflected both in the "gaudy baroque" of the island's architecture and in the very velocity of the revolutionary process.[29] He sees in that velocity an absence of gradualism in the island's recent historical process, the worst expression of which was the cry of "paredón" ("to the firing squad!") and the occurrence of "mítines relámpagos" (spontaneous political gatherings), both of which, he felt, articulated a "violence," a lack of Christian "compassion," and an "animal spirit," indicating the "horrible danger that exists under the surface of the most worthy of revolutions."[30] In Frank's view, Cuba's rebirth, as propelled by the revolutionary process, should more ideally unfold in a measured process of cultural maturation within a tradition of "Hispanic Americanism" inherited from Bolívar and Martí, and from the Mexican Revolution and the Spanish Republic.[31]

It is precisely at this point in his book, in tracing what he considers the Cuban Revolution's ideology and evaluating its role in the island's relations with the United States, that Frank introduces the ideas that the Cuban leadership would have found the least palatable. Frank quotes Castro's own claim that his revolution was

> not red but olive-green. One step ahead of both right and left. This is a *humanist* revolution, because it does not deprive man of his essence, but holds the whole man as its fundamental aim. Capitalism sacrifices the man, the Communist state by its totalitarian concept sacrifices the rights of man.[32]

Although the passage is a translation of Castro's own words, Frank's choice of a citation recalling the humanist and other-than-communist justificatory aims of Castro's revolution was not well received in Havana in February 1961—and even less so in September of that year, when the Spanish-language edition of *Cuba, isla profética* appeared in Buenos Aires.

Thus, unlike Sartre, Frank did believe, or at least wanted to believe, that the Cuban Revolution possessed an ideology (even while conceding in his private notebooks, much to his own chagrin, that the French philosopher had been right).[33] That ideology, which Frank found enshrined in the First Havana Declaration of August 1960, was nationalist and anticolonialist, was critical of the limitations of representative democracies monopolized by the hegemony of political parties, and was also opposed to the consumerism created by the most privatized versions of capitalism. However, his exposition in *Cuba: Prophetic Island* begins to warn that this ideology that had originated in the Cuban Revolution, and that was inscribed in twentieth-century Latin American leftist nationalism, was increasingly incorporating elements of the communist Left. At times, his argument adopts an accusatory tone, a warning to Castro:

> Castro has understood the inadequacies and the falsities of elections in states where the choice of candidates is rigged by a system to ensure its own continuance. But Castro must know that a mass meeting also has its limitations. He perhaps has read Gustave Le Bon's *Psychology of Crowds* or Freud's analysis of the individual's regression into the dark unconscious when he becomes part of the crowd which so readily becomes the mob. Surely he knows that under crowd pressures the individual loses his capacity to ponder, to choose, even to observe.[34]

In Frank's view, in contrast to the views of many other socialist and Marxist intellectuals of New York (such as the members of the *Monthly Review* group, for example), the border between these two versions of leftism was not only geopolitically inconvenient but was also one that should not be ideologically traversed. Like C. Wright Mills, he based his entire argument for a friendly US policy toward Cuba on this ideological definition of the island's revolutionary process. Frank had been a member of the Communist Party in the United States at the beginning of the 1930s when he made his journey to the Soviet Union. His book *Dawn in Russia: The Record of a Journey* (1932) recounts his itinerary from Leningrad to Moscow and his pilgrimage to Lenin's tomb in Red Square and concludes with a "Meditation on the Atlantic," in which he argues that the values of Marxist-Leninism were not in conflict with Western Christian civilization.[35] In 1936 he had supported the presidential candidacy of communist leader Earl R. Browder, and in the 1940s he had backed the congressional reelection campaigns of American Labor Party leader Vito Marcantonio. But starting at the end of the 1930s, after the Moscow Trials, Frank had begun to gradually distance himself from communism, severing from it in

1956 when the Soviet invasion of Hungary was added to denunciations of Stalin's crimes.

By the time the Cuban Revolution broke out in January 1959, Frank, like many New York leftist intellectuals, had repositioned himself in the US Cold War political spectrum as a socialist democrat or as a liberal progressive. Within this orientation, whose doctrinal expression can be read in the humanism of *The Rediscovery of Man: A Memoir and Methodology of Modern Life* (1957), Frank's vision of the problems in Spain and Latin America weighed heavily. He possessed extensive knowledge of these cultural contexts thanks to his constant travels in Hispanic countries between 1920 and 1950. Those travels had resulted in books, such as those read by the Cuban revolutionary leaders, in which Frank made common cause with the Mexican Revolution and the Spanish Republic, and with Lázaro Cárdenas and Rómulo Betancourt. The point of departure of Frank's Hispanic Americanism, which has been studied by Frank Ninkovich, Michael A. Ogorzaly, and Ricardo Fernández Borchardt, was a call for a noncommunist leftism in the two mid-twentieth-century Americas, which might recuperate the hemispheric dialogue initiated by early nineteenth-century republicanism.[36]

It was for this reason that the policy Frank recommended for the United States in 1960 was to hold off from punishing Castro's government militarily and economically and to instead tolerate, with patience and goodwill, the island's growing ties with the Soviet Union and the socialist field. This was the original position, as formulated in New York in April 1960, of the Fair Play for Cuba Committee, an organization Frank headed with Carleton Beals and most of whose American leftist intellectual members—such as Norman Mailer, Truman Capote, Allen Ginsberg, William Appleman Williams, or Lawrence Ferlinghetti—were not communists. It was also the idea that Frank argued in *Cuba: Prophetic Island*—a defense of good relations between Washington and Havana whose aim was to temper the radicalization of the revolutionary process and thereby avoid risking an acceleration of Cuba's integration to the Soviet bloc.

It was not surprising that in Havana Waldo Frank was soon incorporated into a diverse list—originating in the Fair Play for Cuba

Committee—of American writers considered to be "friends of the Revolution." In the October 1959 issue of *Lunes de Revolución*, whose release coincided with Frank's visit to Havana, the young Cuban poet Heberto Padilla interviewed the American writer for this important magazine. Frank used the interview as an opportunity to reaffirm his Americanist humanism and his openness to dialogue between the two Americas but also to communicate a rather critical view of American literature. In his opinion, some of the most prominent writers in the United States, such as Hemingway, Faulkner, and Eliot—figures who were also greatly admired in Cuba—were alien to the great American literary tradition that had begun in the nineteenth century with Poe, Melville, and Whitman, and had continued in the twentieth century with Hart Crane, Sherwood Anderson, and Frank himself.[37] But Frank also used the opportunity to address young Cuban writers and reiterate his defense of intellectual autonomy:

> Writers should work for their countries. If they need to give speeches to peasants, then they should do that, but they should not lose their independence; [political] engagement should not veil their critical function. The duty of writers is to artistically reflect reality, whether that reality is Cuba or Iceland. Propaganda art is the art of traitors. Watch out for that![38]

Frank's republican Americanism and his identification with the noncommunist Left prevented him from espousing a wholly negative view of his country's history. Hence, despite questioning US expansionism and hegemonic control over Cuba, as expressed in the cry of "Remember the Maine" and the establishment of the Platt Amendment, he could recall with pride the Teller Amendment, the product of a joint resolution of the US Congress passed on April 1898, which recognized that the Cuban people had a right to "independence and liberty."[39] Washington's historical stance on Cuba, according to Frank, was "ambivalent" or "ambiguous": that stance asserted Cubans' right to sovereignty but at the same time equally defended the "right of American Business—the anatomy and live organs of the country—to do what it wanted to do with Cuba."[40]

This very notion of "ambivalence," however, also harbored a certain positive view of the US liberal and democratic tradition, a view that the Cuban leadership found uncomfortable at a moment when the island was immersing itself in Soviet Marxist-Leninism. In his book, Frank reclaimed the US liberal-democratic tradition both in order to call for American tolerance of the island's increasingly close ties with the Soviet Union and to exhort Castro and his government to resist importing "alien" or "strange" doctrines and to remain faithful to Christian humanism—or, more precisely, to the "democratic Judeo-Christian vision of the complete man."[41] If such an exhortation still resonated somewhat in both Washington and Havana in the spring of 1960 when the Fair Play for Cuba Committee was formed, by the beginning of 1961, when the English edition of Frank's book appeared, the exhortation fell on deaf ears in both governments.

Such a disencounter prevented the Cuban leaders from taking advantage of certain points of agreement—rather conservative ones—between Frank's ideas and those of the Cuban revolutionary ideology. For example, the New York writer's view of Cuban popular culture was in fact quite close to the official perspective that would be responsible in that same year, 1961, for censoring Sabá Cabrera Infante and Orlando Jiménez's film *PM* and closing *Lunes de Revolución* magazine. While walking on the beach with Nicolás Guillén—the "greatest of the Afro-Cuban poets, who has built from the matrix of his forebears' fierce rhythms a passionate, contemporary living substance"—Frank hears a conga being played and proceeds to associate it with decadence and frustration.[42] He comments similarly on a Havana nightclub performance by singer La Lupe, whom he calls "mad Lupe," who "flings herself into an orgasm of motions" and "bespeaks a decadent Cuba whose explosive senses express frustration."[43]

Out of his Judeo-Christian humanist perspective, Frank was in agreement with a communist diagnosis of Cuban popular culture, which was beginning to circulate among the island's ruling elite. In the most orthodox of those diagnoses, the popular culture in question represented a burden of the bourgeois past that needed to be overcome by the new socialist order. This regenerative logic of socialism strongly attracted Frank, who found a certain consonance between the "new man" promoted by the Cuban revolutionaries and the "integral, total man" of his own humanistic philosophy. Despite his clear distance from communism, Frank continued to believe that some final Marxist religiosity would be capable of dialoguing with American democracy.

THE FINAL BOOK

Although he was born in Long Branch, New Jersey, Frank grew up on the Upper West Side of Manhattan in a family of second-generation German Jewish immigrants. After brief periods spent in Lausanne and Paris, the young Yale graduate established himself in Greenwich Village, where he would write his first novels.[44] New York, "The City," features as a protagonist in many of his fictional works, such as *The Unwelcome Man* (1917), where young university students move between Manhattan and Long Island, read Cicero, and undergo the sufferings of love and friendship.[45] In *City Block* (1922), Manhattan's urban modernity provides a setting of religious and racial diversity as Christmas serves as the occasion for the emergence of faith and charity in the lives of Jews, Catholics, and Protestants.[46] *Holiday* (1923) is set in the US South, but its story strongly reflects the thematic concerns of the Harlem Renaissance. Written after a journey Frank took to the South in the company of his friend and Harlem Renaissance writer Jean Toomer, the novel recounts the protagonist's pilgrimage from the white section of a southern coastal town to its black section, called "Nigger Town."

The Dark Mother (1920), one of the more stylistically coherent of these early novels, is a bildungsroman that recounts the story of a young outsider from the American Midwest who, like Frank himself, grew up in Manhattan between the end of the nineteenth century and the beginning of the twentieth. The novel reconstructs the newspaper debate in New York that transpired during Cuba's final war of independence (1895–98, organized by José Martí), and recounts how New Yorkers experienced the explosion of the

USS *Maine*, their nation's intervention in that war, and the subsequent US military occupation of Cuba, Puerto Rico, and the Philippines.[47] In the heat of this experience, the protagonist develops a leftist Americanist ideology in which readings of Walt Whitman and Peter Kropotkin are interwoven.[48]

Frank's own ideological evolution was quite similar to that of this character in *The Dark Mother*, as can be observed in his posthumous *Memoirs* (1973), edited by Alan Trachtenberg, and *Our America* (1919), his first book of essays. In his *Memoirs*, Frank recalls that close to his home on the Upper West Side, there lived a family of Cuban exiles who failed to return to the island after the defeat of Spain.[49] The essays of *Our America*, which Peruvian Marxist José Carlos Mariátegui read as a double critique of American expansionism and narrow-minded Hispanic American *Arielismo* (anti-US Hispanic Americanism that imagined the United States as a utilitarian nation lacking in culture and spirit), sought to define a nonimperialist, republican-democratic tradition based on the work of Whitman, Thoreau, Emerson, and Lincoln.

In his *Memoirs*, Frank would confess that he had not read José Martí's essay *Nuestra América* (1891) prior to writing *Our America* (1919) but that after he did read it, he felt that his ideas converged with those of the Cuban poet, who was likewise an admirer of Emerson, Whitman, Lincoln, and Thoreau.[50] The Spanish-American War (1898), viewed from Manhattan, was no doubt a formative experience for Frank and led to his gravitation toward Hispanic America over the following decades. No other American intellectual of the mid-twentieth century attained Frank's level of familiarity with Hispanic American culture. No other intellectual of his era established such a broad network of contacts and friendships in the Hispanic sphere, which extended from José Ortega y Gasset and the *Revista de Occidente* in Madrid to José Carlos Mariátegui and the journal *Amauta* in Lima; from Jorge Mañach and the *Revista de Avance* in Havana to Jorge Luis Borges and the journal *Sur* in Buenos Aires; and from the Mexico of Alfonso Reyes and José Vasconcelos to the Caracas of Rómulo Betancourt and Rómulo Gallegos.[51]

In his many references to his friend and frustrated poet Hart Crane (1899–1932), Frank always insisted on considering himself a member of the "génération perdue," the lost generation made famous by Gertrude Stein, which included writers of the American avant-garde of the 1920s, such as T. S. Eliot, Ezra Pound, Ernest Hemingway, and F. Scott Fitzgerald.[52] However, Hemingway, who popularized the expression, deliberately ignored Frank in *A Moveable Feast*, ridiculed him in *The Sun Also Rises*, and even dedicated an offensive verse to him in his 1924 poem, "The Soul of Spain": "Democracy is the shit / Relativity is the shit / Dictators are the shit / Menken is the shit / Waldo Frank is the shit."[53] Frank was likewise attacked by Fitzgerald in "A Note on My Generation" (1926), where the latter wrote that "the prose of Joyce in the hands of, say, Waldo Frank becomes as insignificant and idiotic as the automatic writing of a Kansas Theosophist."[54]

This mention of theosophy was perhaps a reference to Frank's interest in the mystical ideas of Russian exiles George Gurdjieff and Piotr Uspenski during a curious spiritual phase of his life prior to his communist period in the 1930s. In any case, Frank's lateral membership in the aesthetic canon of the lost generation had to do both with factors of aesthetic discordance and modes of assuming political engagement. In contrast to the "cool" politics of Hemingway and Fitzgerald, Frank's direct solidarity with the Mexican Revolution or with the Spanish Republic, or his own adherence to the liberal tradition of ideologically grounded politics—which stemmed from John Dewey and, above all, from the pacifist and cosmopolitan ideas of Randolph Bourne and his magazine the *New Republic*, of which Frank would later serve as contributing editor—situated him in the sphere of what Edward Abrahams has called the "lyrical left."[55]

Frank's cosmopolitanism—his constant depiction of multiethnic and multireligious communities—was inconceivable without New York. As a character in *The Dark Mother* (1920) comments, "the City is run on schedule. On schedule. That's why it's a great City. That's what makes a great City out of a piece of country."[56] It was his status as a mouthpiece of the New York microcosmos that constituted Frank as a privileged interlocutor for Latin American intellectual and political elites at the middle of the twentieth century. It was also this status that led to the Cuban leadership's decision, in 1959, to hire Frank to write a biography of the island that would provide a historical justification for the Cuban Revolution in the eyes of New York public opinion.

What Frank failed to realize is that his book would end up being read, not as a historical justification of the Cuban Revolution but as a defense of the island's alliance with the Soviet Union and the expansion of communism in the region. By the time the English edition of *Cuba: Prophetic Island* was published in February 1961, a US Senate Subcommittee on Internal Security presided by Senator James O. Eastland of Mississippi had already spent months conducting hearings on the Fair Play for Cuba Committee, which had been formed in 1959 by Robert Taber and Alan Sagner and was led by Frank since 1960.[57] One of the witnesses in those hearings was veteran journalist-writer Carleton Beals, author of *Mexico: An Interpretation* (1923) and *The Crime of Cuba* (1933), the latter of which was illustrated with photographs by Walker Evans. In his testimony, Beals acknowledged that he had invited Frank to chair the Fair Play for Cuba Committee because he felt Frank's moral authority would draw the support of many intellectuals of the American Left.

In Beals's testimony during the hearings, one reads the singular position of a mid-twentieth-century American dissident who made common cause with Latin American nationalist leftists and revolutionaries while at the same time maintaining independence from Moscow.[58] Beals, who refers to books by Frank such as *Virgin Spain* (1926), presented both himself and Frank as activists for Latin American causes in New York who perceived no contradiction between their activities and US interests in the hemisphere due to the fact that they were working to prevent Latin American leftists from drifting toward communism and alliances with Moscow. Beals further argued that the role he had played in Mexico during the 1930s and 1940s should be rearticulated in the Cuban context in order to prevent the revolution from becoming Sovietized.

The Cuban government's public adoption of Marxist-Leninism as its revolutionary ideology during the months prior to and following the Bay of Pigs invasion had the effect of turning Frank's book into something it was not. Cuba's Marxist-Leninist turn also distorted the author's own positions, as strong anticommunist

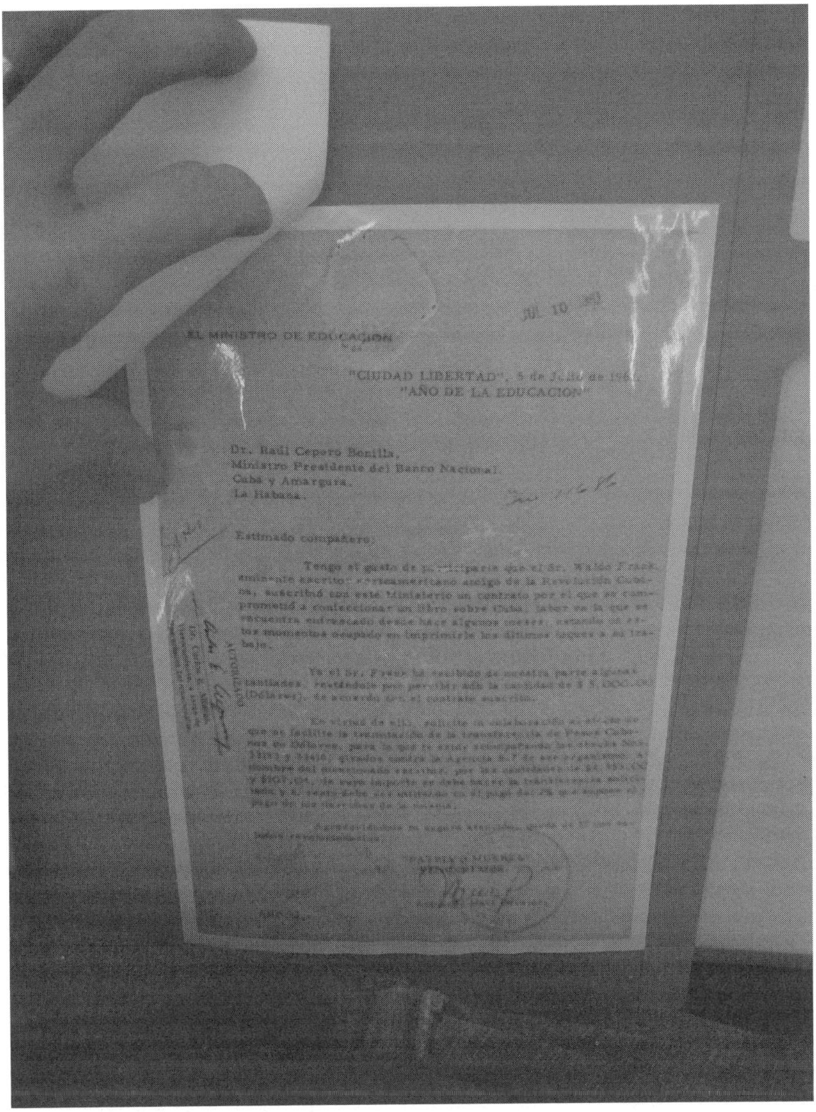

EL MINISTRO DE EDUCACION

"CIUDAD LIBERTAD", 5 de Julio de 1961.
"AÑO DE LA EDUCACION"

Dr. Raúl Cepero Bonilla,
Ministro Presidente del Banco Nacional.
Cuba y Amargura.
La Habana.

Estimado compañero:

Receipt of payment made by the Cuban government to Waldo Frank for his book *Cuba: Prophetic Island* (1961). (National Archives, Washington, DC)

opinion in America indicted him as an agent of international communism. Reviews of *Cuba: Prophetic Island* by Joseph Newman in the *New York Herald Tribune Books* and Daniel James in the *Saturday Review* were negative, and a McCarthyite reporter from the *Evening Independent* even recalled Frank's former membership in the Communist Party, his collaborations in leftist magazines, his support for Earl Browder and Vito Marcantonio, and his defense of the Rosenbergs.[59] With the intention of presenting Frank as a communist agent, some recalled his participation in antifascist organizations such as the League of American Writers and his articles in the *New Masses* or the *Nation*, such as "The Anti-Communist Peril," a denunciation of McCarthyism published in the latter magazine in 1954.[60]

Cuba's alignment with the Soviet Union heightened polarization in the New York public sphere and led to fractures within the Left itself. Just as Frank's article in the *Nation* had come under criticism from the communist Left due to its liberal-democratic rejection of anticommunism and McCarthyism, *Cuba: Prophetic Island* was now criticized by communist and socialist leftists who supported the island's integration to the Soviet bloc. Although J. P. Morray's article "Cuba and Communism" in the summer 1961 issue of *Monthly Review* did not mention Frank, it questioned the liberal Left for denouncing the communist radicalization of the revolutionary government even while rejecting harsh US policies toward Havana.[61] New York anarchist-unionist Sam Dolgoff, however, reproached Frank for his tolerance of Castro's Stalinist vocation:

> Waldo Frank's *Cuba: A Prophetic Island* (New York, 1961) is particularly disappointing because he had always been a consistent anti-state communist, strongly influenced by libertarian ideas, which he amply demonstrated by his sympathetic attitude towards the CNT (anarcho-syndicalist union confederation of Spain). That Frank with 40 years study of Spanish and Latin American history should have allowed his pro-Castro euphoria to becloud his judgment to the point where he could not recognize the obvious earmarks of a dictatorship in the making is unpardonable. Although Frank was granted a two year subsidy by the Cuban government to write his book, he insists that his "only obligation was to seek the truth as I found it" (Preface). Nevertheless Frank's "unbiased" evaluation of Castro's personality and achievements rivals the tributes heaped upon Stalin by his sycophants.[62]

Perhaps the best-formulated New York leftist critique of the partisans of the Cuban Revolution was that of Theodore Draper, a friend of Frank's since the 1930s when the two writers had published in the *New Masses* and who, like Frank, was a former communist. Writing for *Encounter* and *Commentary*, Draper criticized a number of books on the Cuban Revolution published in New York in 1960, subsequently compiling these critiques in his book *Castro's Revolution: Myths and Realities* (1962). At a time when the Cuban revolutionary government's pro-Soviet turn was becoming more and more evident, Draper denounced the Sartrean idea that the Cuban Revolution lacked an ideology and criticized writers such as C. Wright Mills in *Listen, Yankee* (1960), Paul Johnson in the *New Statesman*, and Samuel Shapiro in the *New Republic*, who persisted in casting the Cuban revolutionary process as noncommunist.[63] Although Draper no longer shared the theoretical and ideological perspective of Paul M. Sweezy and Leo Huberman, he felt that these Marxists, who had openly supported the socialist profile of the Cuban Revolution in the *Monthly Review* since the summer of 1960, were more accurate in their analysis of the island.

Draper did not share Sweezy and Huberman's argument that the Cuban Revolution constituted a "peasant revolution," nor did he see a socialist program in the text of Castro's 1953 speech, *La historia me absolverá* (1954).[64] But he believed it was more honest to acknowledge the revolution's Marxist turn than to persist in attributing to it a "humanist" ideology that was alien to both blocks of the Cold War, as Herbert L. Matthews in the *New York Times* and Stuart Hall in the *New Left Review*—two figures he debated in mid-1961—had continued to do.[65] When Frank's book began to circulate, Draper had already advanced too far in his debate against the thesis of the Cuban Revolution's noncommunist identity. For this reason, in addition to enumerating the errors in *Cuba: Prophetic Island*, he also referred to the book's conclusions as "anachronistic" and recognized very little value in Frank's cautious efforts to distance himself from Havana's growing authoritarianism:

> Though he was admittedly subsidized by Castro's government, I doubt whether the latter can be sure that it got its money's

> worth. It may not be enough for Fidel to read of himself as a "genius," a "presence," and "less the politician than the *poet and the lover.*" It may mean little to him at this late date that anyone should explain on his behalf that elections would be a "bothersome delay" and an opposition press a "nuisance." For this book happened to appear, at least in its American edition, after Castro had labored for hours to explain that he had become a Communist and how inevitable it had been. Not only did Waldo Frank fail to foresee the avowal of his hero, but his book is full of earnest admonitions and exhortations against it.[66]

In the appendixes to the Argentine edition, Frank acknowledges that the revolutionary leadership's deliberate abandonment of the 1940 constitutional platform—which Castro had defended throughout the insurrection and even during the first revolutionary year—was the "most serious" of the charges levied by Castro's intellectual critics.[67] As he argues, however, the school of thought that was articulating this charge—which Frank identifies with Draper—was committing the error of "anticipating" that Cuba would collectivize agricultural production as had occurred in communist experiments such as the Russian and the Chinese.[68] According to Frank, Draper—whom he disparages as "not demonstrating any contact with the people of Cuba or its leadership"—was merely assuming that Cuban farmers would be subjected to a nationalizing process similar to that of the Soviet Union or China.[69] Curiously, what Frank thus considered an error on Draper's part was also precisely what Sweezy and Huberman were defending in the *Monthly Review* in their writings on socialist agrarian reform.

From the moment it was published, Frank's book was launched into crossfire from the Right and the Left, as well as from the various factions within the Left itself. The alliance between Castro and Khrushchev, which would become evident a year later with the installation of Soviet missiles on the island of Cuba, situated Frank's position on a no-man's-land. In American public opinion—even within the New York liberal Left—Cuba had come to be perceived as a Soviet satellite, and any call for dialogue and respect vis-à-vis the Cuban government was now viewed as intellectual ingenuousness at best and complicity with the enemy at worst.

In his final years of life, and despite his long experience in public debate, Frank expressed his resentment for the interrogations he was subjected to after the revelations that he had received payment from Havana to write his book. In his posthumous *Memories*, edited in 1973 by Alan Trachtenberg, Frank defended the intellectual independence he had maintained throughout his career. As he argued, the books he had written in support of twentieth-century Hispanic American leftist causes, whether produced independently or under contract, had all responded to a historical and personal vision that at times, although not always, had converged with socialist or communist policies of organizations and states. In his view, that convergence had not distorted the personal development of his convictions nor had it mechanically turned him into an unconditional ally of the organizations and states in question. However, not even Frank could fail to acknowledge that the polemic unleashed by his book on Cuba had damaged his moral reputation as an intellectual:

> I could write what I wished on any subject little or large, until my defense of Castro's Cuba lost me that commission. The trend was wide-spread. A tide was ebbing, and I alone on the sands. To celebrate this new solitude, I wrote two brief novels, which have not yet seen the light; and one of which, at least, may be among my best.[70]

Cuba: Prophetic Island (1961) was the last book that the prolific Waldo Frank would publish during his lifetime. Produced for publication in New York and Havana, and for the purpose of persuading minds in both cities, the book never saw a Cuban edition. Frank's desire was to reach readers in New York and Havana, not readers in Fidel's government, and that government's objective was to develop currents of sympathy for the Cuban Revolution in New York and at the same time limit the circulation of democratic-leftist ideas left on the island. Curiously, with the Argentine edition of the book, Frank gained readers on the left in this South American city, and those readers communicated their admiration for the American writer to the Cuban government. One of them was writer Julio Cortázar, who in a well-known letter to Roberto Fernández Retamar, informed the latter that his reading of *Cuba: Isla profética* had convinced him to support the Cuban Revolution.[71]

Sadly, Theodore Draper had been right: the very ideological and political evolution of the Cuban revolutionary project refuted Sartre, Mills, Frank, and other intellectuals of the Western Left who had imagined the development in Cuba of a socialism substantially different from the Soviet model.[72] The failure of books such as Frank's to reach audiences in Havana during the 1960s was one of the many factors that conspired to prevent an alternative socialism from taking root on the island. Those who should have read *Cuba: Prophetic Island* were not only intellectuals from Manhattan, Brooklyn, Buenos Aires, or Córdoba, but the youth who were constructing socialism in the Caribbean island cities that had so astounded Frank.

3

SOCIALISTS IN MANHATTAN

★

The debate over the Cuban Revolution on the New York Left during the 1960s would be incomprehensible without *Monthly Review*, a journal founded by Marxists Paul M. Sweezy and Leo Huberman in 1949. At Harvard, Sweezy had been a student of the liberal Austrian American economist Joseph Schumpeter (1883–1950), author of *Imperialism and Social Classes* (1919), and of historian Francis Otto Matthiessen (1920–50), an erudite, gay scholar of nineteenth-century American culture and author of *American Renaissance: Art and Experience in the Age of Emerson and Whitman* (1941). Sweezy inherited analytic discipline from Schumpeter and a leftist vocation from Matthiessen. It was the latter who provided Sweezy with the initial funds to start a socialist publication critical of capitalism but distant from pro-Soviet communism.

Sweezy would coedit *Monthly Review* for more than half a century, first with his friend Leo Huberman until the latter's death in 1974, and then with coeditor Harry Magdoff until Sweezy's own death in 2004. Born into a family of Manhattan bankers in 1910—his father served as an executive at the First National Bank of New York for many years—Sweezy was drawn from an early age to critical views of the modern economy through his study of the mutations of industrial capitalism and his readings of alternative economic and financial policies that circulated within the American and European Left from the middle of the 1930s onward.

Sweezy's formation at Harvard coincided with the reorientation of American social and economic policies following the crash of 1929. The market implosion led to applications of the Keynesian paradigm to the political economy and bolstered attempts to articulate a state social policy during the two final presidential terms of Franklin Delano Roosevelt. The period from the end of the 1930s to the beginning of the 1940s was also a time of great impetus for a broad spectrum of leftist activity in Europe, Latin America, and the United States, as well as for the formation of alliances between communist parties and other progressive forces oriented toward countering the rise of fascism in Europe and supporting the Mexican Revolution and the Spanish Republic against domestic and foreign enemies.

During a visit to London in the mid-1940s, Sweezy gave final shape to a manuscript he had been working on since the time of his studies at Harvard, a book that would be published under the title *The Theory of Capitalist Development* (1946). From that point onward, Sweezy's Marxism would open a fundamental dialogue with the Latin American theoretical Left. By situating economic development at the center of an economic theory that today could be understood as radical Keynesianism, this New York socialist inaugurated one of the most fertile dialogues between leftists in the United States and Latin America in the twentieth century.

Starting with their first editorial in *Monthly Review* in May 1949, Sweezy and Huberman presented the magazine as an independent socialist publication, defending a socialism derived more from the direct application of Marx's ideas to the concrete realities of global capitalism—such as those experienced by colonial and postcolonial nations—than from the acritical adoption of a political or ideological line from Moscow. Significantly, the editorial in question is followed by an article by Albert Einstein that argues for a humanist and pacifist socialism.[1] In his text, Einstein does not cite Marx, Engels, or Lenin, but rather American sociologist Thorstein Veblen (1857–1929), who had called for abandoning exploitative capitalism in order to advance beyond "the predatory phase of human development." Curiously, Sweezy had expressed strong criticisms of Veblen three years prior in the *New Republic*.[2]

Writing four years after Hiroshima and Nagasaki, Einstein argued in his article that science and ethics in the era of the atomic bomb should mutually assist each other in forging a mode of social development that would preserve the human species. His article did not fail to call for improving conditions for workers and combatting poverty and unemployment, but just as he saw certain advantages in the implementation of the principles of economic planning, he also feared for the loss of individual liberties under a totalitarian state. More like Weber or Veblen himself than Marx or Lenin, Einstein believed that democracy still constituted the mechanism best prepared to counteract the growth of bureaucracy and the increase of state regulatory control over the economic and political realms:

> Nevertheless, it is necessary to remember that a planned economy is not yet socialism. A planned economy as such may be accompanied by the complete enslavement of the individual. The achievement of socialism requires the solution of some extremely difficult socio-political problems: how is it possible, in view of the far-reaching centralization of political and economic power, to prevent bureaucracy from becoming all-powerful and overweening? How can the rights of the individual be protected and therewith a democratic counterweight to the power of bureaucracy be assured?[3]

A reading of the essays collected by Sweezy in the book *Socialism* (1949), which was published the same year as the founding of *Monthly Review*, persuasively demonstrates that his concept of socialism was different from that held by Einstein.[4] Sweezy and Huberman's sympathies for models of economic planning and their objections to the representative democracies of the West were, of course, greater than those of the legendary German scientist who had discovered the theory of relativity. Nonetheless, Einstein's conceptualization of socialism served the two editors as a way to situate the magazine's space of theoretical and ideological legitimization beyond that of a direct subordination to Moscow.

This decentering, which would be reinforced by a notable editorial focus on China and other zones of conflict for the Stalinist and pro-Stalinist USSR, such as Latin America and the Caribbean, accentuated the non-pro-Soviet communism of these New York socialists.

As we will see, although *Monthly Review*'s socialism did not maintain an acritical stance toward the "popular democracies" of Eastern Europe, it would also be incorrect to identify this socialism with the liberal and democratic socialism that openly criticized totalitarian communism and that was espoused by certain New York intellectuals in the early years of the Cold War, such as Irving Howe, Lionel Trilling, the members of the *Partisan Review* group, and, later, the *Dissent* group. These sectors of the liberal Left were characterized by a resolute adherence to Trotskyism and democratic socialism, which is nowhere found in the articles of *Monthly Review*, a publication that, in the end, had the support of the US Communist Party.

In the pages that follow, I will reconstruct the character of Marxist reflection on the capitalist economy, particularly in relation to developing nations, in the work of Paul Sweezy and Leo Huberman, and, of course, in the pages of *Monthly Review* during the first decade of its publication, from 1949 to 1959. Subsequently, I will explore certain elements of the history of the relations between Sweezy, Huberman, and *Monthly Review* with the Cuban Revolution. Above all, I am interested in inscribing those relations within the larger history of encounters and disencounters between the New York Left and Cuban socialism during the 1960s. Although Sweezy and Huberman's support for the Cuban Revolution was unwavering during that decade, it was not without conflicts.

WHAT SOCIALISM?

The fact that Sweezy and other intellectuals of the New York Left maintained direct relations with the US Communist Party—although not always holding memberships in that party—is insufficient for explaining the type of socialism that was espoused and defended in Manhattan during those years. Since the time of Earl

R. Browder, the Communist Party in the United States had itself been characterized as one of the most flexible expressions of the concepts of "broad front" and "class alliance," and furthermore the party had been forced to defend itself against McCarthyism and anticommunism during the 1950s. In the case of Sweezy and other American Marxists of his generation, the historical peculiarity of American communism was further accentuated thanks to its fluid contact with liberal economists, sociologists, and functionalists, and the adherence of many American communists to more heterodox modes of Western Marxism, particularly the British variant.

As a disciple of Schumpeter, Sweezy debated the latter's economic ideas and those of the Keynesians of the previous generation without entirely rejecting liberal ideas in the way Soviet orthodoxy demanded. Already in *The Theory of Capitalist Development* (1942), it was evident that Sweezy sought to challenge liberal economic policy at its point of greatest intersection with Marxism, a point that, in his judgment, was most evident in the work of authors like John Maynard Keynes and Schumpeter himself.[5] The Keynesians and the Schumpeterians had achieved the greatest advances in liberal economic theory since the time of Smith and Ricardo, but in Sweezy's view, they were overly stubborn in their refusal to accept Marx's theory of value.

From Matthiessen's studies of Walt Whitman, Henry David Thoreau, Ralph Waldo Emerson, and the nineteenth-century transcendentalists, Sweezy had learned the importance of recalling the ideological diversity of the past and maintaining a historical perspective on the present.[6] He put these two principles to work in his study of US mid-twentieth-century capitalism from the perspective of democratic and American socialism—in the sense that Matthiessen's Christianity had given these adjectives. Unfettered by Matthiessen's religiosity, and possessing his own, more positive view of the Soviet Union and Eastern Europe, Sweezy sought to defend a socialism that would be capable of debating and dialoguing with the progressive liberalism of Keynes and Schumpeter or of A. C. Pigou and Alvin H. Hansen. One notes the friendly tone with which Sweezy debated these figures as compared to the more confrontational stance he adopted in his arguments with, for example, F. A. Hayek's *The Road to Serfdom* (1944).[7]

Like many British Marxists of his generation (such as Raymond Williams, E. P. Thompson, or Eric Hobsbawm), Sweezy argued from the outset of his career for the importance of reading the texts of Marx and Lenin directly and without special regard for the mediations of Soviet Marxism. The distinction between "Marxian theory" and "Marxist theory" served him as a way to privilege classical sources and avoid seeking Moscow's approval. This choice drew him toward Marxism as an economic and political theory and distanced him from the idea of Marxism as philosophy or even as dialectical and historical materialism. He shared this stance on Marx and Lenin with other American thinkers such as C. Wright Mills and Edmund Wilson. The approach ensured him a plural engagement with the Marxist tradition in which the formulations of such figures as Eduard Bernstein, Karl Kautsky, Rosa Luxemburg, and Rudolf Hilferding could be considered without regard for the habitual excommunications of Marxist orthodoxy.[8]

Sweezy's proximity to Mills's work and his criticism of Oskar Lange's theory of fascism as a "popular imperialism" show the limits of this theoretical flexibility.[9] While approving the move of a Weberian like Mills toward a postfunctionalist analysis of social class, he distrusted interpretations of fascism that cast it as a mode of imperialism substantially different from liberal or democratic imperialism. Like Lenin or Hilferding—whom he employed in an appendix to *The Theory of Capitalist Development* (1942)—Sweezy believed that imperialism was linked to the rise of financial capitalism as a global phenomenon that was destined to precipitate a crisis after World War II, particularly in the colonial or postcolonial Third World.[10]

Without ceasing to be a communist publication, *Monthly Review* managed to maintain an editorial line notably independent from Soviet dogmatism during the 1950s, a decade that was characterized by the rise of anticommunism in the public sphere, driven by the campaigns of Senator Joseph McCarthy and the Smith Act. Sweezy was personally opposed to the application of this act against communist leaders such as Carl Marzani and was a tenacious critic of McCarthyism and other witch hunts that targeted socialist leftists. At the same time, *Monthly Review* also did not restrain itself from questioning the imperial elements of Soviet policies in the "era of Stalin," Moscow's treatment of the Soviet Jewish community, or Marxist-Leninism's rejection of psychoanalysis.[11]

In the mid-1950s, following the death of Stalin and the denunciations of his crimes, which were voiced during the Twentieth Congress of the US Communist Party, Sweezy reaffirmed in *Monthly Review* the idea of a "Marxian socialism" directly related to Marx's theory of capitalism, which provoked a debate over the future of the communist Left in the United States.[12] The formula of "Marxian socialism" also allowed Sweezy to not only conveniently extricate himself from the legacy of Soviet Marxism—from Nikolai Bukharin in the 1920s and early 1930s to V. Afanasyev, F. V. Konstantinov, P. Nikitin, and other writers in the 1950s, none of whom are the least bit present in his work—but to also free himself from the dissensions provoked by Trotskyism, which, despite the force it maintained among New York intellectuals, likewise failed to penetrate the pages of *Monthly Review*.

The growing importance that Sweezy gave to underdeveloped nations during the 1950s was a major factor for his insertion in the debate over the Cuban Revolution and Latin American socialism. Notably, in 1959, *Monthly Review* did not devote a single article to the Cuban process, even as other publications of the New York Left celebrated the Caribbean revolutionary event. The magazine's central topic that year was China, and particularly the economic and social dynamics of Chinese communism at the moment of the Great Leap Forward led by Chairman Mao.[13] This interest in China, coinciding with a moment of clear distancing between Moscow and Peking, had to do both with Sweezy and Huberman's rejection of Soviet orthodoxy and with the importance that the two editors gave to Third World socialism.

Although they did not devote space in the issue to Cuba in 1959, the editors of *Monthly Review* initiated certain theoretical discussions that year that would have a central importance for the New York Left. In the summer issue, the journal featured articles by Ralph Miliband on the "new capitalism" and by

William Appleman Williams on the "new imperial style," both of which reinforced the Third World perspective in the debate on capitalism and imperialism.[14] Along that same line was an interesting study by Hobert P. Sturm and Francis D. Wormuth, "The International Power Elite," an application of this well-known concept of C. Wright Mills to the corporate system of global financial capitalism.[15] The theoretical redefinition of capitalism in *Monthly Review* was accompanied by a redefinition of Marxist theory itself.

In the final issues of 1959, Paul Baran, a key figure in the journal, promoted two debates, one on Marxism and psychoanalysis and the other on Marxist theory itself, that highlight certain characteristics of this redefinition. Joseph Starobin and Stanley Moore took part in the latter debate, which was dominated by a criticism of the doctrinal status of Marxist-Leninist philosophy in the Soviet Union and the bureaucratization of socialism in Eastern Europe.[16] During this period, *Monthly Review*, without subscribing to the positions of democratic socialism or Trotskyism—such as that of Max Shachtman in *The Bureaucratic Revolution: The Rise of the Stalinist States* (1962)—also reflected the desertion from pro-Soviet camps that took place in the wake of the USSR's invasion of Hungary and the dispute between Mao and Khrushchev.

It was in this ideological and theoretical climate that Sweezy and Huberman began to interest themselves in Cuba. That interest was awakened precisely at the moment when Moscow and Havana began to align, when Cuba's conflict with the United States was accelerating, and as the revolutionary leaders began to publically position themselves in favor of socialism. As long as the Cuban Revolution had maintained itself within the liberal democratic horizon, it did not interest the editors of *Monthly Review*, but as soon as the Cuban leadership's aggressive nationalization policy opened the door to a model of economic planning and toward having an effect on the capital of large American companies, Cuba became a central topic in the magazine.

That topic was introduced in the May 1960 issue with an interesting essay by Manuel Pedro González, a Cuban literary critic born in the Canary Islands who was now a professor at the

University of California in Los Angeles. González was an expert on the work of José Martí, especially on the Cuban poet's journalistic chronicles written in New York at the end of the nineteenth century. During this period, González was compiling the essays on Martí that he would include in his book *Indagaciones martianas* (1961), published by the Universidad Central de las Villas in Cuba. González's article in *Monthly Review*, entitled, "Why Cubans Resent the US," sought to offer a simple historical explanation for growing "anti-Yankee" sentiment on the part of Castro and other leaders of the Cuban Revolution.[17]

As González argued, Cuban resentment toward the United States was justified by historical events, such as the 1898 military intervention and American occupation of the island from 1898 to 1902 and 1906 to 1909; the Platt Amendment (1901–34); the appropriation of Cuban territory by US agricultural companies; and Washington's backing of the unconstitutional regime of Fulgencio Batista during the first period of his final term in power. Like Mills and Frank, González insisted that the Cuban Revolution was primarily a nationalist rather than a communist movement, and therefore if the United States would tolerate Cuba's recuperation of sovereignty, relations between the two nations might be reoriented sooner rather than later.

Historically, US policies toward the island had two faces, like Janus, González suggested. One of those faces was democratic, as expressed by the Teller Amendment, but the other was imperialist, exemplified by the Platt Amendment. Now that the Cuban Revolution had taken place, the democratic face needed to predominate and the imperialist face had to be restrained from punishing the former, as the Jacobo Arbenz movement in Guatemala had punished it in 1954.[18] Washington, according to González, needed to understand that the more hegemonic its policies were toward Latin America, the more leftist and rightist dictatorships would arise in the region, and the more Latin American anti-US nationalist resentment would grow. Against the editorial line of *Monthly Review* itself, González presented the communist radicalization of nationalist leftist movements as an evil that could be avoided through a nonimperialist policy.

In the summer issue, Sweezy and Huberman entered the Cuban debate in full force by reproducing in *Monthly Review* the entirety of their cowritten book, *Cuba: Anatomy of a Revolution* (1960), a work that sought to introduce another way of thinking about the Cuban topic within the New York Left. This work was also one of the very few—or perhaps the only one—of the dozens of books on Cuba published in the United States at that time that was also printed in Cuba, by the Vanguardia Obrera press, in 1961. Although Sweezy and Huberman's book did not fail to recognize the weight of the historical hegemony of the United States toward Cuba, particularly in the construction of a dependent and underdeveloped capitalist economy, they did not focus their argument on nationalist revindications for the revolution but rather on the "socialist" content of some of that revolution's measures, such as agrarian reform, industrialization, urban reform, universal access and promotion of literacy, health and education, and the accelerated diffusion of a leftist ideology and a vanguard culture.

According to these authors, what was new about the Cuban Revolution was not nationalism, which was already manifest in twentieth-century Latin American populist leftist movements, but the appearance of a state that prioritized the egalitarian distribution of income, economic equality, and social justice. Sweezy and Huberman called this process "socialism" without engaging in excessive terminological disquisitions and by extending to the Cuban process the meaning they had given this concept in the early years of *Monthly Review* and in the above-cited essay by Sweezy from 1949. They identified this particular type of socialism even in the text of Castro's *History Will Absolve Me* (1954), as well as in the initial program of the 26th of July Movement that was issued following the invasion of the Moncada barracks, despite the fact that the doctrinal referents of both Castro's speech and the 26th of July Movement program had been liberal-democratic rather than Marxist-Leninist.[19]

Huberman and Sweezy cited some of the first reports and books on the Cuban Revolution published in the United States between the middle of 1959 and the middle of 1960—such as the writings of Ray Brennan and Jules Dubois—to argue that the Cuban economy

Special issue of *Monthly Review* dedicated to the Cuban Revolution.

had undergone an "impoverishment" as a result of its dependence on the United States during the most recent decades of republican rule.[20] In fact, Cuban economic historiography produced both on and outside the island had indicated economic growth rather than recession during the decades in question, but Huberman and Sweezy sought to stress the social deterioration in Cuba's experience of underdeveloped and dependent capitalism. Therefore, in their view, if the Cuban revolutionary leaders were conscious of that deterioration and were attempting to confront it with concrete policies, they could not be called anything but socialists.

In contrast to the majority of intellectuals of the New York Left, who argued either that the Cuban Revolution lacked an ideology (following Jean Paul Sartre) or that the revolutionary ideology in question was humanist, agrarian, nationalist, or anti-imperialist yet not Marxist (the position of Carleton Beals and Waldo Frank), Huberman and Sweezy defended the socialist identity of the Cuban process. They directly criticized Sartre's idea and also denounced the "humanist" thesis, which they attributed to Joseph Newman, editor of the *New York Herald Tribune*.[21] Like Mills, Huberman and Sweezy defended Cuba's right to align itself with the Soviet Union, and furthermore the concept of socialism they appealed to was not entirely disconnected from Marxist-Leninism or from the communisms of Eastern Europe. Their recurrent reminders that Cuban socialism was undergoing a "transitional" phase as a step prior to increasing economic statification remitted directly to the experience of the USSR and the "popular democracies":

> For our part, we have no hesitation in answering: the new Cuba is a socialist Cuba. This does not mean that all or even the majority of the means of production are now publicly owned. Undoubtedly, they are not. But, as previous chapters have surely made clear, the dynamic and in this sense overwhelmingly decisive sector in the Cuban economy today is the public sector. Furthermore, while no comprehensive economic plan has as yet been formulated, there can be no question that the government's economic policies and actions, far from being haphazard and uncoordinated, are directed by a supreme central

authority—now in the process of being institutionalized in the Planning Commission and its Secretariat—with a view to optimizing their effects on the economy as a whole.[22]

Sweezy and Huberman wrote these words in the summer of 1960 at a time when relations between the United States and Cuba had not even yet been severed, and when the majority of the revolutionary leaders, starting with Prime Minister Castro and President of the Republic Osvaldo Dorticós, were still at great pains to not present themselves as Marxists or socialists.

Huberman and Sweezy's viewpoint, shaped over the course of various trips to the island and meetings with Cuba's principal leaders, was a clear reflection of the perspective on the Cuban process held by the old leaders of the Popular Socialist Party, such as Blas Roca, Carlos Rafael Rodríguez, Aníbal Escalante, Joaquín Ordoqui, and Edith García Buchaca, with whom they had been acquainted since the 1930s and 1940s. Huberman and Sweezy's conception that the revolutionary government had initiated a "structural change" in the island's social and economic order that could be considered a socialist transition—one not led by the Communist Party but that merely included that party in a process of unified political forces—was a notion that had already appeared in texts and declarations made by the old communist leaders of the island. [23] In fact, the *Monthly Review* editors made efforts to dismiss both the notion of the "revolution betrayed" and the idea of "communist infiltration of the government," which the first Cuban opposition had promoted as part of its argument that the socialist transition was deliberately pushed by Castro as a way of leading to the Communist Party's full incorporation in, and leadership of, the revolution and therefore to the creation of a new, single political institution. [24]

Huberman and Sweezy's interpretation of events in Cuba had a number of questionable aspects from a historical point of view, as Theodore Draper would argue.[25] Almost all of these aspects were related to the *Monthly Review* editors' conceptualization of the 26th of July Movement's program and of the ideological goals expressed by the revolution's principle leaders (up to at least 1960) as socialist. However, although Draper considered Sweezy and

Huberman's thesis ideologically questionable from his liberal democratic perspective, he acknowledged that the thesis in question at least had the advantage of coinciding with the declarations of the revolutionary leaders between the second half of 1960 and the invasion of the Bay of Pigs.[26] Due to its insertion in the center of New York public debate over the island, Sweezy and Huberman's intervention was sufficiently effective to open a Cuban chapter within *Monthly Review*.

A few months following the publication of *Anatomy of a Revolution*, the editors published an article by Castro entitled "A Real Democracy," in which the Cuban premier announced an indefinite postponement of democratic elections on the island with the argument that basic social rights first needed to be distributed among the Cuban population before any electoral competition could take place.[27] Several issues later, the magazine published Nancy Reeve's article, "Women of the New Cubans," which inscribed the Cuban phenomenon within one of the themes of the New York Left's ideological repertoire: women's liberation.[28] *Monthly Review* covered the topic of Cuban socialism perhaps more consistently than any other periodical of the Anglophone New Left. (One recalls, for example, editor Stuart Hall of the *New Left Review* arguing in the pages of his magazine that the Cuban Revolution needed to radicalize its original humanism, its olive-green color, and avoid turning red under the mantle of the Communist International.[29])

At the beginning of 1961, when tensions between the United States and Cuba had increased to the point where the project of a CIA-organized invasion began to be publically mentioned, *Monthly Review* directed its critique toward the US Cuban policy. With John F. Kennedy assuming the US presidency, the journal's editors began to speculate on the possibility that the new president might abandon the hostile policy of the previous administration. In January of that year, *Monthly Review* featured an article on Cuba written by Carl Marzani, an old militant communist, a friend of Sweezy, and the publisher of Waldo Frank's book on Cuba. In his article, Marzani called for a peaceful coexistence between the two nations, building his argument on a discussion of Guatemala and

Cuba, and a consideration of the possibility for an understanding between Kennedy and Khrushchev.[30]

The debate continued over whether the Cuban Revolution was "socialist," as Huberman and Sweezy were arguing, and *Monthly Review* itself subsequently published a number of articles on the question that, while not questioning the thesis, nonetheless gave it greater nuance and development. Paul A. Baran, in his "Reflections on the Cuban Revolution," called for the Western Left to employ greater flexibility in the notions with which it categorized the political processes of underdeveloped nations, and Herbert Matthews and Adalgisa Nery reviewed Sweezy and Huberman's *Cuba: Anatomy of a Revolution*, not without some objections.[31] In April 1961, after news of the Bay of Pigs invasion broke and Castro subsequently announced the revolution's "socialist character" and confessed that he had always been a Marxist-Leninist, the editors of *Monthly Review* confirmed the Cuban leader's thesis. Their May editorial, entitled "The Criminal Plan," was a denunciation of the Kennedy administration's support for the CIA's project.

In its summer issue, the magazine returned to the topic of the ideology of the Cuban Revolution as viewed from a postinvasion perspective. In an article published in that issue entitled "Cuba and Communism," J. P. Morray went beyond Sweezy and Huberman's book and Baran's "Reflections" in formulating an argument that would subsequently be adopted by many members of the New York Left and would later serve as the point of departure for the author's forceful book, *The Second Revolution in Cuba* (1962), published by Monthly Review Press. Morray argued in his article that although the Cuban Revolution was not originally communist, the radicalization of the social process on the island, on the one hand, and—especially—the disloyal opposition of the United States, on the other, had been responsible for setting the nation on the path to communism.[32] A few pages preceding Morray's article, *Monthly Review* featured a translation of Che Guevara's classic essay, "Cuba, excepción histórica o vanguardia de la lucha anticolonialista" (1961), which had originally appeared in April of that year in the journal *Verde Olivo*.[33] Guevara's piece sought to explain the socialist character of the revolution within a broad perspective determined not by East-West tension, nor by the escalation of conflict between Cuba and the United States, but rather by the struggle of Third World peoples against colonialism and imperialism. According to Guevara—voicing an observation shared by Sweezy, Baran, and Huberman in their own studies of monopolistic global capitalism—that struggle constituted the fundamental global contradiction following the Second World War.

From the end of 1961, Guevara gradually began to displace Castro as the central figure representing the Cuban process in the pages of *Monthly Review.* Guevara's celebrated speeches at the United Nations and Punta del Este, Uruguay, situated Cuban socialism within a larger Third World revolution. His argument would subsequently receive theoretical backing in the economic scholarship of Sweezy, Huberman, and, above all, Baran, whose impactful study of "monopoly capitalism" as the "American economic and social order" (largely a condensation of arguments from his earlier works, *The Political Economy of Underdevelopment* [1952] and *The Political Economy of Growth* [1957]) began to be published in *Monthly Review* precisely in 1962.[34] At the end of that year, when the Cuban Missile Crisis accelerated the island's integration within the Soviet bloc, Sweezy and Huberman seem to have understood that Guevara personified the idea of the Cuban Revolution that was the closest to the New York Left's global view.

FROM KEYNES TO GUEVARA

It is notable that just as American capitalism was entering a lengthy period of sustained deregulation from the 1960s onward, which would lead Marxists such as Sweezy and Baran to reconsider the Keynesian legacy, the positions of the Latin American Left defended by these Marxists were the most radical on the continent. In order to understand the encounters and disencounters between the Cuban Revolution and progressive Western thought during this period, it is useful to enumerate the different reactions of New York's New Left to Cuban socialism's strong incorporation within the

Soviet orbit after the Bay of Pigs invasion of April 1961 and the missile crisis of October 1962.

Harper's Magazine, for example, which had published an advance selection from C. Wright Mills's *Listen, Yankee* in December 1960 and had often featured the work of writers such as Norman Mailer and Tom Wolfe, subsequently distanced itself from any support for the Cuban revolutionary government starting in the spring of the following year. A few weeks after the Bay of Pigs invasion, in its May 1961 issue, *Harper's* began publishing a series of articles that were critical of the repression of dissident intellectuals in the Soviet Union. Soviet expert Richard Pipes began the series with "The Public Mood," an article that questioned the anti-Americanism of Soviet propaganda.[35] The magazine also published a long report on dissident university students in the USSR that denounced the Communist Party's control of the Soviet Academy of Sciences.[36]

In that same issue of May 1961, *Harper's* featured a posthumous interview between Patricia Blake and writer Boris Pasternak (1890–1960) in which the author of *Doctor Zhivago* and winner of the 1958 Nobel Prize for Literature confessed that he had not "breathed easily" in the final years of his life.[37] Alfred Kazin, an important voice of New York liberalism, wrote a piece for the same issue on Soviet relations with Russian Jews, concluding that persecutions against Jewish culture and religion had not disappeared or diminished after Stalin's death.[38] Like his friend Hannah Arendt, Kazin argued that anti-Semitism was one of the irreducible components shared by Soviet and Nazi totalitarianisms.

Harper's Magazine continued to publish Russian dissident writers in subsequent issues. In September, for example, it featured a brief anthology of poems by Pasternak and Akhmatova translated by Robert Lowell, and the magazine gradually began adopting a critical view of Soviet influence in Latin America as well. The July issue featured an article by Peter Ferdinand Drucker, entitled "A Plan for Revolution in Latin America" (1961), which expressed clear support for Kennedy's Alliance for Progress initiative and warned against the sympathies that Latin American radical leftist movements were awakening.[39] According to Drucker, those

Marxist editors of the *Monthly Review* defended the socialist path taken by the Cuban Revolution.

sympathies, although well intentioned, ran the risk of supporting the introduction of communist regimes and reinforcing Soviet influence in the hemisphere.

Cuba's placement at the center of Cold War tensions between 1961 and 1962 led to a recasting of the New York leftist debate over intellectual engagement. From the perspective of the majority of influential liberal opinion in the city, the Cuban Revolution was defensible as a recuperation of the island's lost sovereignty and as an occasion for the implementation of state policies in favor of social justice, but not as an introduction of a one-party political regime with an exclusively Marxist-Leninist cast similar to the Soviet model, and much less as a pathway toward increasing Moscow's influence over Latin America. By means of Baran's eloquent essay, "The Commitment of the Intellectual" (1961), *Monthly Review* situated itself in a singular position within this debate. The role of the critical intellectual in a phase of financial monopolization of global capitalism, Baran argued, should not be put in the service of "liberty" in the abstract but should instead favor policies that confront this new world order:

> The desire to tell the truth is therefore only *one* condition for being an intellectual. The other is courage, readiness to carry on rational inquiry to wherever it may lead, to undertake "ruthless criticism of everything that exists, ruthless in the sense that the criticism will not shrink either from its own conclusions or from conflict with the powers that be" (Marx). An intellectual is thus in essence a *social critic*, a person whose concern is to identify, to analyze, and in this way to help overcome the obstacles barring the way to the attainment of a better, more humane, and more rational social order. As such he becomes the conscience of society and the spokesman of such progressive forces as it contains in any given period of history. And as such he is inevitably considered a "troublemaker" and a "nuisance" by the ruling class seeking to preserve the *status quo*, as well as by the intellect workers in its service who accuse the intellectual of being utopian or metaphysical at best, subversive or seditious at worst.[40]

Together with its support for radical American leftist movements that fought for black civil rights, peace in Vietnam, women's liberation, and university and union struggles, *Monthly Review* promoted an idea of intellectual engagement, one of the main features of which was solidarity with the decolonizing processes of Asia, Africa, and Latin America: the so-called tricontinental revolution. Baran, Sweezy, and Huberman's economic theory of global financial and monopoly capitalism found a fertile reception among new intellectuals of the Latin American or Latin Americanist Left, such as Argentine Adolfo Gilly and German-American Andre Gunder Frank, who wrote frequently in the journal in the mid-1960s.

While Frank's writings initiated *Monthly Review*'s dialogue with the defenders of dependency theory (which had just begun to be formulated by Ruy Mauro Marini, Theotonio Dos Santos, Vânia Bambirra, Celso Furtado, Enzo Faletto, Fernando Henrique Cardoso, and others), Gilly's writings for the magazine and its press promoted interest in Latin American guerrilla movements and dialogue with libertarian, Trotskyite, and Maoist leftist movements. Examples of the latter turn included the contributions of Isaac Deutscher and the interpretation of the Cuban Revolution proposed by Gilly himself at the end of 1964 in his book *Inside the Cuban Revolution*, published by Monthly Review Press.[41] Gilly had traveled to the island before involving himself in the Guatemalan guerrilla movement, which he was unable to join in person because he had been incarcerated in the Lecumberri penitentiary in Mexico City in 1966.

In the view of the young Trotskyite Argentine, the Cuban Revolution in the middle of the 1960s was marked by a conflict between two irreconcilable ideas about socialism, as reflected in the Sino-Soviet confrontation on the island.[42] The first of these ideas, defended by the pro-Soviet leaders of the old Cuban Communist Party, gravitated toward a centralized economic model structured around an axis of industrialization, in which, in the manner of the Soviet Union and the popular democracies of Eastern Europe, the state held the reins of monetary and trade policy while also maintaining rigid control over worker and peasant organizations. This "tendency"—as Gilly referred to it—was countered by the second idea, defended by Guevara and characterized, in Gilly's view, by points of contact with Trotskyism and Maoism, which sought to eliminate monetary and trade relations and to promote agrarian cooperatives and worker autonomy.[43]

Gilly's assessment accurately reflected the debate that was taking place in Cuba between Guevara and Carlos Rafael Rodríguez over how the economic policies of Cuban socialism would be conducted and the schism that was occurring at the heart of the revolutionary leadership between a pro-Soviet wing (Aníbal Escalante, Joaquín Ordoqui, Edith García Buchaca, and others) and critics of that wing from a number of fronts, including the 26th of July Movement, the Revolutionary Directorate, and the new Guevarist current.[44] Although Gilly's ultimate message was an expression of resolute support for the revolution's continuity and Castro's ability to maintain that continuity, his book for Monthly Review Press did not fail to observe the disquieting signs favoring the bureaucratization of Cuban socialism, which risked the drowning of Cuban national or regional initiatives in the Soviet bloc's international schema.

When Guevara disappeared from the island's political class in 1965 and reappeared shortly later in the Congo and subsequently in the jungles of Bolivia, Manhattan socialists determined that the time had come to join all the Latin American guerrilla movements within the same political project, one that, in addition to leading the Latin American New Left to power, would work to definitively exorcize the bureaucratizing tendencies in Cuban socialism. *Monthly Review* was the Anglophone press that published French Marxist Régis Debray's essay *Revolution in the Revolution?* (1967) in London and New York, a work that was published that same year in Paris by François Maspero and in Havana by Casa de las Américas.

Just as Roberto Fernández Retamar, in the Cuban edition, pointed out Debray's antecedents as a disciple of Louis Althusser, Sweezy and Huberman highlighted, in the English-language edition, Jean Paul Sartre's support for the ideas of the young French socialist, who was then being held captive in a Bolivian prison.[45] Debray thus joined the debate of the New York New Left with strong authorizations from the Western Left. Sweezy and Huberman did not hesitate to present Debray's "foquismo" theory—the notion that small cadres of paramilitary forces could garner popular support and thereby jump-start revolution—as a theoretical development of the ideas of Castro and Guevara: "We have here for the first time a comprehensive and authoritative presentation of the revolutionary thought of Fidel Castro and Che Guevara."[46] The editors of *Monthly Review* assumed that Debray's defense of a socialist "third way" in Latin America, one different from the Soviet and Chinese models and personified by the Cuban Revolution, was consonant not only with the thought of Guevara, who was fighting in Bolivia, but also with that of Castro, who was governing on the island.

Despite the fact that Debray was imprisoned as a collaborator of Guevara's guerrilla warfare and had spent more than five years traveling to Cuba, *Revolution in the Revolution?* was no more than a Latin American application of Guevara's ideas as expressed in the Argentine guerrilla's works, such as *Guerrilla Warfare* (*La guerra de guerrillas*), *Cuba: ¿Excepción histórica o vanguardia en la lucha anticolonialista?*, or *Socialism and Man in Cuba* (*El socialismo y el hombre en Cuba*). Debray's point of departure was a denunciation of the idea that the Cuban Revolution constituted an exceptional and unrepeatable phenomenon in Latin American political history. He argued that a similar triumph was possible throughout the region by means of the employment of a guerrilla *foquismo* effort to spread the struggle to every geographical and social region of a country. Although neither Debray nor Guevara excluded the communist parties from this process—as Castro himself had not excluded the Cuban Popular Socialist Party from the struggle in the Sierra Maestra—both thought that given Moscow's prejudice against armed struggle in Latin America, it would not be these old institutions but new leaders on the left who should lead the guerrillas.[47]

Sweezy and Huberman supported the thesis of the French Marxist's book from the office of *Monthly Review* in New York, just as Robin Blackburn and Perry Anderson of the *New Left Review* did so from London. The latter journal not only featured one of the most laudatory reviews of *Revolution in the Revolution?* but had also published numerous essays by Debray between 1965 and 1967.[48] In the view of these four editors, Debray's criticism of Latin American communist parties was backed by the authority of Che himself, as well as that of Castro, who in the closing speech of the

Latin American Organization of Solidarity conference in Havana in August 1967 had questioned the indifference or the rejection of the Soviets toward Latin American guerrillas.[49] The two publications' backing of Debray's book sparked multiple adverse reactions from a broad spectrum of the New Left. The year after the publication of *Revolution in the Revolution?*, Sweezy and Huberman found themselves obliged to produce the volume *Régis Debray and the Latin American Revolution* (1968), featuring a dozen critiques of the guerrilla *foquismo* thesis, and those critiques would multiply after Guevara's death in October 1967.

For example, Andre Gunder Frank, who up to this time had ascribed to dependency theory in dialogue with the Guevarist Left, reproached Debray for relegating the Latin American economy to a feudal status, which dependency theory had refuted since the beginning of the decade, and for failing to understand the economic and social structure of the region's diverse capitalisms in proposing the same revolutionary strategy for every Latin American country.[50] Brazilian sociologist Cléa Silva found similar "errors" in Debray's guerrilla *foquismo* thesis, and Manchester sociologist Peter Worsley, citing texts of Marx, Engels, and Lenin, recalled that local historical contexts were basic to the formulation of a global revolutionary theory, and unjustly cast Debray's work as a mere vulgarization of Guevara.[51]

Yet Debray did not lack defenders during the fraught and emotionally tense period following the death of Che in Bolivia. Dominican revolutionary Juan Bosch and Marxist historian William Appleman Williams lauded Debray's bravery and cited evidence that the socialist movement had often advanced in the absence of a communist vanguard, as the Cuban case itself had demonstrated. Bosch reiterated Huberman and Sweezy's own thesis in *Anatomy of a Revolution* (1960), although adding the nuance that the Cuban revolutionary leaders had produced a socialist revolution without themselves being socialists but radical nationalists.[52] Williams, for his part, recognized the importance of Debray's focus for comprehending the mobilization of a non-Marxist-Leninist Left, such as the student movement of 1968 and that of young African American radicals.[53]

Perhaps what Sweezy and Huberman never suspected is that one of the harshest criticisms of Debray's theory of guerrilla *foquismo* would come directly from Havana. Two Cuban revolutionaries, Simón Torres and Julio Aronde—whom Argentine historian Néstor Kohan identifies as "pseudonyms" for Cuban Communist Party collaborators of Manuel Piñeiro (Commander Barbarroja)—sent *Monthly Review* a detailed refutation that termed Debray's thesis "sectarian."[54] Among the first signals of the new ideological turn taken by Castro's government in 1968 with the so-called Revolutionary Offensive, which resulted in the near total statification of the island's economy and accelerated the island's definitive insertion in the Soviet bloc, were official criticisms of Guevara's voluntarism and Havana's expression of support for the Soviet invasion of Czechoslovakia.

Sweezy and Huberman traveled to the island in February and March 1968 with the goal of refreshing their view of the Cuban process seven years after *Anatomy of a Revolution* (1960) and at a moment of evident ideological and political reorientation. In November, while cowriting a new manuscript on Cuba with Sweezy, Huberman died, and Sweezy had to finish the text on his own, publishing *Socialism in Cuba* (1969) at the beginning of the following year. From the perspective of intellectual and political history, this work continued to be faithful to the parameters of *Anatomy of a Revolution*, asserting that the six central demands of the Moncada program, as articulated by Castro in *La historia me absolverá* (1954)—land, industrialization, housing, employment, education, and health—constituted the project of a socialist society in Cuba and had already been established there.[55]

In education and health, above all, Cuban progress had been extraordinary, the two authors asserted, but in the economic and political realms, the Revolutionary Offensive had introduced disquieting elements. With an economy now fully integrated within the socialist field's system of investments, credits, and trade, Cuban productivity, they noted, had not surpassed numbers from prior to the revolution and was falling behind those numbers in certain indicators. In the middle of the 1960s, the sugarcane harvest had fallen below the level of five million tons, and even below four million tons, and the production of nickel was growing very slowly and in some cases decreasing.[56] Huberman and Sweezy were now insinuating the failure of certain hypercentralized economic policies, such as that pertaining to cattle, with the drastic decline of milk production in the spring of 1968.[57]

In the debate over Cuban economic policies, Sweezy and Huberman subscribed to the view Trotskyite Ernest Mandel had proposed in the journal *Partisans*, one that reiterated, in turn, Adolfo Gilly's central idea. In the argument between those supporting the budgetary financing of state enterprises (Guevara's position), and those who believed in maintaining the financial autonomy of those enterprises (the position of Carlos Rafael Rodríguez), Mandel seemed to sympathize with the latter. However, when the debate moved to questions of what kinds of work incentives should predominate, Mandel sided with Che, asserting that moral stimulation was more important than material stimulation.[58] As Sweezy and Huberman noted, however, Guevara had been outside of the Cuban political class since 1965, and his influence, although still perceptible in certain aspects of the Revolutionary Offensive, was weakening.

Like Mandel, Sweezy and Huberman reviewed the polemic between alternative models of political economy in Cuba between 1963 and 1964 with a melancholic, defeatist tone. These economists lamented the fact that although Cuban treasury minister Luis Alvarez Rom had defended the system of budgetary financing designed by Guevara, two other ministers, Alberto Mora of Commerce, and Cuban National Bank president Marcelo Fernández Font, had supported economic calculation and entrepreneurial autonomy. The influential French economist Charles Bettelheim had also backed the latter policies, against Guevara and Mandel, based on the premise that in the transition to socialism monetary-commercial relations did not disappear and that it was necessary to make room for state capitalism. Well-positioned figures in the new Central Committee of the Cuban Communist Party, such as Rodríguez himself or Blas Roca, were supporters of this latter model, viewing it as better adjusted to the economic policies of the Soviet Union and the real socialisms of Eastern Europe.[59]

The final message of *Socialism in Cuba* (1969)—a book dedicated to Guevara yet whose opening epigraph was taken from the classic liberal work, John Stuart Mills's *Principles of Political Economy*—was a series of critical interrogations on the future of economic and political socialism in Cuba. In the view of Sweezy and Huberman, the worst effect on the island's public sphere that the absence of Guevara and other critics of the Soviet system could have was an indiscriminate statification of Cuban economic, social, and cultural life, since it would result in the bureaucratization of socialism that Che feared. Sweezy and Huberman felt that in order to avoid this result, the revolutionary government should keep turning left, in a Caribbean variation of the permanent revolution, yet they conceded that the current point of departure, from the institutional point of view, was not favorable:

> Cuba's governing system is clearly one of bureaucratic rule. Power is concentrated in the Communist Party, within the Party in the Central Committee, and within the Central Committee in the Maximum Leader. The structure was built from the top down: first came the leader, then the Central Committee, then the regional and local organizers, and finally the membership.[60]

The Cuban leadership's habitual way of compensating for this bureaucratic rationality was not to encourage the autonomy of the workers but to reinforce the charismatic tie between Castro and the masses:

> The revolutionary leadership might have seen in this situation an opportunity to attempt the difficult feat of bringing the people more directly into the governing process, forging institutions of popular participation and control and encouraging the masses to use them, to assume increasing responsibility, to share in the making of the great decisions which shape their lives. In practice, however, the relationship between government and people continued to be a paternalistic one.[61]

Unlike their *Anatomy of a Revolution* (1960), Huberman and Sweezy's *Socialism in Cuba* (1969) was not published on the island. The only Spanish edition of the book was published by Nuestro Tiempo press in Mexico. The authors' apprehensions regarding the Sovietization of insular socialism would be confirmed over the following years, when the island's failure to achieve the ten-million-ton sugar harvest goal of 1970 was followed by Cuba's joining the Eastern Bloc's Council for Mutual Economic Assistance and the start of an institutionalizing process on the island that was inspired by the Soviet model. With Cuba's Sovietization, the island lost its centrality in the theoretical and ideological debates of *Monthly Review* and of the New York Left in general. In the 1970s, the magazine founded by Sweezy and Huberman devoted more attention to other Latin American topics—the Popular Unity Coalition in Chile and its leader Salvador Allende, the urban guerrilla movements in Argentina and Uruguay, and the Sandinista Revolution in Nicaragua—than to Cuban socialism.

The attention Sweezy and Huberman devoted to Cuba in the 1960s contributed greatly to the modernization of New York's New Left, broadening its global perspective and incorporating into its agenda critical values such as the rejection of US hegemony over Latin America and opposition to centralized and hierarchical models for socialist states. The Cuban experience, despite its Soviet denouement in the 1970s, paradoxically helped to shape critical viewpoints regarding the USSR and real socialism among the Marxists of Manhattan. It was not in such a Mecca or in such a Rome where, according to Sweezy, the responses to the great interrogations of the Latin American Left would be found.

The fact that Sweezy, Huberman, Baran, and *Monthly Review* were present in the New York Left resulted in the formation of a heterodox view of the Cuban Revolution, one that was distinguishable from Marxist heterodoxy itself (the latter of which was advancing only with great difficulty on the island). Their activities and publications prevented New York Marxists from subscribing rigidly to either of the two opposing currents in the debate over Cuban economic policy in the 1960s.[62] The *Monthly*

Review collaborators' distance from the Cuban project, and above all, their inscription of that project within the framework of the Latin American Left, gave them an intellectual autonomy that permitted them to both accompany and critique the island's socialist experiment.

4

THE CULTURAL APPARATUS OF THE EMPIRE

★

DURING THE LAST TWO YEARS OF HIS LIFE, AMERICAN SOCIOLOGIST C. Wright Mills joined the intense debate that the Cuban Revolution had sparked in New York public opinion. Born in Waco, Texas, and educated at the University of Texas at Austin and the University of Wisconsin-Madison, Mills had been a professor at Columbia University since 1945. It was in New York where he wrote the principal works of his important career: *The New Men of Power: America's Labor Leaders* (1948), *White Collar: The American Middle Class* (1951), *The Power Elite* (1956), and *The Sociological Imagination* (1959). These works constituted a requisite tetralogy for the study of the recomposition of social class in the United States during World War II and the first decade of the Cold War.

The intellectual solidity of Mills's project granted him access to the center of the American public discourse. As his object of study—labor leaders, the middle class, bureaucrats, business leaders, and politicians—gained prominence among American elites, the Columbia sociologist grew ever more convinced of the importance of public opinion and the media in the formation of consensus. Already in *White Collar* (1951), he examined the role of public discourse in the development of what he called "models of consciousness," a concept that highlighted the dispute between liberal and Marxist persuasions for the soul of the middle class.[1] One of the central references of his work was liberal public intellectual Walter Lippmann, who had critiqued the power of stereotypes in American public opinion and defended the transparency of the press since the 1920s.[2]

Mills observed in *White Collar* that during the postwar period, the rise of the service economy and the spread of consumerism that accompanied the growth of a middle class of bureaucrats, lawyers, managers, doctors, and professors had resulted in paradoxical situations, including the mixed acceptance and rejection of labor unions and political parties, and the coupling of greater enlightenment with growing political indifference.[3] As he observed, public opinion now constituted a fundamental theme for the social sciences insofar as it played an ever more articulatory role for citizens in complex democracies. To this first proposition, Mills added an analysis of the role of "celebrity" in mass society, as well as a critique of the mechanisms of control employed by US economic and military elites during the transition to the Cold War.[4] As he argued, the mixture of "conservatism" and "immorality" that characterized these elites was reflected in the projection of corporate interests in the media.[5]

The Sociological Imagination (1959) represented a synthesis of Mills's intellectual project. The book summarized his observations about social change in the United States and at the same time announced his intention to increase his own public activism as a sociologist, an activism whose intellectual basis was motivated in large part by his proposal for dialogue between liberalism and Marxism as outlined in the section of his book entitled "On Reason and Freedom."[6] Since the Renaissance and the Enlightenment, as he argued in that section, modern thought had debated between knowledge of human reality and the liberation of that reality, between reason and freedom. In ideologies and in the social sciences, this tension seemed to discharge itself in the Cold War, without, according to

Mills, the binary polarization of the latter being able to reproduce itself in the former. In his view, Max Weber and Karl Marx, whom he considered the two central figures of Western thought, exemplified the necessity of assimilating the best legacies of both traditions.

It was necessary to develop the art of sociological imagination, Mills argued, in order to evade the false alternatives of the Cold War. At stake in this effort were the fortunes of humanity itself, but also something more immediate and tangible: intellectual politics. As Stanley Aronowitz recalls, Mills played those politics to their final consequences.[7] While Jean Paul Sartre was developing his idea of intellectual engagement in Paris, in New York Mills was proposing another variation of that engagement, which he called "intellectual craftsmanship."[8] He argued that the increased complexity of the public sphere in advanced democracies compelled intellectual labor to perfect its technical or artisanal elements and to hone its areas of specialization within the division of labor of mass society. This artisanal dimension, however, did not reduce the moral content of the public interventions carried out by the intellectual—a figure Mills conceived more as a politician than as a Weberian scientist—but instead broadened it.

In January 1959, just as Castro was making his triumphal entry to Havana, Mills was delivering a series of lectures at the London School of Economics entitled "The Cultural Apparatus, or the American Intellectual."[9] More than one scholar of Mills's work has noted the convergence of his ideas with those of Sartre, as well as the shared sources of both of these intellectuals' ideas in important conceptual formulations of the 1960s, such as Louis Althusser's notion of "ideological state apparatuses" or Jürgen Habermas's "public sphere."[10] Mills's travels to Latin America and the Soviet Union convinced him that it was necessary to conceptualize the cultural apparatus with greater sophistication if one aspired to destabilize the commonplaces of the Cold War binary mentality.

In his texts from these years, such as *The Causes of World War Three* (1958) or the famous "Letter to the New Left," which he sent to the London journal *New Left Review* in the summer of 1960, Mills began to conduct a double critique, on the one hand repudiating liberal rhetoric for declaring the "end of ideologies"—a position characterized by such figures as Arthur Schlesinger Jr. and Daniel Bell of the Congress for Cultural Freedom or by the journal *Encounter*—and, on the other, denouncing "vulgar Marxism" and Soviet "socialist realism" for promoting a mechanistic idea of history and culture.[11] Due to this orientation of his intellectual and political interests, Mills would inevitably focus his attention on a phenomenon that would shake American public opinion in general, and New York liberal and socialist circles in particular, during those years: the Cuban Revolution.

THE VOICE OF CUBA

Daniel Geary and Stanley Aronowitz have effectively questioned the established notion of Mills as a "lone wolf" or as American liberalism's "maverick on a motorcycle."[12] In fact, Mills was not the only liberal of his generation who read Marx through Weber, who traveled to the Soviet Union, China, and Cuba, and who sought to overcome the Manichean logic of anticommunism and the Cold War. Mills was, however, one of the most emblematic intellectuals of that radicalization and perhaps the figure who most vehemently called for abandoning both Marxism's Stalinist orthodoxy and liberalism's anticommunist orthodoxy.[13]

Unlike other American public intellectuals who sympathized with the Cuban Revolution in its early years, such as Waldo Frank and Carleton Beals, Mills did not have a lengthy experience with Latin America. His first trips to Brazil and Mexico during the 1950s had been academic in nature and were largely motivated by the interest that his sociological work had garnered in these countries. In 1957, Mexico's Fondo de Cultura Económica publishing house, then led by Argentine Arnaldo Orfila Reynal, published a Spanish translation of *The Power Elite* (*La élite del poder*), which would become an important point of reference for Mexican social sciences. The connection with Mexico led to Mills's friendship with some of the most important intellectuals of the Mexican Left at the time, such as Carlos Fuentes, Pablo González Casanova, Enrique González Pedrero, and Víctor Flores Olea.

However, prior to the Cuban Revolution, the Latin American country that Mills knew the best was not Brazil or Mexico but Puerto Rico. At the end of the 1940s, Mills and his colleagues Clarence Senior and Rose Kohn Golden conducted a field study of Puerto Rican immigrants to Manhattan's Spanish Harlem and Morrisania in the Bronx, with the objective of better understanding New York's Hispanic community. After more than a thousand interviews and various trips to San Juan, the researchers revealed the results of their survey, which, while demonstrating the overall "adaptation" of these immigrants, also foregrounded their strong cultural identification.[14]

The sociologists observed that Puerto Rican immigrants in the mid-twentieth century were undergoing changes, just like the population of the American society where they had settled. The proportion of white-collar workers among working-age Puerto Rican immigrant males and females was increasing—in 1948 it had risen to 45 percent of the male population and 22 percent of the female immigrant population—and constituted the aspiration of the majority of "skilled wage workers."[15] Educational levels of the Puerto Rican community in New York were also growing: 61 percent of this population had graduated from high school and 35 percent from college.[16] These immigrants' growing social mobility toward middle-class status was not dissolving their cultural identification but accentuating it, as could be seen in their conflicts with other communities—particularly with African Americans—but also in multiple examples of their practices of solidarity.[17]

Mills and his colleagues argued that this migratory community of New York was incomprehensible without studying and understanding the social and political history of Puerto Rico. They conceived this Caribbean nation as a "bifurcated" culture that had resulted from the clash between its Spanish colonial and slaveholding history—which they characterized as "agricultural," "patriarchal," "static," "preindustrial," and "predemocratic"—and its subjection to American hegemony since 1898, a period they described as a process of incomplete modernization.[18] The Columbia researchers' view of this American hegemony was not acritical. They considered it contradictory and unjust that Puerto Ricans had not elected their own governor until 1948, were unable to vote in US presidential elections, and lacked US congressional representation: "the incoherent political position of the Puerto Ricans symbolizes the discontinuity of their total situation."[19]

Mills, Senior, and Kohn attributed great importance to the racial and religious makeup of Puerto Ricans in their formation of a migratory identity in New York. They interpreted the decreasing proportion of black and Catholic immigrants in the Puerto Rican emigrant community as a reflection of an intensification of a process of transcultural miscegenation that had occurred on the island since the end of the nineteenth century.[20] That transculturation, similar to the phenomenon named and formulated by Fernando Ortiz in the Cuban context, did not prevent Puerto Ricans, both on the island and in New York, from identifying on a broader level as "Hispanic."[21] Machismo and racism were factors in this tradition, but they were reinforced by the government's limited educational and cultural policies.[22]

The sociologists recognized that since the end of the 1940s, the Puerto Rican government's education budget had significantly increased—education would be one of the priorities of Governor Luis Muñoz Marín and University of Río Piedras rector Jaime Benítez—and they concluded that the island's social indicators were relatively high in Latin American terms.[23] Modernization, however, was resulting in a population increase that the state was unable to manage due to its limited resources. The researchers therefore anticipated a steady increase of emigration to the United States, particularly to Spanish Harlem and Morrisania, where more than two hundred thousand Puerto Ricans resided at the time.[24]

At the moment when the Cuban Revolution triumphed in January 1959, and when Mills began to interest himself in the Cuban process, his two principal Latin American referents were Puerto Rico and Mexico. The archive of his approach to Cuba and Latin America consisted primarily of American and Mexican works, including Oscar Lewis and Edmundo Flores's studies of post-Cardenist Mexico, Lewis Hanke's *Mexico and the Caribbean* (1959), J. J. Johnson's *Political Change in Latin America* (1958), and Edward Lieuwen's *Arms and Politics in Latin America* (1960).[25]

However, his direct contact with the Puerto Rican experience a few years before led Mills to situate Cuba's colonial relation with Spain and the United States at the center of his Cuban analysis.

The American bibliography on Cuba that Mills consulted prior to his 1960 trip to Havana—including *Our Cuban Colony* (1928) by Leland H. Jenks; *Problems of New Cuba* (1935), a famous report by the Foreign Policy Association; *Rural Cuba* (1950) by Lowry Nelson; and the *Report on Cuba* (1950) of the International Bank of Reconstruction and Development—conformed to historical views of the Hispanic Caribbean that were similar to those developed in *The Puerto Rican Journey* (1950).[26] It is likely that Mills had even read some of those books during the 1940s while conducting his research on the Hispanic community of New York. The centrality of the colonial theme in *Listen, Yankee* (1960) in large part had its origination in that Puerto Rican project.

The anticolonial discourse was gaining ground in New York in those years, thanks to the convergence of critical voices of Hispanic leaders, black nationalists, and many members of the leftist Beat Generation, which would give rise to the hippie movement. Even in ex-Trotskyite and democratic-socialist sectors of the liberal Left, such as the collaborators of *Dissent* magazine, the idea that Latin American revolutions represented a decolonizing challenge to the United States similar to what the Asian and African nations presented for Europe came to be comfortably established. The young Michael Walzer, for example, would develop the decolonizing argument in an essay on Cuba that, curiously enough, was not inspired by Mills but by old Rooseveltian liberalism.[27]

Unlike Waldo Frank, Carleton Beals, and other liberals of the New Deal generation, Mills's reading of the Cuban Revolution was not accompanied by an exploration of the island's own intellectual tradition. His book did not feature quotations from Ramiro Guerra, Fernando Ortiz, or Jorge Mañach, nor disquisitions on the ideas of José Martí. His objective was less intellectually ambitious yet at the same time more politically sophisticated. For Mills, as important, or more important, than the comprehension of the Cuban Revolution itself was the critique of prejudices toward this revolution that were reflected in public opinion in the United States.

In the introductory pages of *Listen, Yankee*, which was written in September 1960, the sociologist disclosed that his travels to the island and his research had been "facilitated" by journalist Robert Taber, a CBS correspondent who, like Herbert L. Matthews, Ray Brennan, and Jules Dubois, had reported for the American media on the Castro-led insurrection against the dictatorship of Fulgencio Batista in the Sierra Maestra. Taber, however, was one of the few of these reporters and correspondents who backed the socialist radicalization of the island at the end of 1960 and, in particular, during the spring of 1961.[28] Taber had become the central operating figure of the Fair Play for Cuba Committee, the association financed by the Cuban government, and had in fact been responsible for organizing Mills's trips and those of other New York leftist intellectuals to the island.

Despite the importance for Mills of the distinction between elites and the masses, when it came to societies as stratified as those of the Hispanic Caribbean, he was rather less observant of this distinction, proposing in *Listen, Yankee* a dissolution of the boundary between the Cuban leaders and the island's people. Within his objective of rearticulating the voice of the "Cuban revolutionaries," Mills claimed to have interviewed "rebel soldiers, intellectuals, officials, journalists, and professors."[29] In fact, however, his interview subjects were members of the revolutionary government, starting with President Osvaldo Dorticós and Prime Minister Fidel Castro, including various ministers (Ernesto "Che" Guevara, Raúl Cepero Bonilla, Armando Hart, Enrique Oltuski, and others), and finally the heads of economic, cultural, and educational institutions, such as medical doctor René Vallejo, the director of agrarian reform in the eastern region of the island, and Carlos Franqui, director of the magazine *Revolución*.[30]

For Mills, the Cuban Revolution was such a popular phenomenon on the island that it was impossible to uncouple the nation's collective will from the particular interests of its government. In his view, the nation's leaders therefore articulated the voice of Cuba. As a result, in reconstructing the arguments of Cuban government figures, Mills felt no need to distinguish among their individual opinions in the articulation of that collective voice. Whether Castro or Guevara, Dorticós or Hart, Oltuski or Cepero Bonilla, all spoke

Cover of the first English edition of *Listen, Yankee*, by C. Wright Mills. (Ballantine Books, 1960)

as one. Amassed together as the voice of a single parliament, these figures all explained to the American public, through Mills's writing, what "Cuba" signified, what the meaning of the US-backed "counterrrevolution" was, what the contours of the island government's economic project were, what its position vis-à-vis communism was, and above all, what the revolutionaries understood by the term "Yankee."[31]

The tone of *Listen, Yankee* is that of a group interpellation in second person addressed by a small Caribbean nation to the economic, political, and military power of American imperialism. That interpellation takes its point of departure in the lengthy accumulation of complaints against US hegemony in Cuba since the nineteenth century, now mobilized specifically against the immediate and concrete escalation of conflict with the Cuban exile opposition and Washington's growing hostility toward the revolutionary government's accelerating radicalization. The "Yankee" that Mills and the Cuban leaders interpellated was also a subject manipulated by the mighty US communications media, which was starting to present Cuba as an island coming under the growing influence of the Soviet Union.

Such was the tone established from the book's first phrase, brilliantly maintained to its conclusion: "We Cubans know that you believe we are all led by a bunch of Communists, that the Russians are soon going to set up a rocket base, or something like that, here in Cuba, aimed at you."[32] Mills then proceeds to express, in the mouths of the island's leaders, the nationalist and egalitarian meaning of the Cuban Revolution as exemplified in specific projects—such as agrarian reform or the literacy campaign—and attempts to identify the ideological orientation of Cuban government figures in these measures rather than in the language of abstract doctrines. By chapter 5, "Communism in Cuba," Mills fully enters the debate over the ideology of the Cuban Revolution in the terms in which this debate was playing out in New York public opinion.[33]

The Cuban revolutionaries, and Mills through them, defend the island's right to maintain economic, commercial, and, of course, diplomatic relations with all nations of the world, including the Soviet Union, China, and the socialist nations of Eastern Europe. But while reiterating that these relations did not have a particular defensive agenda against the United States, the revolutionaries communicate with clarity that neither Castro nor the revolutionary government were communists. The Communist Party, they insist, comprised but one political force among many within the revolution; it was not the hegemonic current in that project. The actual hegemonic current was not communist but neither was it anticommunist, that is to say, McCarthyist. At one point, the island's leaders even speak of their own "opposition to communism," one that is different from that encouraged by Washington in the Cold War:

> Our Cuban opposition to communism doesn't mean the kind of McCarthyism that you've put up with in your country. That kind of hysterical anticommunism is very much the kind that prevails among your top Government people today, and they are trying very hard to make it come about in our country, and other countries all over the world. But we're not having any of that panic and ignorance in Cuba.[34]

The simultaneous declarations that the Cuban Revolution had a noncommunist character but also rejected prohibitions against communism on the island acquires great dialectical effect in Mills's book. The rhetorical counterpoint in question reaches a culminating moment in the formulation "anticommunism as counterrevolutionary," which had been rapidly advancing in official Cuban discourse since the end of 1959, when the desertion of aviator Pedro Luis Díaz Lanz and the resignation of President Urrutia was followed by the incarceration of revolutionary commander Huber Matos, a politician who, like Díaz Lanz and Urrutia, had accused the government of incorporating communists in its ranks and reorienting the revolution's ideology.

In these same pages, Mills's interlocutors pose the possibility that the Cuban Revolution would undergo even greater radicalization and that the Communist Party of Cuba would gain greater power within the island if US policies continued in the direction of confrontation. The Columbia University sociologist had warned of this in his introduction, stating, "It is possible to entertain about Cuba several nightmare hypotheses."[35] The voice of Cuba was a voice of anger, but one capable of assuming a pragmatic tone in the midst of its threats and invectives. At times in Mills's book, the Cuban leaders almost invite the US government to join a pact of complicity: if the Cubans were well treated, they would not turn toward communism. This was the conviction that Mills transmitted in his book:

> The Cuban Government, as of mid-1960, is not "communist" in any of the senses legitimately given to this Word. The Communist Party of Cuba, as a party, does not pose any serious threat to Cuba's political future. The leading men of Cuba's Government are not "Communist," or even Communist-type, as I have experienced communism in Latin America and in research work in the Soviet Union.[36]

But evidently Mills did not conceive ideologies as elements of negotiation but instead as social values. Unlike Jean Paul Sartre, Mills believed that the Cuban leaders did possess an ideology, and unlike Waldo Frank, he argued that this ideology was not democratic and humanist but Marxist, although neither Stalinist nor pro-Soviet. During the months that followed the debate over *Listen, Yankee*, Mills worked on an anthology of leftist thought precisely entitled *The Marxists* (1962), a work in which he featured all the ideological currents derived from *The Communist Manifesto* from the second half of the nineteenth century to the beginning of the twentieth: anarchists, Bolshevists and Menchevists, Bernstein and Bakunin, Kautsky and Lenin, Luxemburg and Gramsci, Trostsky and Mao, Fidel and Che.[37] The view of Marxism that Mills reflected in this anthology was as flexible as the one that he had reflected from Max Weber and his followers at the start of his career in the mid-1940s.[38]

At various moments of *Listen, Yankee*, a superimposition of voices takes place between the Cuban leaders and Mills in which it becomes difficult to distinguish between the latter and the former. In its passages of greatest aggressivity, the book's interpellation is directed toward the elites of US economic and military power, the same subject that Mills had criticized in his earlier books. In the final pages, when the geopolitical implications of Cuba's proximity to the United States is discussed and parallels are established between this zone of geographical proximity and other conflicted borders such as those shared by Turkey and Afghanistan with the Soviet Union, or Taiwan and Japan with China, the speaker could just as easily be Castro as Mills, who just two years before, in *The Causes of World War Three* (1958), had pointed out the precariousness of "international realism" during the Cold War.[39]

This interpretation of the blending of voices in *Listen, Yankee* also applies to the way in which the work positions itself on the question of the ideology of the Cuban process. The Cuban leaders use Mills's voice to denounce Washington's hostility toward the island, but at the same time Mills uses the Cuban Revolution to position himself as a noncommunist socialist in the American public sphere. There are moments, however, in which the voice of the island's leaders is clearly differentiated from that of their New York translator. When those leaders cite a phrase from Fernando Ortiz's *Contrapunteo cubano del azúzcar y el tabaco* (1940)[40]—"thick broth of civilization which bubbles on the Caribbean fire"—it is not in order to emphasize the transcultural character of Cuban identity but to rearticulate the nationalist myth of the island as a "major center of world affairs," and it is clear that the Cuban leaders are speaking in this instance, not Mills.[41]

The voice of Cuba, according to Mills, was not exclusively Caribbean or national but global. Cuba spoke in the name of a "hungry-nation bloc," an expression Mills used in a number of his books at the end of the 1950s and in his correspondence from the beginning of the 1960s.[42] This bloc of nations differed from developed capitalist nations and also from the nations characterized by the Soviet or Chinese systems of socialism. In some of his texts from this period, Mills referred to the NATO states and the Warsaw Pact states, delineating the two blocs in accordance with their military alliances. In practice, what Mills sought to do was to point out that revolutions like the Cuban one were occurring and would continue to occur in the Third World, as could be seen in Asia and North Africa.

Those revolutions were therefore not strictly national or regional phenomena, but responded to the rising conflicts between advanced capitalist nations and impoverished colonial or postcolonial nations. In Mills's judgment, this peripheral conflict was drawing the attention of the real socialisms of Eastern Europe, particularly the Soviet Union, and the Second World would therefore begin to draw closer to the emerging countries in order to encourage their revolutions. By warning Washington that the Soviet Union was moving toward Cuba and that Havana would end up aligning itself with Moscow if the United States failed to soften its policies toward the island, Mills was behaving like a loyal liberal who shared Washington's desire to check the growth of Soviet power.

In the debate on the Cuban Revolution in New York public opinion, Mills was one step ahead of Waldo Frank, Herbert L. Matthews, and other intellectuals who considered the ideology of Castro and his government to be "humanist" rather than Marxist. Mills thought that Castro was Marxist, although of a different stripe than the Soviet model. The Columbia sociologist's position was closer to that of Leo Huberman, Paul Sweezy, and Paul Baran, who, as of the summer of 1960, argued for the socialist character of the Cuban Revolution in the pages of *Monthly Review*. In *Listen, Yankee*, Mills referred to Sweezy and Huberman's *Anatomy of a Revolution* (1960) as the best book that had been written on Cuba in the United States.[43] Like these two authors, Mills supported Havana's right to maintain relations with the socialist camp, but he disapproved of any introduction of the bureaucratic and authoritarian mechanisms of the Eastern European regimes on the island.

The subtle contrast between Mills's position on Cuba and that of the *Monthly Review* can be more clearly perceived in J. P. Morray's eloquent and astutely entitled book, *The Second Revolution in Cuba* (1962). Morray, a graduate of the Harvard School of Law and professor at the University of California, Berkeley, was an admirer of Mills and joined *Monthly Review* in praising *Listen, Yankee*, but his aforementioned book and his article "Questions and Answers on Cuba" (published in the summer of 1962), expressed clear support for Havana's alignment with Moscow as seen in the revolutionary government's ideological shift from its initial "Jacobin restoration" period to its "Marxist-Leninist" turn, the latter of which was already clearly evident from November 1960 when

Castro and his government broke with the World Bank.[44] More overtly than Mills, Morray refuted the "revolution betrayed" motif voiced by the first revolutionary government's dissenters, by Arthur Schlesinger Jr., and by the Department of State during the Kennedy administration.

Morray believed that the ideological shift in question had been a natural result of the escalation of class conflict generated by the early revolutionary measures and by US opposition to those measures.[45] In other words, the ideological radicalization of the new Cuban elites reflected the material reality of a fracture in Cuban society and the global polarization of the Cold War. Over the course of two years, Castro and his closest followers had ceased to be liberal and democratic leaders in the cultural-political mold of other Latin American leaders such as Lázaro Cárdenas, Luis Muñoz Marín, Rómulo Betancourt, Alberto Lleras Camargo, and José Figueres (albeit with some clear differences from these other leaders), and had become more like Lenin or Mao.[46] The island's adoption of communism, and the incorporation of Soviet elements in its social and political system, was therefore part of a historical reality that Washington needed to adjust to.

ON THE EDGE OF THE NEW LEFT

In September 1960 Mills submitted the manuscript of *Listen, Yankee* to Ballantine, the New York publisher that would also produce *Sartre on Cuba* (1960). Mills's book was released at the end of that year, preceded by an advance selection in *Harper's Magazine.* As New Yorkers began reading *Listen, Yankee*, the conflict between the United States and Cuba was undergoing a considerable escalation. At the end of September, Castro had traveled to New York, where he held his famous meeting with Nikita Khrushchev, and on his return to Havana the tone of his rhetoric against the United States had harshened. Earlier, in the spring of 1960, the CIA was authorized by President Eisenhower to begin training a contingent of Cuban exiles in Guatamala. The group would land in the Bay of Pigs in April of the following year.

The release of Mills's book thus coincided with a sudden elevation of the debate over the ideological orientation of Castro and his government. *Listen, Yankee* sold several hundred copies within just a few months, and within a year Ballantine would release two further editions. Between the printing of the first and third editions, the Bay of Pigs was invaded and Castro pronounced his declaration of the "socialist" character of the Cuban Revolution during an April 16, 1961, speech that also denounced the bombings that had preceded the invasion and lauded the scientific prowess of the Soviet Union for having sent the first man—cosmonaut Yuri Gagarin—into space. Although one of the central arguments of Mills's book was an avowal of the revolution's pro-Soviet yet nonetheless Marxist character, Mills would not alter his opinion in light of these events of 1961.

In the Spanish edition of the book, which was translated by Julieta Campos and Enríque González Pedrero and issued in August 1961 by Mexico's Fondo de Cultura Económica press, several appendixes were included that are useful in reconstructing the history of the book's reception. In a "Segunda advertencia al lector" (Second Note to the Reader), Mills anticipates the responses of his critics by debating certain authors who had sought to define the ideology of the Cuban Revolution prior to his book. Mills mentions an article by Rooseveltian political figure A. A. Berle that had appeared in the October issue of *Foreign Affairs*. Berle, who would join the Kennedy administration at the beginning of the following year as a strategist for the Alliance for Progress, argued that it was becoming more and more clear that the Cuban Revolution, in both its internal structure and its foreign policy, was being oriented toward the Soviet model.[47]

Mills refuted Berle's claim, arguing that the increase of trade between Cuba and the Soviet bloc, and the indefinite postponement of democratic elections, would not automatically turn Cuba into a communist country. He admitted that the Cuban Revolution was more radical than the Mexican Revolution but assured that it bore more resemblance to the latter than to Russia's Bolshevist revolution of 1917. In any event, he argued, if the United States wished to prevent Cuba from falling into Soviet hands, then it needed to carry out policies of collaboration and tolerance toward the island. Mills then cited an old essay by Bertrand Russell, *The Theory and Practice of Bolshevism* (1920), and Edward Hallett Carr's monumental *A History of Soviet Russia* (a multivolume work whose publication began in 1950) to support the assertion that Western hostility toward Bolshevism had facilitated the rise of the Stalinist dictatorship.[48]

Not unexpectedly, one of the first detractors of Mills's book was Adolf A. Berle himself, who had previously written a negative review of *The Power Elite* (1956) in the *New York Times*.[49] In December 1960 Mills and Berle were scheduled to debate each other on the NBC television network, although the event had to be canceled when Mills suffered a massive heart attack the night before. One month earlier, in November, in a debate organized by Americans for Democratic Action, Mills confronted Kennedy administration liberals who sought to justify Washington's policies based on their identification of the Cuban Revolution as a communist project. In the appendix to the Spanish edition of his book, Mills denounced Berle and Arthur Schlesinger Jr. as "ignorant about everything related to Latin America," "first-class obfuscated liberals," and "historically doctrinaire anticommunists" who were badly advising Kennedy on policies related to Cuba.[50]

Although Mills was not without his defenders in New York public opinion, such as the editors of *Monthly Review*, Carleton Beals at the *Nation*, or Joseph Hansen at the *Militant*, his book was met with loud denunciations from both the conservative Right and the liberal Left, which only increased as the Cuban government more clearly aligned itself with the Soviet Union starting in the spring of 1961. Criticisms of the book by journalists who had initially backed the Cuban Revolution—and whom Mills had used as sources in his book, such as Jules Dubois—were followed by objections printed in liberal magazines such as *Dissent* and *Encounter* from liberal and Trotskyist voices associated with the Congress for Cultural Freedom and by the explicit or implicit disapproval of intellectuals allied with social democracy or democratic socialism, including Max Lerner, Theodore Draper, Irvine Kristol, and Irving Howe.[51]

The reaction against *Listen, Yankee* was sufficiently vehement that Mills's Mexican friends, led by Carlos Fuentes, published a letter of support for him in the *Saturday Review* in January 1961, signed by director of the Fondo de Cultura Económica Arnaldo Orfila Reynal and by other leftist Mexican intellectuals, such as Pablo González Casanova and Enríque González Pedrero. In February of that year, *Evergreen Review* printed a long interview between Mills and these Mexican intellectuals designed as a response to the attacks.[52] The Mexican Left, with its long-standing intellectual tradition of solidarity with the revolution in its own nation and with the Spanish Republic, came out in strong defense of Mills in New York public opinion.

As evidenced in his letters during these months, Mills felt wounded by the liberal attacks. His reaction in the appendix "Escucha otra vez, yanqui" (Listen again, Yankee), also printed in the Fondo de Cultura Económica translation of his book, was overly irate, referring to both his liberal and conservative detractors as "brothers" in anticommunism.[53] As he also argued in this text, the Cuban Revolution had helped to unmask liberalism by revealing its fundamental complicity with conservativism with regard to democracy and the democratic response to totalitarianism. Perhaps even Mills himself was conscious of his own injustice in making this claim: Max Lerner's criticism of Cuba's alliance with the Soviet Union was definitely not of the same order as the rabid anticommunism of a Nathaniel Weyl, as Mills had argued.[54]

Mills was also unjust in referring to all Cuban dissidents who had supported the Bay of Pigs invasion—whether on the island or in exile—as soldiers of the CIA. Mills did not acknowledge the possibility of any autonomous will on the part of political dissident figures, such as José Miró Cardona, Manuel Ray y Rivero, Manuel Artime Buesa, José Ignacio Rasco, and others, most of whom had opposed Batista, backed the revolution, and had even served in the new Cuban government during its first year. Despite his harsh anticommunism, historian Herminio Portell Vilá, a nationalist critic of American annexation and expansionism against Cuba, was correct in reproaching Mills for refusing to recognize any legitimacy on the part of the Cuban opposition movement and exile community.[55]

Yet while strongly attacking liberals of his generation for rejecting the pro-Soviet turn of the Cuban Revolution, Mills, in the midst of this debate, continued to claim the banner of liberalism for himself. In a passage of *Listen, Yankee*, for example, he adopts as his own L. T. Hobhouse's declaration of liberal principles (originally made in a work precisely entitled *Liberalism* [1911]), stating, "I cannot give unconditional loyalties to any institution, man, state, movement or nation. My loyalties are conditional upon my own convictions and my own values."[56] Mills's continued identification with liberal values despite his resolute acceptance of Marxism and his passionate defense of the Cuban Revolution no doubt had to do with the elaboration of the concept of the "New Left" and critiques of the Cold War "cultural apparatus," initiatives in which he would become involved during his final years.

Mills's letters written between 1960 and 1962 in the midst of his Cuba debate with liberals and conservatives describe the consolidation of his interest in the diversity of twentieth-century Marxisms and the possibilities of dialogue between that rich tradition and liberal thought. One of Mills's friends and epistolary correspondents during this period was British Marxist historian Edward Palmer Thompson (1924–93), founder of the journal *Past and Present* and one of the central figures of twentieth-century British Marxism. At the time, Thompson had become close to the *New Left Review*, a magazine founded in 1960 and directed first by Stuart Hall and then by Perry Anderson. The celebrated "Letter to the New Left" addressed by Mills to his British friends had provided the journal with its name.

In his correspondence with both Thompson and Ralph Miliband, Mills disclosed his displeasure over the aggressivity that the debate over Cuba had adopted in the United States. In letters to Thompson and Miliband at the end of 1960 and the beginning of 1961, he suggests that the first heart attack he had suffered in December 1960 was due to the emotional tension of the debate.[57] Both Thompson and Miliband proposed that Mills travel to London, as a sort of therapy, to give a course on the "Varieties of Marxism," a project that would subsequently result in his book *The Marxists* (1962). Mills also commented to Thompson that he had written a letter to Castro requesting that Thompson be hired in Cuba as an adviser to the National Institute of Agrarian Reform (Instituto Nacional de Reforma Agraria [INRA]), given the British Marxist's growing interest in rural European history, and suggested that Thompson also teach a course in Havana similar to the one Mills planned for London.[58]

The work that Mills imagined for Thompson in Havana made sense for the American sociologist as one more means of reinforcing the heterodox character of Cuban socialism. Like a number of Marxists of his generation, Thompson had resigned from the British Communist Party in 1956 as a protest over the Soviet invasion of Hungary. He had also demonstrated this intellectual autonomy in his first book, *William Morris: Romantic to Revolutionary* (1955), which proposed a rereading of British utopian socialism against the predominant interpretation maintained by Soviet "scientific socialism," as well as a positive assessment of the British Romantic tradition (Keats, Carlyle, Ruskin, and so on), which would lay the groundwork of Thompson's poetics of English history.[59] The book exemplified Thompson's interest in highlighting the diversity and ideological flexibility of the nineteenth-century Socialist League moment, in which anarchists, unionists, communists, Fabians, and social democrats rejected different modes of theoretical and political "purism."[60]

Thompson's reaction against Soviet-style Marxist-Leninism would be manifested more clearly in his next book, *The Making of the English Working Class* (1963), a classic of twentieth-century Marxist historiography.[61] Thompson's reflections on the "tree of liberty" and the socialist tradition, on the role of "moral machinery" in the capitalist exploitation of wage labor, or on the plurality of radical culture, which was characteristic of the class consciousness of English workers during the nineteenth century, owed very little to the dogmatic historical materialism that predominated in the Soviet Union and in the "popular democracies" of Eastern Europe.[62] It was while Thompson was working on the manuscript of this work that he received Mills's letter informing him of the upcoming invitation to Havana—one that would never materialize.

Unlike other British Marxists associated with the *New Left Review*, such as Perry Anderson, Robin Blackburn, and Eric Hobsbawm, who published in the Cuban journal *Pensamiento Crítico* or who, like Miliband, would attend the Cultural Congress of Havana in January 1968, Thompson maintained a distance from Cuban socialism.[63] It is perhaps noteworthy to observe that during Thompson's debates with Perry Anderson, Louis Althusser, and French structuralism, spurred by the *New Left Review*'s support for structuralism, *Pensamiento Crítico* chose to side with the Althusserians, which was the variant of Western Marxism that maintained perhaps the strongest ties with Soviet dialectical and historical materialism during the 1960s.[64] Thompson's sympathy with terms such as "libertarian communism" or "humanist socialism," as demonstrated by Gerard McCann and Brian D. Palmer, in addition to his resolute pacifism and his critique of paternalistic or indulgent views of European leftists vis-à-vis Third World decolonizing nationalisms (which would lead him to interpellate Sartre's prologue for Frantz Fanon's *The Condemned of the Earth*, Keith Buchanan's anticolonialist articles in the *New Left Review*, and even Mills's *Listen, Yankee*), placed him outside of the dialogue between the Cuban Revolution and the New Left.[65]

Thompson's distance from orthodox Marxist-Leninism, his eloquent anti-Stalinism, and his rejection of American and British, but also Soviet, participation in the arms race, helped to reinforce the intellectual autonomy of Mills himself. When Thompson defined himself as "libertarian" or "humanist," he sought to distinguish his positions from Moscow and the communist parties, similar to the way Mills sought to identify himself with the term "liberal."

Mills's anthology *The Marxists*, his final intellectual project, was proof of this desire to promote the construction of a New Left, one critical of the hegemonic world powers and at the same time distinguished in its discourses and practices from the Cold War communist and liberal Left. It was this historical framework that the New Left imagined by Mills and Thompson sought to overcome. In selecting the pieces he would feature in *The Marxists*, Mills employed extraordinarily inclusive selection criteria, which allowed him to recuperate and emphasize the plurality of the Marxist tradition since the middle of the nineteenth century. The anthology excluded no one, at least from the Euro-American context. It featured communists, anarchists, and social democrats; Marx, Engels, Bakunin, Lassalle, and Bernstein; the Bolsheviks and their enemies; Lenin and Kautsky; Trotsky and Luxemburg; Gramsci and Lukács; Korsh and Sartre; Mao and Stalin. However, the only Latin American Marxists that Mills devoted space to in the anthology were Castro and Guevara, an inclusion, and an exclusion, which was highly symptomatic of Mills's own ignorance—shared by many European leftist intellectuals—of the rich Latin American Marxist tradition, which, by the middle of the twentieth century, included such notable figures as Juan B. Justo, José Carlos Mariátegui, and Julio Antonio Mella.

In Mills's anthology the variant of Marxism that was most clearly presented in a negative light was the Leninist and/or Stalinist variety of Soviet orthodoxy. The Columbia University sociologist's sympathy for Western critical Marxism was evident in the collection: in his view, it was in the diverse currents of Western Marxism where a dialogue with noncommunist liberalism could be produced. This inclination would cause problems for Mills when, between the end of 1961 and the beginning of 1962, the Cuban government began to take concrete steps toward the adoption of Soviet-style institutions, such as the institution of single-party rule, the shuttering of public debate, the elimination of autonomy in civil society, and the imposition of state control over the economy. Daniel Geary and Stanley Aronowitz argue that Mills was bothered by Castro's sudden avowel of identification with Marxist-Leninism because it undermined a part of his argument.[66]

In light of this final chapter of the Columbia sociologist's relation to the Cuban Revolution, the place that Mills assigned to Cuba within the New Left perhaps requires a reassessment. A careful reading of Mills's "Letter to the New Left" (1960), a programmatic document with regard to the renewal of Western socialist thought in the 1960s and 1970s, reveals that, against what some authors have argued, there was no full consensus about Cuba's place in the New Left.[67] As Holger Nehring and Wade Matthews recall, Mills was led to write his letter out of his favorable reaction—although one that did not lack detailed objections—to reading E. P. Thompson's edited volume *Out of Apathy* (1960), a collection of articles on the status of socialism in British and global contexts written by Stuart Hall, Alasdair MacIntyre, R. Samuel, Peter Worsley, K. Alexander, and Thompson himself. [68]

The volume's authors constitute the group of British Marxists who in January 1960 founded the journal *New Left Review*, of which the Jamaican Stuart Hall served as the first editor. As reflected in the editorial in the journal's seventh issue, "The Siege of Cuba" (1960), Hall's view of the Cuban Revolution shared the sense of puzzlement and speculation that characterized the response of the European and American critical Left at that time. In February 1961, two months prior to the invasion of Girón and the declaration of the socialist character of the revolutionary government, the British Marxists, in the aforementioned editorial, pondered the type of socialism Cuba would eventually adopt. Would it be "olive-green" or "Comintern red"? Would Castro consolidate his personal leadership and become a "Tito" of the Caribbean, or would the Cuban Communist Party reproduce a bureaucracy similar to the Soviet or Euro-Oriental model? Would Cuba play a role of "active neutrality" in the world order, or would it turn into a kind of "Formosa" off the southeastern coast of the United States? Would "humanist and libertarian" values predominate on the island, or would Havana succumb to Cold War realism?[69]

Mills's letter did not participate in posing these questions, instead designating the Cuban Revolution as a New Left phenomenon independent of any consideration of the type of socialism that might be adopted on the island. In a way, Mills's letter responded avant la lettre to the "Siege of Cuba" editorial, since it reacted to the "ambiguities" encountered by the British Marxists in recent global experiences of leftist political change—such as the Cuban Revolution itself or the installation of Cemal Gürsel's government in Turkey following the coup d'état of May 1960—where the political system might evolve either toward totalitarian or authoritarian forms of state organization.[70] In *Listen, Yankee* (1960), he himself had recognized these ambiguities and had not discounted the possibility that Cuban socialism might become just another dictatorship. But rather than focus on this kind of speculation, the sociologist preferred to consider that the Cuban Revolution's place within the New Left was ensured, at least during its first three years, due to its contribution to the articulation of a third bloc voice different from that of NATO or the Warsaw Pact: the bloc of the hungry Third World nations.[71]

The reference to Cuba in the "Letter to the New Left" was no more than marginal, limited to Mills's comment on the ideological uncertainty surrounding the Cuban or Turkish contexts. The letter's central argument was Mills's attestation of the rise of a New Left different from the traditional communist and liberal leftisms that had formed in the wake of the Bolshevik Revolution of 1917. The argument in question was an extension of the ideas Mills presented that same year in *Listen, Yankee*, where he precisely argued that it was unnecessary to wait for the Cuban Revolution to define itself ideologically in order to support it, since the support itself would help prevent the island's Sovietization.

The letter to Thompson and the British Marxists therefore opened a front of interrogation of the communist—particularly the pro-Soviet—Left, which was also an implicit effect of *Listen, Yankee*. When the Cuban project shifted toward the Soviet model, the move represented not only an assault on the image of the Cuban Revolution that Mills sought to communicate but a challenge to the very alliance between liberals and Marxists that the Columbia University sociologist was proposing. Against *Listen, Yankee*'s message that the Cuban Revolution had helped to unmask rightward tendencies among American liberals, the effect provoked by Cuba's alignment with the Soviet bloc would only be a sense of disappointment among liberals, Trotskyites, Social Democrats, humanists, libertarians, pacifists, and many others, a disappointment that Stuart Hall would effectively summarize in his influential essay *The Hippies: An American Moment* (1968).

Mills did not get the opportunity to fully experience this American moment of the Western Left that unfolded during the 1960s, although he contributed to the theoretical profile of that moment like few others of his generation. Without doubt, his eloquent invective against the cultural apparatus of the United States during the most fraught years of the Cold War is an example of intellectual courage during a dangerous and convulsive period. Critical socialists at the time had to confront not only their traditional enemies on the conservative Right but also their adversaries on the dogmatic Left, who persisted in subordinating international conflicts, particularly the dilemmas of socialist societies with regard to material and cultural production, to the rigid paradigms of what Mills himself recognized as the ontology and aesthetics of "socialist realism."

Mills's 1961 correspondence with two Latin American friends, the Mexican writer Carlos Fuentes and the Argentine director of the Fondo de Cultura Económica press, regarding the Fondo's reeditions and reissuings of *Listen, Yankee*—which reached a total press run of 70,000 copies and for which the publisher paid the author more than 10,000 Mexican pesos ($800 US dollars in 1961)—help one to better understand the somewhat unstable place that Mills granted the Cuban experience within the New Left. Since October 1960 Fuentes had proposed to Orfila Reynal that the book be published by the Fondo, and when the translation by Enrique González Pedrero and Julieta Campos was ready at the beginning of 1961, Mills suggested that he should perhaps travel to Cuba to gather new information about the revolution's communist shift and incorporate it into the book.[72] But in May of that year, following the Bay of Pigs invasion and the declaration of the revolution's "socialist character," Orfila wrote to Mills, telling him that since the 20,000 copies of the first and second editions had already sold out, it was necessary to issue the third edition with an epilogue:

> this led us to prepare a third edition, which we deemed should be ready for the end of June, but in view of the dynamics of the Cuban Revolution, we have thought that it would be most interesting to add a foreword or appendix, with reference to the fundamental events of the last months, particularly the recent aggression.[73]

Mills's original idea was to make another trip to the island, in the winter of 1961, to find out what kind of Marxism or socialism the Cuban leaders had in mind. In the summer, Fuentes met with Mills in Prague, and the two seem to have agreed that the third edition should appear with more than just the new preface that Mills had already written and sent to the translators. It was for this reason that, starting in September 1961, Mills began to request that Orfila issue a fourth edition featuring substantial modifications to the original text of *Listen, Yankee.* At that point, Orfila responded by suggesting that Mills abandon the idea, since after the third edition, "the market for this book could already be satisfied."[74] During those months, Orfila commented to Mills, who was now in London, that the Cuban revolutionary government's minister of foreign trade, Raúl Cepero Bonilla, was interested in communicating with him in order to send him some materials related to the new Cuban economy.[75]

During the final months of 1961 Mills's health had deteriorated and the aggressive attacks levied on him by the anticommunist right-wing press in the United States led him to consider a temporary exile. Fuentes and Orfila encouraged him to accept an invitation from a Mexican university: "they would be very happy if you accept to teach as permanent professor and maybe, from here, you would contemplate the events of the world with a different perspective."[76] One of Mills's final letters to Orfila allows one to conclude that, despite accumulating new material on the socialist transition that had been initiated in Cuba, which would adjust or alter some of his points of view about the Cuban Revolution and its growing relations with the Soviet bloc, Mills decided to leave the manuscript as it was and to abandon the focus and format he had employed in *Listen, Yankee*, now considering them limited:

> I'm not now able to plan another journey to Cuba, as much as I'd like to, but even if I did, I rather doubt that we could do much more than we have with this particular book. Next time I write about Cuba, it will have to be another book, and it will have to be about more Latin America, not just Cuba.[77]

Mills's death in 1962 prevented him from further developing his vision of Cuban socialism through an interrogation of the process of the Cuban system's institutionalization during the 1960s and 1970s. Many aspects of his conceptualization of the New Left were discordant with such a process of institutionalization and the specter of what it would soon lead to in the Cuban context. The bureaucratic structure of Cuban socialism would end up reproducing not a few of the principles of the Soviet model of government and state organization. Those principles were already distancing Mills from Havana even while his criticism of the US cultural apparatus during the Cold War tied him to the Cuban Revolution and to a strong defense of Cuba's right to construct a social and political order that would differ from capitalism and democracy.

5

MOONS OF THE REVOLUTION

★

When the Cuban Revolution triumphed in January 1959, another revolution was brewing in American literature: the aesthetic revolt of the Beat Generation. In 1956, Lawrence Ferlinghetti at San Francisco's City Lights Press had published Allen Ginsberg's *Howl*, a book that provoked a reaction that led to an obscenity trial in the US court system. The following year, as the critics were still digesting Ginsberg's collection, Jack Kerouac's *On the Road* was published by Viking Press in New York. In 1959, William S. Burroughs's *Naked Lunch*, the story of junkie William Lee's travels through the United States, Mexico, and Morocco, was published in Paris; obscenity trials back in the United States delayed the release of an American edition until 1962, two years after Castro's forces took power in Havana. As Todd F. Tietchen has observed, it was inevitable that the paths of these two revolutions would cross only to immediately diverge.[1]

Many members of the Beat Generation were enamored with the Cuban Revolution and traveled to the island in order to directly experience its social and political process. Tietchen's study particularly emphasizes the Cuba sojourns of Lawrence Ferlinghetti, Amiri Baraka (LeRoi Jones), Marc Schleifer, and, of course, Allen

Ginsberg.[2] All four of these writers were members of the Fair Play for Cuba Committee (FPCC), which was founded in 1960 and led by veteran Latin Americanists Waldo Frank and Carleton Beals. The group's membership comprised intellectuals, journalists, and politicians who worked to encourage nonpunitive US policies toward the island. During the widely followed US Senate hearings on the FPCC's activities, CBS journalist Robert Taber confirmed that the group had received financing from the Cuban government and that, as part of its objectives, it had organized travels to the island in which Ferlinghetti, Baraka, and Schleifer had taken part.

These were the years (1960–62) when US policies toward Cuba were turning increasingly hostile, as reflected in the American-supported Bay of Pigs invasion, other violent US actions against the Cuban regime, and the Kennedy administration's subsequent declaration of a trade embargo against the island. These were also the years in which the Cuban Revolution radicalized its own ideology, abandoning its original liberal humanism, canceling numerous agreements with the Western New Left, and aligning itself with Moscow. The writings of Ferlinghetti, Jones, and Schleifer on Cuba during this period reflect these writers' strong sense of identification with what they viewed as a process of social and political change in a postcolonial nation of the Hispanic Caribbean, a process that would reverse that nation's dependent and underdeveloped status by deterring US hegemony and without reproducing the bureaucratic models of socialism of the Soviet Union and Eastern Europe.[3]

In a blurb written for the back cover of *The Cubalogues* (2010), Ferlinghetti defines himself "as an early supporter of the original non-Communist revolution" in Cuba. In his texts on Cuba during these years, one finds no defense of socialism as a political system or of Marxism-Leninism as a social ideology. For Ferlinghetti, as for Baraka and Schleifer, to express solidarity with Cuba meant supporting primordial political values anterior to or independent from the ideological polarization of the Cold War, such as recognition of Cuba's sovereignty, rejection of the obscene exercise of US hegemony around the globe, and even respect for the life of Castro.

The last, in fact, was the theme of Ferlinghetti's poem "One Thousand Fearful Words for Fidel Castro" (1961), in which the beat poet reacts against the psychiatric discourse of the American Right with respect to Castro:

> I'm sitting in Mike's Place trying to figure out
> what's going to happen
> without Fidel Castro
> Among the salami sandwiches and spittoons
> I see no solution
> It's going to be a tragedy
> I see no way out
> Among the admen and slumming models
> and the brilliant snooping columnists
> who are qualified to call Castro psychotic
> because they no doubt are doctors
> and have examined him personally
> and know a paranoid hysterical tyrant when they see one
> because they have it on first hand
> from personal observations by the CIA
> and the great disinterested news services[4]

A similar inscription of the Cuban theme is found in the poetry of Allen Ginsberg at the beginning of the 1960s. But from the earliest writings on Cuba by the author of *Howl*, one also notes a sense of ambivalence about the revolution, an ambivalence similar to that of Waldo Frank, who, as Michael A. Ogorzaly recalls, wrote in his notes regarding Castro, "his hysterical speeches sicken me," while at the same time publically opposing US policy against the island.[5] Ginsberg's public and private texts during these years show a similar vacillation, between the fantasy of a revolutionary Cuba and a rejection of communism in the Caribbean. The vacillation in question merits a closer exploration. Ginsberg, unlike Ferlinghetti, Baraka, and Schleifer, did not travel to the island during the first years of the revolution but rather in 1965, when he was invited to serve on the jury for the Casa de las Américas poetry award that year. Not for its belatedness was Ginsberg's Cuban experience any less intense.

Ginsberg's trip to Havana, his contact with gay and black poets of the city's El Puente group, and his subsequent deportation from Cuba can be situated within the plot line of encounters and frictions that was traced between Havana and New York during the 1960s. Those encounters and frictions would involve discourses and cultural practices that were decisive for leftist activity in both cities, including sexual and corporeal freedom, the consumption of drugs, the formation of autonomous associations, and the practice of automatic reading and writing—a "raptured" practice, as Germán Labrador Mendez refers to it ("letras arrebatas") in his study of the literature of the post-Franco political transition in Spain.[6]

Letters sent by Burroughs from his hotel in the Latin Quarter of Paris to his writer friends in New York and San Francisco provide a good example of the view of the Cuban Revolution held by members of the Beat Generation. Burroughs, who had already published works that were developing a cult following, such as *Naked Lunch*, *The Soft Machine*, and *Nova Express*, surveyed the Cuban experiment with a mixture of curiosity and skepticism from a life lived on the edge, between drugs and sex, between Tangier and Paris.[7] As expressed in his letters, Burroughs felt that socialism on a Caribbean island was a good thing for decolonization but that if it failed to explode the walls of moral bourgeois containment and ended up merely reproducing the structures of communist totalitarianism, then it did not represent a truly liberating option.

PINK CASTRO

Ginsberg's poetry, as his best critics have demonstrated, constituted a veritable machinery of absorption and reproduction of public messages from the mid-1950s onward. *Howl* (1956), and particularly *Kaddish* (1961) and *Empty Mirror* (1961), are characterized by a pop mood that processes cultural icons and commercial messages, ideological stereotypes, and moral dogmas. Ginsberg gave poetry a new capacity for political aggression, one directed fundamentally against American bourgeois social and sexual conservatism. His work's capture of a multiplicity of characters and topics from the New York public sphere, in particular, did not exclude the figures of Castro and Guevara, the Cuban Revolution's two most visible leaders, and who visited New York on various occasions at the beginning of the 1960s.

Cuba made an appearance in Ginsberg's poetry before the revolution ever did. A journey to Havana taken by the poet in 1953 produced a work, later published in *Reality Sandwiches, 1953–60* (1963), that conveys a nocturnal vision of the island capital under the old regime. The vision is populated with bar patrons, including the poet himself, drinking Cuba libres at dawn under the radiance of illuminated signs. The poem's city is an impressionistic Havana of nightwalkers, police, prostitutes, and *chulos*: "In walks a weird Cezanne / vision of the nowhere hip Cuban: / tall, thin, check grey suit, / gray felt shoes, / blaring gambler's hat."[8] A Havana, in short, not unlike the vision of the city captured by Sabá Cabrera Infante and Orlando Jiménez Leal in the film *PM*, whose censorship would lead to the closing of *Lunes de Revolución*, the magazine that published Ginsberg's first texts in Cuba.

Already involved in the FPCC starting in 1960, Ginsberg began to incorporate Castro and Guevara in his *Journals* and poetry notebooks. However, the way in which these figures appear in his printed works is quite different from the view disclosed in his private notes. For example, in November 1960 Ginsberg wrote the following verses in his *Journals*: "I'm smarter than Eisenhower . . . He, whoever, Castro, Kennedy, whosever Elected King."[9] In a poem of January 1961, Ginsberg undoes the symbolic equivalence between Castro and Kennedy, insinuated in the note by means of a well-known homoerotic coquetry: "Che Guevara has a big cock / Castro's balls are pink."[10] Another composition written in February 1961 proposes a gaze similar to Ferlinghetti's, in which Castro's figure is presented as a scapegoat of the American imperialist Right:

> the Pharisees are US Congress & Publicans is the American
> people who have driven righteous bearded faithful pink new
> Castro 1961 is he mad?
> Who knows—Hope for him, he stay true

and his wormy 45-year dying peasants teach Deaths beauty
sugar beyond politics, build iron children schools. . . .[11]

The writers of the New Left, particularly those related to the Beat Generation and the civil rights movement, were impressed with Castro's four-hour speech before the United Nations in September 1960, and by the Cuban leader's gesture in moving the Cuban delegation to the Hotel Theresa in Harlem, where he met with Malcolm X. In the gestures and language of the revolutionary leaders—who at the time were at pains to not position themselves as favorable to communism—there was a dialogue with the Left's symbolic repertoire that interested the young Americans. The pink color that Ginsberg observed on Castro's skin was a metaphor for an ideology of the Left, neither red nor white but tinged with both red and white elements. This pink Castro was also a symbol of the subjects that the white ideology of Yankee imperialism might sacrifice, if it chose to do so, in the United States, Latin America, Asia, or Africa.

From his journal notes, we know that Ginsberg came under great pressure during the US hearings against the FPCC at the beginning of the 1960s. That pressure only increased when Castro declared the "socialist" character of the revolution just hours before the Bay of Pigs invasion. As the revolutionary leaders pronounced their public declarations of Marxist-Leninist ideology, the position of figures like Ginsberg and Ferlinghetti, who had defended the Cuban Revolution as standing for another kind of Left, was put in a state of suspense. It was this state, compounded by reports from the island on the censorship of the film *PM* and the closing of *Lunes de Revolución* magazine, directed by Guillermo Cabrera Infante, that led Ginsberg to write his first clearly critical notes on Cuban socialism. In December 1961, for example, he penned the following lines:

Allessandri [*sic*] of Chile, trickery and oily manners, Castro of
Cuba, a big cigar and he wants to be a hero too,
He thinks of his name in the future & shuts down the Moons of
the Revolution.—
The Moon of the Cuban Rebellion's gone under the laughing
Carib![12]

Already here in Ginsberg's work, Castro is portrayed as one more Latin American caudillo, a political figure whose manner might differ from that of the civil president of Chile but who is nonetheless capable of authoritarian moves such as the closing of *Lunes de Revolución*. In a few months, the revolutionary leader had ceased to be a homoerotic symbol for Ginsberg and had instead become a personification of machismo. In a poem devoted to the closing of *Lunes de Revolución*, Ginsberg definitively foregrounds this change in his view of Cuban socialism by juxtaposing communism and capitalism as hegemonic equivalences. The poem reiterates the comparison between Castro and Kennedy suggested in the November 1960 *Journal* entry, but this time it inserts the Cuban leader's revolution into the Cold War Soviet bloc:

The Moon of the Cuban
Revolution's gone under
the Laughing Carib—
I told you so!

Pierrot Lunaire's been
banned from the stands
for seraphim tender cries
Wouldn't you know!

What'll we do for new
hope for the masses now
politics shows its tricks
How should I know?

Communists, Capitalists
play up to the masses
and both are sincere but
Business is slow!

Le Roi Jones President
I'll be the Treasury
We'll reform the world with
our stupid noses in a row!

Cut up the world, and
You'll see the right answer

Words are the weapons,
the weapons must go![13]

Ginsberg appeals here to a pacifist formula that allows him to situate communism and capitalism on the same level of threat to world peace and the survival of the human species. This was a frequent argumentative trope in Western humanism at the time, one associated as much with Albert Einstein as with Bertrand Russell, but in Ginsberg's voice the trope shifts toward the horizon of the New Left thanks to the poet's antiauthoritarian discourse, which was concerned with racial, sexual, and religious subjectivities. Ginsberg's pacifism, which would soon be aimed against the Vietnam War, shared its strong conviction of the interpellative potential of the written and spoken word with other discourses of the New York Left at the time, such as the Black Panthers or the Puerto Rican Young Lords. In Ginsberg's work, pacifism comprises a kind of violent call to peace, further characterized by resonances of the decolonizing thought of Frantz Fanon and Che Guevara, and involving marginalized and repressed communities such as homosexuals, bohemians, and addicts.

However, the rhyme scheme of Ginsberg's poem also seems to parody the poetry of Nicolás Guillén and other Cuban communist poets who were beginning to be associated with the growing cultural dogmatism of Cuban institutions—the very dogmatism that had provoked the closing of *Lunes de Revolución*. The ironic tone of the poem as a whole seems to convey Ginsberg's unease with maintaining public support for the Cuban Revolution—or his displeasure with the idea of writing work favorable to that revolution—in a New York public sphere associated with anticommunism and at a moment when the first signs of incorporation of the discourses and practices of real socialism were beginning to appear in Cuba. The caprice of suggesting a "Le Roi Jones President" serves to present the black poet as the community's alternative prince, as a statesman alien to the great chess match of the Cold War.

There was a growing friction between the libertarian politics projected in Ginsberg's poetry and the revolutionary and socialist morality postulated by the Cuban Revolution. The beat poet attempts to convey this friction in his "Prose Contribution to the

Cuban Revolution" (1961), a text written in October of that year and published in the first issue of *Pa'Lante* (1962), a magazine produced by the League of Militant Poets of New York, an ephemeral association of socialist and communist writers led by Hispanic writer José Yglesias and in which numerous beat poets collaborated. Ginsberg conceived of prose as a more public type of text than even printed poetry and therefore the ideal medium for exploring the theme of the ideology of the Cuban Revolution that pervaded New York public opinion during those years.

The first pages of the text, however, are not dedicated to Cuba or the revolution but to the literary memory of the Beat Generation. Ginsberg expresses his conviction that the two events, the triumph of the Cuban Revolution in Latin America and the emergence of the Beat Generation in American literature, were connected. He begins by announcing his topic: "this will have to be long junk letter so might as well relax and get to the point that's bothering me, you maybe right now, jump in, what to do about politics, Cuba, human history, what I should do, what you are doing."[14] However, the first six pages of the text's total of eight pages are devoted to a reconstruction of the poetics and ethics of Ginsberg's intellectual generation. He writes of his homosexual encounters in the streets of Manhattan and San Francisco or with young Greek men as in the age of Plato. He remembers Peter Orlosky, Neal Cassidy, Jack Kerouac, William Burroughs, Lucien Carr, Gregory Corso, and Herbert Huncke, his companions in love and literature.[15]

Ginsberg subsequently recalls the readings during his youth of the works that constructed his generation's imaginary: Shakespeare, Blake, Rimbaud, Whitman, Dostoyevsky. He evokes opposition to Hitler, solidarity with the republican struggle during the Spanish Civil War, the tense relation with Russian communism, the rejection of anti-Semitism from the Right and the Left, his initiation to Buddhism, and his experience with drugs.[16] Finally, he turns to the topic of Cuba, a country that, because it was governed by a group of young communists, Ginsberg states, should be naturally thought of just as one thought of the problems of Russia or China.[17] In Ginsberg's text there is an implicit acceptance of Cuban communism as an act of sovereignty on the part of the Cuban government, although this acceptance is expressed with reservations that denote the poet's lack of sympathy with the type of state that such a system would construct in Cuba.

Ginsberg observes a global tendency toward the development of mechanisms of social control, which were manifested as much in communism as in capitalism. The implicit human problem presented by this "universal monopoly on reality," which he believed was established through the rationality of a transcendent Logos alien to historical subjects, had no solution in either of the two models that were confronting each other in the Cold War. In fact, the poet argued, those models only further demonstrated that the principles of vigilance and punishment of consciousnesses were becoming ever more global, imposed through rigid laws and moral codes and restricting individual freedoms by penalizing beliefs, habits, and life practices, such as homosexuality or drugs. The Cuban Revolution's communist turn, he asserted, reduced emancipatory expectations in the island's political process:

> I see no reason why no government on earth is really alive in this evolutionary direction. All governments including the Cuban are still operating within the rules of identity forced on them by already outmoded means of consciousness. I say outmoded since it has brought all governments to edge of world destruction. No government, not even the most Marxian revolutionary and well-intended like Cuba presumably, is guiltless in the general world mess, no one can afford to be righteous any more. Righteous and right and wrong still fakes of the old suicidal identity.[18]

Ginsberg recalled that in a New York conversation with *Revolución* magazine's editor Carlos Franqui, prior to the censorship of its literary supplement, *Lunes de Revolución*, directed by Guillermo Cabrera Infante, the *Revolución* editor had made the following comment to him: "It should be easier for a poet to understand a revolution than for a revolution to understand poetry."[19] The phrase led Ginsberg to articulate the point where his literary poetics found itself unable to communicate with Cuban revolutionary politics. The point in question was psychic experimentation, as illustrated by the freedom to use marijuana, which he believed was poets' right. By subscribing to the most rationalist arguments against the use of marijuana, he asserted, the Cuban government had fully inscribed itself within the bureaucratic dogmatism of both the American Right and the Soviet Left. Ginsberg's view of the Cuban Revolution was merciless: "No revolution can succeed if it continues the puritanical censorship of consciousness imposed on the world by Russia and America."[20] What "success" was Ginsberg referring to? Success "in liberating the masses from domination by secret monopolists of communication."[21]

The end of "Prose Contribution to the Cuban Revolution" (1961) adds to this vast interpellation a deliberate abandonment of the moral suspension of criticism that "solidarity" with Cuban socialism presupposed. Although Ginsberg defended the sovereign right of the Cuban people to construct whatever political system they chose, and rejected all forms of limitation on their independence, he asserted at the same time that Western intellectual relations with the island should not be acritical. Support for Cuba's right to independence and Cuban socialism, he argues, must not be assumed as a moratorium on criticism in relation to a nondemocratic political system that resorted to censorship and repression in order to sustain itself. It was better, he asserts, for American poets who were not opposed to the Cuban Revolution to nonetheless speak their minds about life and literature rather than silencing their critiques: "Big statements saying Viva Fidel are/would be meaningless and just two-dimensional politics."[22]

Ginsberg's text is continually marked by the dilemmas reflected in the New York debate over the Cuban Revolution during the 1960s: sovereignty versus empire, communism versus anticommunism, dictatorship versus freedom, totalitarianism versus democracy. The use of the term "prophecy" in his prose no doubt came from reading Waldo Frank's *Cuba: Prophetic Island* (1961), which had just been published in New York in February of that year. Ginsberg's was a "prophecy without death as its consequence," a "giggle into paradise" that made the poet both a defender and a critic of utopias.[23] When Ginsberg calls for transcending the "two-dimensional" logic of politics, he is doing no more than giving his poetics a public role that could move from the topic of Cuba to that of Vietnam, Algeria, civil rights, or sexual freedom.[24]

Conceived as a letter to the editors of *Pa'Lante* magazine, Ginsberg's text concludes with a challenge: "publish as much of this letter as interests you, as prose contribution to Cuban Revolution."[25] The magazine, whose name was inspired by a line from a Havana conga song—"somos socialistas / palante y palante / y al que no le guste / que tome purgante" (we are socialists, forward ever forward, and whoever doesn't like it can go take a laxative)—was presented by its editors (Howard Schulman, Elizabeth Sunderland Martínez, and José Yglesias) as an organ for New York socialist writers associated with the League of Militant Poets to which other beat figures belonged, such as Michael McClure, John Wieners, Joel Oppenheimer, LeRoi Jones, and photographer Leroy McLucas, all of whom had already traveled to Havana.[26] Ginsberg's aspiration was for his prose to read with a dissonant effect in a publication where the discourse of solidarity with Cuba predominated.

"Prose Contribution to the Cuban Revolution" (1961) was one of the first texts where Ginsberg formulated his public poetics. From this moment onward, his attack on the binarisms of politics ("two-dimensional politics") began to proliferate in a multiplicity of interventions, which ranged from criticism of the US party system and a denunciation of wars in the Third World to protests against laws prohibiting the use of drugs, censorship of sexual liberation, measures of surveillance and persecution by the security apparatuses of democratic societies, and the repression of dissidents in the Soviet Union and Eastern Europe.[27] Cuba and its revolution thus came to constitute an experience that allowed Ginsberg to formulate the politics that his literature demanded.

EXPELLED FROM PARADISE

In 1965 Ginsberg traveled for the first time to revolutionary Havana, where he had been invited as a member of the jury for the Casa de las Américas literary prize that year, which would be awarded to Argentine poet Víctor García Robles for his *Oíd mortales* (1965).[28] The other members of the jury were Chilean poet Nicanor Parra, British critic J. M. Cohen (translator of Boris Pasternak and Octavio Paz), Mexican poet Jaime Sabines, and Cuban poet, narrator, and essayist José Lezama Lima. All five of the jurists were writers who by the mid-1960s had come to adopt a critical view of the political system that would be constructed on the island. Parra and Lezama Lima would subsequently experience explicit differences with Castro's government, resulting in the Chilean writer's break with that government and the Cuban writer's relegation to a life of social ostracism in his native country.

Ginsberg's work was known and admired among the island's young writers at the time. In 1960, *Lunes de Revolución* magazine, under the editorship of Guillermo Cabrera Infante, published a fragment of *Howl* in its April issue, within a dossier entitled "USA vs. USA."[29] The following month, in its May issue, devoted to the theme of the Atom bomb and the nuclear threat, *Lunes de Revolución* published a short sample of the poetry of the Beat Generation, including works by Ferlinghetti and Corso, and a fragment from Ginsberg's poem "America."[30] In addition to his aesthetic following among new generations of Cuban poets, Ginsberg was no doubt also well received by members of the Cuban political elite, due to his denunciations of the war in Vietnam and Cambodia and his writings from Southeast Asia—where he had traveled as an activist—which had featured some friendly allusions to Castro.[31]

In the "USA vs. USA" issue of *Lunes de Revolución*, although editor Cabrera Infante cited Ginsberg in a list of figures (including Eliot, Faulkner, Saroyan, and Salinger) that he considered to represent "intermediate solutions" to the dilemma of writers in the United States (in Ginsberg's case the solution of "marijuana"), another of the magazine's collaborators, Oscar Hurtado, wrote a vehement defense of beat writing for the same issue, interpreting the American movement's engagement with Buddhism, the Orient, existentialism, drugs, and sexual freedom as reactions against US militarism and imperialism, particularly in Asia.[32] After reviewing the fundamental works of Jack Kerouac, Allen Ginsberg, and Carl Solomon, Hurtado concluded that the "beatniks" were the "barbudos" (bearded revolutionaries) of the North:

> The bearded Northerners are brothers bonded in rebellion with the bearded revolutionaries of Cuba; and this is important,

> because Cuba is the beginning of the end of Yankee imperialism in America. In order to triumph in this struggle against the Colossus of the North every assistance is necessary, and the "beatniks" help by pointing at the ulcers from within the monster's belly.[33]

For this issue of *Lunes de Revolución* Hurtado also contributed a sample of beat poetry that featured his own translations of LeRoi Jones's poem "The Death of Nick Charles" ("Nick Charles habla desde la muerte") and Ginsberg's *Howl* (1959) ("Alarido"). Although the translation of Jones's long poem featured the work in its entirety, characterizing it as evidence of "the struggle of a black man of the North against the society he lives in," Ginsberg's *Howl* was translated in a fragmentary fashion.[34] Hurtado's version included the initial stanzas of part 1 of the work and then skipped to passages on Moloch and the culture of death in America in part 2, eliminating moments in the work where Ginsberg refers to drugs, homosexuality, jazz, and the working-class neighborhoods of Manhattan, Harlem, and Chinatown. This mutilation of Ginsberg's text demonstrated both the importance that Cuban ideologues gave to the critique of imperialism and racism in the United States and the limits that the revolution's new moral orthodoxy was imposing on the Cuban reception of beat vanguardism and counterculture.

In his 1965 trip to Havana, Ginsberg came into contact with the poets of the El Puente group, an independent publishing project consisting of a group of young writers, many of them gays, blacks, and women, who were interested in beat literature. The El Puente imprint had begun in 1960 with the release of *El grito* (1960) by José Mario (Rodríguez) and *La marcha de los hurones* (1960) by Isel Rivero, two collections that condensed the aesthetic aspirations of this generation of Cuban poets. Against the epic and politically engaged poetry predominant during the early years of the revolution, the poets of *El Puente* favored an aesthetics of difference centered on individual solitude and collective rejections of sexual and moral freedom. In their attempt to found a new literary lineage in Cuba, these writers also resisted both the poetic models inherited from Cuban literary magazines—such as *Orígenes* and *Ciclón*, which focused on consecrated literary figures such as José Lezama Lima and Virgilio Piñera—and those of the socialist vanguard promoted by *Lunes de Revolución* and its editor Cabrera Infante.[35]

In *La marcha de los hurones* (1960), for example, Isel Rivero lyrically describes the process of political mobilization generated by the revolution as a paradoxical affirmation of the self in the middle of the crowd. According to her poetry, the poet felt even more alone, in intimate dialogue with the self, during that time of constant marches and parades, literacy and agricultural initiatives, military training and ideological confrontation. To be placed among the masses did not result in a blurring of the subject's personal identity but instead put that identity into greater relief, distinguishing it from the community. The construction of a collective subject that the revolutionary process aspired to, Isel's work suggests, was an illusory enterprise whose finality was not communion but solitude. The revolution, according to Rivero,

Es como una marcha donde todos vamos separados
Acentuando nuestra absoluta soledad
Porque a una sola flexión de nuestra mente
a una sola palabra
proclamamos las enormes diferencias que nos envuelven
borramos existencias, sentimientos
y quedamos frente al Ego imperecedero
el indestructible
el primitivo Ego
de donde se desprendió la raza humana.[36]

[Is like a march where we all proceed separately
Accentuating our absolute solitude
Because with one flexion of our mind
with one word
we proclaim the enormous differences that surround us
we erase existences, feelings,
and are left facing the imperishable
the indestructible

the primitive Ego
from where the human race was pulled.[37]]

In his work, José Mario persisted in defending the individual's freedom within the communitarian apotheosis generated by the revolution. He portrays the latter as a rending experience, one that forced subjects to confront others as well as themselves. But at the same time, José Mario's poetry posits that the revolution had failed to repress personal drives despite its great capacity to gather up bodies and minds into its process. For all the drama of the revolution's transformation and displacement of values and customs, it could not alter—much less "correct"—those passions constitutive of the human being, such as homosexual love. For young El Puente poets like José Mario and Rivero, the revolution would only make sense if it did not aspire to neutralize the drives of modern man:

Las revoluciones
Comprenden en sí
Anidan como potros reflejados
Las facciones de los rostros vivaces.
Transitar.
Una guagua en que él,
Ese que amamos,
Suda destripa, el inasequible
Complemento de los músculos y su destreza.
Transitar.
La piedra se humilla,
Porque ese que va en el carro
De nuestros ojos apreciado
Visa en su centro las espaldas.
Transitar.
Echar los cabellos
A los sembrados
Apresar en el pecho
El jugo alterado de los simientes
Las revoluciones
Escalan por sí
El furor de los que la sienten.[38]

[Revolutions
Comprehend in themselves
They shelter like reflected horses
The factions of lively faces.
Motion.
A city bus on which he,
That one we love,
Sweats eviscerates, the unreachable
Complement of muscles and their skill.
Motion.
The stone bows,
For the one who is passing
Esteemed in the vehicle of our eyes
Aims at the center of the back.
Motion.
Cast the locks of hair
To the sowing fields
Seize in the chest
The agitated, altered juice of the seeds
Revolutions
Scale by themselves
The furor of those who feel them.]

José Mario and translator David Bigelman had attempted to contact Ginsberg prior to his trip to Havana, seeking his authorization for the production of a Spanish edition of *Howl* in the *El Puente* collection.[39] When José Mario heard of Ginsberg's arrival in the city, he contacted him and introduced him to other members of his group, including poet Manuel Ballagas, who was also working with José Mario on a translation of poems from Ginsberg's *Kaddish* collection. These writers brought Ginsberg up-to-date on recent repressive actions on the island: the "purging" of unorthodox youth in Cuban art schools; the persecution of homosexuals; the official rejection of certain kinds of music, such as "groove," that were considered "extranjerizantes" (conducive of negative foreign influence); the repression of popular Afro-Cuban religions; and the classification of a broad range of cultural subjects as "unhealthy."[40]

According to testimonies from José Mario and Ballagas himself, the latter had been detained by the police outside of the Riviera hotel and arrested for "accompanying foreigners."[41] Just a few days later, the police detained another young man who had spent a night with Ginsberg at the hotel, interrogating him for a number of hours.

In his conversations with members of the island's official intellectual circles, Ginsberg denounced these abuses against young writers and spoke out against homophobia, dogmatism, and the penalization of marijuana use. According to his own testimony and that of José Mario, during these conversations, Ginsberg referred openly to the physical beauty of Che Guevara and entertained a rumor that Raúl Castro was gay. Ginsberg's comments, in addition to his close association with the poets of the El Puente group—which was already coming under growing official disapproval—infuriated the State Security apparatus, and the Castro government promptly ordered that Ginsberg be deported on the next flight out of Havana, to Prague. Soon after Ginsberg's expulsion from the island, the Cuban government closed the El Puente press, and many of the writers associated with the group were ostracized or forced into exile.

Ginsberg's clash with Cuban socialism would become a fundamental event of his intellectual and political biography. He spoke of his expulsion from the island in multiple interviews and texts during the mid-1960s.[42] In a 1972 interview with Allen Young—which coincided with the intensification of Cuba's Sovietization following the dogmatic National Congress of Education and Culture of 1971 and the arrest that same year of poet Heberto Padilla—Ginsberg gave a detailed account of the event, recalling how insulted he had been by the official explanation for the prohibition on marijuana use in Cuba: because Batista's soldiers had gotten high on cannabis.[43]

In that interview, Ginsberg also commented that since leaving Havana, he had become informed of the confinement of homosexuals in the system of Cuban labor camps (UMAPs). Ginsberg reported that the UMAP camps, in addition to seeking the isolation of the gay community as a way to prevent the "perversion" of young communists, sought to "humiliate" homosexuals through physical labor, a measure the American poet found doubly perverse as a repressive mechanism imposed by a socialist state.[44] The Cuban leaders, in Ginsberg's view, were a leftist version of "Nixonettes" and Republican "flag-waving kids" who aspired to control the minds and bodies of the state's citizens.[45]

Ginsberg further insisted that the revolutionary event in Cuba had not been a cultural revolution like the Chinese Revolution: "there was no real cultural revolution [in Cuba]; it was still basically a Catholic mentality."[46] He claimed that the Cuban regime's obsessive restrictions on sexual freedom and on the autonomous association of intellectuals were quite similar to those that the American Right sought to impose, likening the reporters of *Granma* and *Juventud Rebelde* to their counterparts at the *Daily News* or the *Wall Street Journal*. During the interview, Ginsberg also recounted the response given to him by Cuban official Haydée Santamaría when he asked her why the music of the Beatles had been prohibited in Cuba: he was told that it was because the British musicians "have no ideology" and "we are trying to build a revolution with an ideology."[47] "What was the ideology they were proposing?" Ginsberg asks, "a police bureaucracy that persecutes fairies?"[48]

In Theodore Roszak's *The Making of a Counter Culture* (1969), one of the most sophisticated theorizations of the countercultural experiment, Cuba fails to be referenced despite the attention this work gives to other important international cultural-political contexts of the 1960s, such as China or India. Roszak's book explores the poetics of liberation from technocratic rationality as read in the work of figures ranging from Herbert Marcuse and Norman Brown to Allen Ginsberg, Alan Watts, and Paul Goodman, as well as in psychedelic art. If Roszak does not mention the Cuban Revolution, nevertheless in his characterization of technocracy, he does not hesitate to include societies organized in accordance with the patterns of the Soviet bloc and the socialist camp.[49] In his discussion of Ginsberg, Roszak observes that the role of utopia, orientalism, Zen, and LSD in this writer's work and activities reflected his search for an antitotalitarian socialism.[50]

After Ginsberg's expulsion from Havana, the image of Cuban socialism as an intolerant and repressive system became consolidated in Ginsberg's memory. As recalled by Ginsberg in the Allen Young interview, on his way to the Havana airport after his forcible removal from the Riviera hotel, he asked the police why he was being deported and what laws he had violated. He observed that the response given to him by the Cuban agents—"You'll have to ask yourself that"—was similar to what Dean Nicholas McKnight at Columbia University had told him "when I got kicked out for staying overnight in my room with Jack Kerouac."[51] As reported by Edward Sanders, Ginsberg also recalled Haydée Santamaría telling him that "too many gays were making public spectacles of themselves and seducing impressionable young boys."[52]

As Sanders suggests, Ginsberg viewed his expulsion from Havana as a convergence of the repressive models of both capitalism and communism. The poet found it highly significant that the FBI and the CIA both opened files on him that same year—1965—classifying him as a "potentially dangerous" person due to his having traveled to Cuba.[53] In several later prose writings, he would refer to this coincidence of two powers imposed on the body as a confirmation of his ideas about personal freedom.[54] Ginsberg notes that the Cuban state security system's categorizations of "peligrosidad" (dangerousness or risk) or "lacra social" (social scourge) were quite similar to categorizations used by the FBI and the CIA and referred to subjects Ginsberg strongly identified with: homosexuals, drug addicts, atheists, and leftists.[55]

This topic of the transideological confluence of the Cold War repressive powers would become an entire motif in Ginsberg's writings. In poems from the 1970s, he would extend his denunciation of censorship and control to the "real socialist" governments of Eastern Europe, with whose literary dissidents—particularly those of Czechoslovakia—he would strongly identify. For example, in "Grim Skeleton," a poem from December 1977, the idea of a convergence of repressive rationalities on the part of the global powers is inscribed within the fears and paranoias of the Cold War citizen. Castro appears in this work, not as a hero of the revolutionary pantheon but as one of the operators of a system of global controls against poetry:

> I'm afraid
> To write my thoughts down lest I libel Nelson Rockefeller; Fidel Castro
> Chogyan Trungpa, Louis Ginsberg and Naomi Kerouac or Peter O.
> Yea Henri Kissinger and Richard Helms, faded ghosts of Power and Poesy
> That people my brain with paranoia, my best friend shall be Nameless.[56]

In another poem, "Capitol Air" (1980), which Ginsberg evidently wrote after hearing Castro's speeches denouncing the Cuban emigrants who fled the island that year through the port of Mariel, the poet is even more explicit in this regard. In Castro's own characterization of the emigrants as "scum" and in the cries of "good riddance" that were hurled against the emigrants—many of whom were homosexuals, including writers such as Reinaldo Arenas—Ginsberg recognized the homophobia he had endured during his own trip to the island. In the poem, shortly before manifesting his usual invectives against imperialism, multinational corporations, the FBI, the CIA, white supremacy groups, the Gulag, and the KGB, Ginsberg writes:

> I don't like Communist Censorship of my books
> I don't like Marxists complaining about my books
> I don't like Castro insulting members of my sex
> Leftists insisting we got the mystic Fix.[57]

By 1980, very little remained of Ginsberg's initial fascination with the Cuban Revolution. Perhaps the only remnant of that early enthusiasm was the poet's still-positive image of Che Guevara, a figure who had by then displaced Castro as an icon of the new Latin American generation for nearly every New York leftist group, including the *Monthly Review* socialists, the Black Panthers, and the Puerto Rican Young Lords. In works from the 1970s and 1980s, Ginsberg continued to evoke Guevara with the passion of the "Elegy" he had dedicated to the Cuban revolutionary leader in November 1967, a month after the latter's death. In that poem, written in Venice, Ginsberg portrays Guevara's life and work as a colossal pressure applied to the region's traditional—communist or nationalist—Left, which refused to take risks in its struggle against the old social order:

> European Trib. boy's face photo'd eyes opened,
> young feminine beardless radiant kid
> lain back smiling looking upward.
> Calm as if ladies' lips were kissing invisible parts of [the body.
> Aged reposeful angelic boy corpse,
> perceptive Argentine Doctor, petulant Cuba [Major
> pipe mouth'd and faithfully [keeping Diary
> in mosquitos Amazonas.
> Sleep on a hill, dull Havana throne renounced.
> More sexy your neck than sad aging necks of Johnson,
> De Gaulle, Kosygin
> or the bullet pierced neck of John Kennedy.
> Eyes more intelligent glanced up to death newspapers
> Than worried living Congress Cameras [passing
> dot screens into TV shade, glass-eyed
> McNamara, Dulles, in old life.[58]

In contrast to other poems where Ginsberg employs a recourse of equivalence and situates Castro among the operators of the Cold War game, here he portrays the figure of Guevara as the antithesis of the global power elite. Guevara's renunciation of the "Havana throne" and his death in defense of his ideas in the Bolivian jungle qualifies him as a genuine symbol of opposition to the institutions of global capitalism, the United Fruit Company, and the corporations of Chicago, Wall Street, and the New York Stock Exchange, and his exemplary life is viewed as having challenged the bourgeois sanctimony of Western intellectuals.[59] In Ginsberg's lines, Che's beauty transports him to territory alien to the operators of the Cold War, such as the Soviet Kosygin and the assassinated Kennedy.

For Ginsberg, Guevara's early death naturalized him not as a leftist leader in the political realm but as an icon in the poetics of the Beat Generation. The allusion to Che's *Bolivian Diary* and to a photo of the fallen hero's body, in a poem written in Venice in November 1967, connected Ginsberg's elegy directly with the celebrated portrait taken by photographer Alberto Kora, which Italian publisher Giacomo Feltrinelli had just produced as a poster a few weeks earlier and which Ginsberg likely would have seen in Italy. His poem was therefore not merely an homage to the fallen hero; it was also a lyrical translation of Guevara's face, a face that the beat poet evoked as the true face of the revolution and as the weapon of a redeeming madness: "one radiant face driven mad with a rifle / confronting the electronic networks."[60]

Robert Anton Wilson describes Allen Ginsberg's poetry as a "radar system" that captures images, sounds, and words in space and gives them form through the imagination.[61] Cuba, its revolution, and its socialism formed part of this world that Ginsberg's writing symbolically absorbed and reproduced. As occurred with many US intellectuals of his generation, Ginsberg's experience of the island critically marked him, with its oscillation between promise and discontentment, between prophecy and frustration. Cuba, the place of utopia as well as dictatorship, strengthened Ginsberg's understanding of the libertarian expression of intellectual engagement and reinforced his wager on poetry that stubbornly resisted the control of capital and the state.

6

NEGROES WITH GUNS

★

During the 1960s, as Cuba advanced rapidly toward its socialist radicalization in the face of growing conflict with the United States, the American Left, for which the Cuban Revolution served as a key, albeit often uncomfortable, reference throughout the decade, was undergoing transformations of its own. In addition to the beat and hippie generations, the rise of the New Left was also manifested in the growth of the civil rights movement during this period, which was likewise linked from its beginnings with the Cuban process. Playing a key role in the civil rights struggle was the Black Panther Party, a political and military association led by such figures as Huey Newton, Bobby Seale, Little Bobby Hutton, Eldridge Cleaver, and H. Rap Brown. The Black Panthers, together with a number of prominent activists and intellectuals associated with the party, including Robert F. Williams, Stokely Carmichael, and Angela Davies, maintained strong ties with the Cuban Revolution throughout the 1960s, and several Black Panther leaders even spent periods of exile on the island.

Scholars such as Van Gosse and Mark Q. Sawyer have stressed the importance of the intersection between the African American Left's rearticulation during this period and the discourse of solidarity with both Cuba and the decolonizing projects of Asia and Africa.[1] Many black leaders became significantly engaged with the Third World struggle against colonialism, and their involvement with that struggle contributed decisively to the internationalization of the civil rights and black nationalist movements back in the United States. Thanks to this dialogue with decolonization, the intellectual discourse of the African American Left acquired a notable sophistication, which was then projected onto its own visions of the reality of Cuban socialism during the 1960s, particularly from 1963 to 1968, the five-year period during which Havana maintained its greatest distance from Moscow.

Like that of other New York leftist movements at the time, the Black Panthers' relation to the Cuban Revolution was not without its disencounters, as has been demonstrated over the last several decades by scholars such as Ruth Reitan.[2] The history of these disencounters is part of the plurality that characterized the American Left during the 1960s, and the tendency to undervalue or avoid this history is detrimental to the study of both American cultural politics of the 1960s and the diverse representations of Cuban socialism that it produced. In the pages that follow, I will propose a reconstruction of the intellectual dialogue between American black leaders and the Cuban Revolution and seek to capture two simultaneous images: that of Cuban socialism in the discourse of the African American Left and that of the Black Panthers in the Cuban public sphere. The conflicts between these two representations comprise one of the most interesting chapters of the intellectual history of the transamerican Left.

A rereading of these American black intellectuals' writings on Cuba, including their occasional interventions in the island's intellectual field itself, demonstrates the plurality of positions within the African American Left, which has so often been subjected to homogenizing historical frameworks in both the United States and Cuba. The differences between Williams's, Newton's, Brown's, Carmichael's, or Cleaver's conceptualizations of the US civil rights movement itself, and that movement's connections with the decolonizing nationalisms of the Third World—and with Cuban socialism in particular—illustrate the ideological richness of the African

American Left. A rereading of the archive of these differences is propitious at the present time, given the current rise of new theories and histories of twentieth-century political violence.

FROM THOREAU TO SOREL

In 1962, Robert F. Williams's volume *Negroes with Guns* was released by Marzani & Munsell, the imprint headed by communist publisher Carl Marzani, who had also produced Waldo Frank's *Cuba: Prophetic Island* one year earlier. Williams was a well-known civil rights leader, the head of the Monroe, North Carolina, chapter of the National Association for the Advancement of Colored People (NAACP), and a World War II veteran who had defended the right of Monroe's African American residents to bear arms against Ku Klux Klan aggression. Williams had formed a black rifle club called the Black Armed Guard, which grew to several thousand recruits, causing the FBI—then under J. Edgar Hoover—to issue an arrest warrant against him in the summer of 1961. In response, Williams made the decision to exile himself to Cuba with his wife Mabel and his four children. At the time, a number of American leftist intellectual and political leaders were supporting the Cuban Revolution through the Fair Play for Cuba Committee and were traveling regularly to the island. In Havana, Williams wrote a pair of articles for an issue of *Lunes de Revolución* magazine devoted to the topic of "Blacks in the United States." In one of these texts, which was focused particularly on denouncing complicity with racism on the part of Catholic and Protestant churches, he wrote:

> The inherent goodness of the Cuban Revolution can be measured by the number of enemies it has created in the senseless capitalist societies lacking in social conscience. It surprises no one that the "democratic" United States has begun a campaign of slander and hatred against the inspired Cuban people in their struggle to free themselves from the economic yoke sanctioned by Wall Street. In order to comprehend the violent reaction of

> the United States against Cuba's struggle for liberation one need only observe the situation of black people in my country and realize that hatred and violence toward those who protest and resist oppression and exploitation is a natural reaction on the part of the North American ruling classes.[3]

Williams's move to Havana opened the route to exile in Cuba for other leaders of the African American Left. His arrival in the island city inscribed itself in a series of encounters between the US civil rights movement and the Cuban Revolution, perhaps most notably illustrated by Castro's September 1960 meeting with Malcolm X at the Theresa Hotel in Harlem and the visits to Cuba that same year of LeRoi Jones and photographer Leroy McLucas, two intellectuals involved in the reconstitution of the African American Left in New York City.[4] Jones and McLucas were two of the dozens of African American activists, intellectuals, and politicians who published a letter in the *New York Post* on April 25, 1961, expressing support for the Cuban Revolution and protesting the Kennedy administration's backing of the CIA-organized Bay of Pigs invasion.[5]

In Havana, Williams was interviewed at his lodgings at the Capri Hotel in the Vedado district by beat writer, publisher, and *Kulchur* magazine editor Marc Schleifer and John Schultz of *Studies on the Left*. He was also profiled on numerous occasions by McLucas, one of whose photographic images featured Williams at the podium of the Plaza de la Revolución.[6] While in Havana, Williams also sent articles to the African American monthly newsletter that he edited, the *Crusader-in-Exile*, which argued for the notion of Cuba as a "land free of America": a nation with black militias led by Castro that banned entry to racist whites from the United States.[7] Many of these writings by Williams, as well as the essays on Williams by Marc Schleifer and historian-novelist Truman Nelson, author of a biography of nineteenth-century abolitionist leader John Brown, were collected in *Negroes with Guns* (1962), an anthology that can be read as a debate on the role of violence in the civil rights movement conducted among members of the African American Left during those years.

Negroes with Guns, in fact, begins with two texts by Martin Luther King Jr., "Hate Is Always Tragic" and "The Social Organization of Non-Violence," in which the iconic civil rights leader summarized the method of peaceful resistance for civil rights. King's central argument in these writings was that the nonviolent interventions of the dominated revealed the violence of the dominators.[8] In a passage of the latter of the two texts, King directly questioned Williams's campaign for the formation of black militias. He acknowledged that violence exercised in self-defense was an inalienable right in all cultures, from the most primitive to the most civilized—a right not even Mahatma Gandhi had opposed—and that Williams's defense of black communities' right to bear arms in self-defense was therefore acceptable. But what was not acceptable, according to King, was the call to violence as a method of political struggle for civil rights—or "advocacy of violence as a tool of advancement, organized as in warfare, deliberately and consciously":

> To this tendency many Negroes are being tempted today. There are incalculable perils in this approach. It is not the danger or sacrifice of physical being which is primary, though it cannot be contemplated without a sense of deep concern for human life. The greatest danger is that it will fail to attract Negroes to a real collective struggle, and will confuse the large uncommitted middle group, which as yet has not supported either side. Further, it will mislead Negroes into the belief that this is the only path and place them as a minority in a position where they confront a far larger adversary than it is possible to defeat in this form of combat.[9]

King's pragmatic tone, in which he appeared to reject a race war between whites and blacks—because the latter group would lose such a struggle due to its lower numbers—concealed his deeply held religious and moral objections to violence as developed in response to Gandhi's legacy and out of King's own experience as a Baptist pastor in mid-twentieth-century America.

Williams's primary objective in featuring King's texts at the beginning of *Negroes with Guns* (1961) was to diminish the ideological and methodological differences between the two leaders in the eyes of African American readers. At the same time, however, he sought to highlight those differences for leaders of the radical Left, to whom the collection's essays by Truman Nelson and Marc Schleifer were aimed. Nelson was an admirer of Henry David Thoreau and a disciple of W.E.B. Du Bois, and had authored several historical writings on John Brown's nineteenth-century abolitionist struggle, such as *The Sin of the Prophet* (1952) and *The Surveyor* (1960) (two works later published together in 1973 as *The Old Man: John Brown at Harper's Ferry*). In his piece for *Negroes with Guns*, Nelson acknowledged the differences between King and Williams but deemed them not irreconcilable.[10] He titled his essay "The Resistant Spirit" and presented Williams as an heir to the ideas of Thoreau and Brown. Citing Thoreau's essay *Resistance to Civil Government* (1848, later reprinted as *Civil Disobedience* or *On the Duty of Civil Disobedience*), Nelson focused on the nineteenth-century writer's double protest against the Mexican-American War and the institution of slavery and his call for citizens to refuse the payment of taxes as a nonviolent means of withholding financial support for the unjust policies in question. However, as Nelson observed, although Thoreau understood civil disobedience as a peaceful act, he also did not reject the right to "revolution" and "resistance" against abuses of power.[11]

Thoreau's central argument, of course, was not a vindication of violent rebellion but an application of the doctrine of natural right to a defense of noncollaboration with the state. Thoreau recalled that eighteenth-century British utilitarian theologian William Paley had defined "submission to civil government" as a duty.[12] In Thoreau's view, however, that duty was always limited by the individual's inalienable right to resist state sovereignty. As he argued in his nineteenth-century essay, the political history of the West from the end of the eighteenth century to the middle of the nineteenth marked a rapid transition, first from absolute monarchy to constitutional and parliamentary monarchy, and then to democratic republicanism—particularly in the Americas—and that this transition reflected an increasing recognition, in the modes of political organization, of individual rights vis-à-vis the state.[13]

While not distorting the liberal framework of Thoreau's reflections, Nelson deliberately nudged those reflections toward a defense of the right to violent rebellion under the aegis of natural right. According to Nelson, Thoreau's true disciple was not Gandhi or King, but John Brown, who had broken with the Christian ambivalence toward abolitionism—as reflected in Harriet Beecher Stowe's *Uncle Tom's Cabin* (1852)—and had risen up in arms against a slavist state.[14] In Brown's 1859 armed raid on the US arsenal at Harper's Ferry, Virginia—an event subjected to a long history of revisionism, including that of Michael Curtiz's 1940 film *Santa Fe Trail*, starring Errol Flynn and Ronald Reagan—Nelson saw the foundational event of a revolutionary tradition that appealed to violence against unjust governments and that dovetailed ideologically not only with Thoreau but also with the 1776 Declaration of Independence and the ideas of the US founding fathers.[15] Nelson's exposition featured no Marxist or Leninist references. It merely defended an American revolutionary legacy against a system referred to not as capitalist but as "continuing feudalism."[16]

In the first of his own chapters for the book, Williams was more cautious than Nelson in entering into his debate with King. He claimed he did not oppose King's notion of nonviolent resistance, stating, "My only difference with Dr. King is my belief in flexibility in the freedom struggle."[17] Williams argued that restrictions on the civil rights of blacks in the United States were so oppressive and cruel that African Americans had a right to make themselves respected by all means necessary. He pointed out that racism in the United States was inscribed in laws and institutions that subsequently reproduced racial inequalities in public life. Because violence by whites against blacks was supported by these laws and institutions, violent defense against the laws and institutions in question was legitimate.

In his own historical and autobiographical reconstruction of his leadership in forming the Black Armed Guard in North Carolina, Williams held to his defense of armed struggle based on the premises of the American liberal tradition, which asserted the right to bear arms in protection of the security and liberty of individuals or groups. Responding to allegations that he was a communist—voiced by anticommunist groups on both the right and the left—Williams assured his detractors that he had never been a member of the Communist Party.[18] While acknowledging that some Marxists had supported the black movement (and pointing out that the few whites who had done so were automatically labeled as such), he argued that Marxism was not the ultimate aspiration of the African American Left because racial discrimination was both anterior to and independent from the exploitation of labor.

Before *The Communist Manifesto* was ever written, before the first labor unions were formed, and before Karl Marx was even born, blacks had not only experienced enslavement and oppression but had also risen up in arms against their oppressors, Williams reminded his readers: "As far back as the 16th century, and the beginning of the 17th century, Negroes were even rebelling on the slave ships."[19] It was therefore neither necessary nor expedient for the black movement to justify its struggle based on exogenous political doctrines or philosophies: "Certainly the Marxists have participated in the human rights struggle of Negroes, but Negroes need not be told by any philosophy or by any political party that racial oppression is wrong. Racial oppression itself inspires the Negro to rebellion."[20]

Williams's radically autonomous view of the black movement in the United States began to change during his Havana exile. His encounter with the Cuban Revolution convinced him that the black struggle was awakening not only in the United States but among every African population around the world. The Cuban Revolution, as he argued during this period, was something "real," not just another coup against the state like those that had occurred so often in South America. The presence of armed blacks in the ranks of the rebel army or in the island's militias was a fact that could not be hidden from the eyes of activists from the civil rights movement.

Williams communicated these impressions in several issues of his newsletter, the *Crusader-in-Exile*, from 1960 and 1961, expressing his conviction that the Cuban experience demonstrated the capacity of blacks to take up arms and resist their exploiters.[21] After the Cuban Revolution had armed the black population, he reported, it had implemented a series of social justice policies encouraging racial equality. US government opposition to those policies, voiced by both political parties under the Eisenhower and Kennedy administrations, went in tandem with opposition to the civil rights movement and the persecution of radical black nationalist leaders. According to Williams, the cry he was hearing in Havana—"Cuba sí, Yanqui no!" (Yes to Cuba, No to the Yankee!)—voiced a direct rejection of the slogan "White, yes, Colored, no!" heard in US racial segregation campaigns.[22] The Cuban repudiation of the powerful, he argued, took on its full meaning when seen as a binary reaction to the rejection of the weak in the United States.

The support of black nationalist leaders such as Williams or Malcolm X for the Cuban Revolution, and for the island government's right to implement socialism even if it led to an alliance with the Soviet Union, was intimately related to these leaders' own struggles against racial, economic, political, and military power in the United States. Their persecution by the FBI only aggravated the injuries of racial discrimination with the addition of anticommunist witch hunts and the ideological attacks of McCarthyism, thereby provoking a doctrinal radicalization of the black leaders' own oppositional strategies. It was this confluence that Williams's interlocutors in the New York leftist beat movement, on the one hand, and within the Cuban socialist leadership, on the other, sought to exploit. Both groups took advantage of Williams's presence in Havana to push the black leader's positions toward their own camps, either toward traditional communism or toward the New Left.

It is in this framework that Marc Schleifer's epilogue to *Negroes with Guns* should be read as a document of the dialogue between the black movement and the New Left during the early 1960s. Schleifer begins by highlighting how scandalous the figure of Robert F. Williams was for American liberalism and even for the "old radicalism" of certain intellectual audiences.[23] But even while inspiring terror in these circles, Schleifer continues, Williams was attracting an increasingly enthusiastic following among bohemian and libertarian youth, as manifested on the streets in expressions of protest against the Vietnam War and support for the Cuban Revolution. Following the argument of C. Wright Mills's celebrated letter to British

Marxist E. P. Thompson, "Letter to the New Left" (1960), Schleifer insisted that the discourse of Williams's African American Left entered into dialogue with his own discourse, that of the leftist beat movement (Jones, Ginsberg, Ferlinghetti), since both groups rejected the gradualist progressivism and moderation that had taken shape on the American Left during the New Deal era.

In Schleifer's view, the point of contact between Williams's armed Negroes and the New York bohemians of *Kulchur* magazine was the "radical insistence on immediacy," the rejection of any notion of deferred time in the social struggle, which only impeded the reclaiming of "Freedom, now!"[24] The use of the word "progressive," according to Schleifer, was a vice of the liberal or communist Left stemming back to the New Deal, which had not integrated the range of values and reflections on American reality voiced by black public intellectuals such as W.E.B. Du Bois prior to the Rooseveltian era. Charting a direct genealogical line between Dubois and Williams, Schleifer introduced a new front within Mills's critique of the Old Left. As he clarified, the New Left did not reject all "styles" associated with the Old Left, but rather those of the "Middle-Aged Left."[25]

Schleifer traced a genealogy that challenged the generation of the fathers—that of the New Deal—and vindicated the generation of the grandfathers: that of the socialist intellectuals and politicians at the turn of the twentieth century who had confronted the birth of American imperialism and had expressed solidarity with the Bolshevik Revolution. The symbolic connection he sought to establish between Williams's project and that of the older leftism was not based exclusively on the black intellectual lineage. Like Truman Nelson, Schleifer highlighted the foundational status of the work of W.E.B. Du Bois, whose *The Souls of Black Folk* (1903) had inaugurated the intellectualization of African American culture for the twentieth century, but he also identified resonances between the radicalism of the African American New Left and the socialism of Bill Haywood, John Reed, Eugene Debs, and Jack London.[26]

In fact, that resonance between early black radicalism and the first generation of American socialism was more a product of Schleifer's own interpretation of Williams's texts than of a literal reading of the essays in *Negroes with Guns.* As we saw earlier, the ideological legitimization of black violence in Williams's anthology was not based on the socialist or Marxist discourse but on the American liberal-abolitionist tradition itself. Nonetheless, Williams—together with his communist-affiliated publisher Carl Marzani—showed his sympathy for Schleifer's reflections by agreeing to include them as the book's epilogue. Even so, Schleifer was careful not to identify early American socialism with US institutional communism, which he viewed as trapped in the same dilemmas of the "Middle-Aged Left" and New Deal liberalism. According to Schleifer, Williams's support for armed struggle against racism put the political category of "progressivism" into crisis in the United States.[27]

From a hermeneutical point of view, Schleifer's boldest intervention in Williams's texts was his effort to establish an intellectual analogy between the latter's ideas about violence and the theories of French socialist philosopher Georges Sorel. Although Schleifer doubted that Williams had read Sorel's *Reflections on Violence* (1908)—since "Williams' sources are not European [but rather] pure expressions of his social existence as a Southern Negro"—he nonetheless observed an "interesting parallel" between the two thinkers.[28] Although he did not develop the parallel in question, what Schleifer had in mind was a possible equivalence between Sorel's notion of class violence and the racial violence defended by Williams. Neither Sorel nor Williams linked these two forms of violence, but Schleifer saw affinities in their conception of this method of struggle.

There were also, in effect, certain similarities between Williams's positions and Sorel's argument for pessimism as a stance of resistance and his rejection of Hegelian theology,[29] even while Sorel's frequent references to Bergson and Renan, and his reflections on the importance of myth for collective action, were too obvious, or alien, for an African American civil rights leader during the Cold War.[30] Nonetheless, Sorel's critique of parliamentary moderation for its constant countering of bullets with votes and his objection to the cult for "social peace" as the exclusive goal of the political economy—a goal that he believed only obscured the "cruel fact" of class struggle—were stances shared by Williams, for whom "racial struggle" was a counterpart to Sorel's "class struggle."[31] These threads, one would have to add, were shared with Frantz Fanon as well. In a well-known passage of *The Wretched of the Earth* (1961), Fanon conceives anticolonial violence as "the perfect mediation," as exemplified in the resistance of the Mau Mau in Kenya or in the "prophetic" violence of the poetry of Aimé Césaire.[32]

In 1962, writing his texts for *Negroes with Guns* from his place of Havana exile, Williams did not share Sorel's idea of violence as a form of struggle that causes the rival's essence to emerge. In one of the most striking passages of his *Reflections*, Sorel refers to proletarian violence as "the only means by which the European nations, stupefied by humanitarianism, can recover their former energy."[33] Proletarian violence, according to the French philosopher, fulfills the paradoxical role of historically perfecting capitalist society and "reestablish[ing] the division into classes," thereby "restor[ing] to the bourgeoisie something of its energy."[34] Sorel thus argued for the regenerative and purifying role of class violence: "The social war, for which the proletariat ceaselessly prepares itself in the syndicates, may engender the elements of a new civilization suited to a people of producers."[35]

Although Robert F. Williams showed no modeling by these ideas in 1962, his later Marxist radicalization demonstrates the effect on his writings by Schleifer's hermeneutics and Williams's own initiation of ideological dialogue with Marxist and anticolonial thinkers and leaders such as Che Guevara and Frantz Fanon. As Mark Q. Sawyer observes, it was from this point onward that Williams's ideological and political position began a shift from black nationalism toward anticolonial Marxism, which led him to identify, significantly, not with the Soviet Union or Eastern Europe but with China and Vietnam.[36] In the Asian socialist nations Williams believed he had encountered greater commonalities with the black movement that he and the leaders of the Black Panther Party, founded in the middle of the 1960s, were attempting to articulate in the United States.

The mutual encounter between Williams and Mao in the mid-1960s took place at a moment of growing conflict between the

Soviet Union and China that favored the spread of Maoist sympathies within the New Left. The displacement of Williams's ideological and geographical alliances followed the turn toward China and Vietnam witnessed among other sectors of the New York Left. *Monthly Review* magazine published numerous articles favorable to Maoism during this period, including pieces by Charles Bettelheim and Keither Buchanan, and in addition to its broad coverage of the Sino-Soviet schism, the magazine also insisted on paying greater theoretical attention to the articulation of socialism and decolonization in countries such as Algeria and Vietnam, contexts that, together with that of Cuba, the editors believed could serve as an inspiration for Latin American revolutionaries.[37]

Williams's exilic trajectory—from the United States to Havana and subsequently from Havana to China in 1965—would open a new horizon of dialogue for the black Left that would subsequently have a deep effect on the radicalization of black Muslim leaders, such as Malcolm X, and the formation of the Black Panther Party in 1966. Leaders of this movement, such as Huey Newton and Bobby Seale, would take Williams's ideas about self-defense and his doctrinal connections with the Cuban Revolution and Maoism and make them their own. Other intellectuals of African American radicalism followed a similar path, including Eldridge Cleaver, the Black Panther leader; H. Rap Brown, chairman of the Student Nonviolent Coordinating Committee; and Trinidadian American black nationalist Stokely Carmichael, all of whose writings retraced the itinerary of encounters and disencounters between the African American Left and Cuban socialism.

In his letters from Folsom State Prison during the summer of 1965, later collected in the volume *Soul on Ice* (1968), Eldridge Cleaver cited Williams's exile in Havana and the assassination of Malcolm X as catalysts for the necessary radicalization of black nationalism.[38] Cleaver signaled his admiration for Guevara and Mao and compared Castro's struggle against the United States to a boxing match between Muhammad Ali and a physically stronger rival: Ali is "the black Fidel Castro of boxing," Cleaver declared; "he is conceived as *occupying* the heavyweight kingdom in the name of dark, alien power, in much the same way as Castro was conceived as a temporary interloper *occupying* Cuba."[39] But Cleaver also defended the appropriation by the African American community of the best of Eastern and Western cultures—Jesus Christ and Buddha, Confucius and Lao-tzu, Muhammad and Aristotle, Voltaire and Marx, Lenin and Merton, and so on—as well as intellectual conversation with liberal white writers such as Norman Mailer, Allen Ginsberg, Albert Camus, and Henry Miller.[40]

Nonetheless, among the intellectual leaders of the Black Panthers, Cleaver's esteem for Robert F. Williams rivaled his admiration of few others. According to Cleaver, the "hot blood[ed]" author of *Negroes with Guns* was nothing less than an "American Lenin."[41] Where the Russian leader had established a foundation for a proletarian politics, Williams had founded a platform for black politics in the broadest sense, Cleaver believed. He recalled his intellectual formation in prison as a process of consciousness-raising, in which his readings of enlightened republicans of the eighteenth century (Rousseau and Paine, primarily) had passed to that of the nineteenth- and twentieth-century socialists (Marx, Bakunin, Necháyev, Lenin, and others), always guided by the example set by Williams, who had the bravery to arm the black citizens of Monroe against the racist gangs of the Ku Klux Klan.[42]

The ideology of the Cuban Revolution during the 1960s rested on the articulation of a series of contradictory political premises, such as the defense of armed struggle, alignment with the Soviet Union, anti-imperialism, support for Third World decolonizing movements, antiracism, and integrationism. Williams's and Cleaver's backing of Cuban socialism dovetailed with some of these premises (revolutionary violence and anti-imperialist nationalism) but not with others (alliance with Moscow or postethnic nationalism). It was therefore inevitable that tensions would begin to emerge between the reading of the Cuban Revolution by these African American intellectual-political figures and that of the revolutionary government itself. Williams's and Cleaver's support for Cuban communism precipitated reactions within the US black nationalist movement, as can be read in *Black Man in Red Cuba* (1970), the memoir of black activist John Clytus, who testified about his own experience of persistent racism in two Latin

American societies impacted by the great revolutions of the twentieth century: Mexico under the PRI Party (Partido Revolucionario Institucional [Institutional Revolutionary Party]) and Cuba under Fidel.[43]

Cleaver himself would offer a testimony similar to that of Clytus in recounting his experience in Cuba to Henry Louis Gates for *Transition* magazine. In this interview, the author of *Soul on Ice* questioned the lingering racism in socialist Cuba, which he saw reflected in the fact that few commanders of the revolution were black.[44] Cleaver had encountered racism in the island's daily life and even in ideological discourses on the Cuban nation and its history, in which white leaders such as José Martí were consistently elevated over black leaders such as Antonio Maceo.[45] In support of his view, Cleaver cited a well-known polemic that took place between black Cuban intellectual Carlos Moore and Haitian poet René Depestre in the mid-1960s, stating that racism in revolutionary Cuba was aided by the integrationist mantra that the island had overcome its racial discrimination following January 1959.[46] Moore's intellectual work in exile would add one more testimony to this ideological disencounter.[47]

The discursive trajectory between Williams and Cleaver in the United States, and between Juan René Betancourt and Carlos Moore in Cuba, allows one to reconstruct—as Ruth Reitan has done—the progression of ideological tension between the black nationalism and Pan-Africanism of Black Power defenders, on the one hand, and the symbiosis of Marxism-Leninism and revolutionary nationalism of socialist Cuba, on the other.[48] Inevitably, the decline of the "radical alliance" between African American civil rights leaders and revolutionary Cuba must be associated with the increasing hegemony of the island's "traditional communist line." That line was established in Cuba in response to the global policies of the Soviet Union, which considered the theoretical questioning of black nationalism to be consubstantial with the philosophical supremacy of class conflict in orthodox Marxist-Leninism and which rejected racial violence in the United States and Guevarist guerrilla initiatives in Latin America as "revisionist" and "ultra-leftist" movements.[49]

FROM FANON TO CARMICHAEL

The founding of the Black Panther Party at the end of 1966 coincided with both an extraordinary rise of leftist global revolutionary violence and the chilling of Havana-Moscow relations that took place following the Kennedy-Khrushchev Pact, which deactivated the 1962 missile crisis. This was the moment when Ernesto "Che" Guevara began his guerrilla movement in Bolivia after returning from the Congo, where he and his ally, Tanzanian leader Julius Nyerere, had fought in support of the anticolonial forces that had survived the assassination of Patrice Lumumba. The guerrilla war in the Congo, which African American leftists had followed with great interest, situated Guevara's figure at the very center of that generation's symbology. Guevara's subsequent execution in Bolivia in October 1967, under CIA orders, had the effect of naturalizing his figure in the ideas, styles, discourse, and fashion of the American Black Panthers.

Certain books and essays published by black intellectuals affiliated with the Black Panthers—such as Stokely Carmichael and Charles V. Hamilton's *Black Power: The Politics of Liberation in America* (1967), Eldridge Cleaver's *Soul on Ice* (1968), and H. Rap Brown's *Die Nigger Die! A Political Autobiography* (1969)—are helpful for understanding the complex relation between African American leftist leaders and the ideology of Cuban socialism at the moment when Castro's government ended its support for the Guevarist guerrilla movements in Latin America to instead immerse itself in the Cold War Soviet bloc. Black leaders like Carmichael, Hamilton, Cleaver, and Brown, some of whom spent periods of exile on the island, lived the ideological transformation of Cuban socialism in a dramatic way. Their relation with the island had begun when the paradigms of decolonization and Third World internationalization held sway over Havana's global politics, but that relation subsequently grew turbulent in the 1970s as the Sovietization of the Cuban project tightened its grip on the island.

An invaluable source for reading the intellectual dialogue between the leaders of the Black Panthers and the Guevarist current of the Cuban revolutionary leadership is *Pensamiento Crítico*'s issue 17 from the year 1968. The journal was edited by a young philosophy professor at the University of Havana, Fernando Martínez Heredia, and its editorial board featured a mix of heterodox Marxists (Aurelio Alonso, Jesús Díaz, José Bell Lara, and Thalía Fung). The journal's issues constitute some of the clearest inscriptions of the New Leftist ideological repertoire in the Cuban intellectual field at the time. Starting with its first issues in 1967, *Pensamiento Crítico* demonstrated a keen interest in numerous topical concerns of the time: the dialogue between existentialism and Marxism that was being led by Jean Paul Sartre; the exploration of links between Marxism and psychoanalysis, particularly following the work of Herbert Marcuse; the review of Western Marxist thought (Trotsky, Luxemburg, Korsch, Lukács, Gramsci) conducted by Polish philosopher Adam Schaff and other Eastern European intellectuals; Maoism; Latin American dependency theory (Andre Gunder Frank, Ruy Mauro Marini, Fernando Henrique Cardoso); British Marxism (Perry Anderson, Eric Hobsbawm, Robin Blackburn); and structuralism.

Despite *Pensamiento Crítico*'s notable eclecticism, the most prominent referential figure in the journal was without a doubt Louis Althusser. This prominence perhaps reflected the fact that Althusser's notion of an "epistemological break" in the work of Marx and the French Marxist's agreement with the philosophical status of dialectical and historical materialism allowed for a less conflictive relation with Soviet Marxist-Leninism, which had begun to spread in Cuban culture and pedagogy. Starting with the virtual homage to Althusser featured in issue 5 of June 1967,[50] *Pensamiento Crítico*'s heterodoxy began to demonstrate a more or less defined profile centered on a critique of the "humanism" and "revisionism" of certain strands of Western leftism, such as that associated with Schaff or E. P. Thompson, and a defense of understanding with both the Soviet Union and China. Many of the journal's theoretical and political treatments of Maoism, such as essays by Maurice Godelier and K. S. Karol, had this accent.[51]

Despite this profile, two issues of *Pensamiento Crítico* were devoted to New Left perspectives. The first of these, issues 25/26 of 1969, was focused on the May 1968 student movement and featured a broad range of authors, particularly from France (André Malraux, Jean Paul Sartre, Roger Garaudy, and others, including the liberal Raymond Aron and Belgian Trotskyite Ernest Mandel). The second was the earlier-cited issue—number 17 of 1968—devoted to the Black Power movement. It included articles and interviews of various Black Panther leaders (Stokely Carmichael, James Forman, H. Rap Brown, Robert L. Allen, and Huey P. Newton) and was preceded by a note of presentation explaining why a social science journal produced by Cuban Marxists had produced an issue on the Black Panthers.

The editors begin the presentation in question by characterizing the global context at the end of the 1960s as a period of structuring for the US strategy of planetary domination and, at the same time, of resistance from the colonial periphery to this relaunching of American imperialism. The cited examples of this resistance include North Korea, Vietnam, and Cuba, three small Third World nations that had confronted US military interventions and had constructed socialism under adverse conditions. As the young philosophers of *Pensamiento Crítico* declared, "the revolutionary struggle of American blacks was demonstrating that it was possible to strike the enemy in its own technologically developed heart."[52] The simultaneous manifestations of the Black Panthers, the European student movement, Latin American guerrilla struggles, and the decolonizing nationalisms of Asia and Africa were proof that the revolution and socialism were establishing themselves on a global scale.

The editors did not hesitate to include all of these scenarios within the scope of a "New Left," which, by "completely rejecting the system's economic, social, cultural, and political structures," ruptured with a "traditional Left" characterized as "captive and impotent as one more component of the bourgeoisie's game."[53] This definition of the New Left, unlike that of C. Wright Mills, was projected not only against the orthodox communist Left but also against the social democratic, humanist, and libertarian leftism that in the Western democracies was still casting its bets on "reform" rather than on "revolution."[54] By rigidly identifying the leftist option with armed struggle and revolutionary violence,

Pensamiento Crítico widened the gulf already opened in Williams's *Negroes with Guns* (1962) between the nonviolent struggle for civil rights led by Martin Luther King Jr. and the Black Panthers' more aggressive assault on racism.

One of the texts included in the issue was an interview with Stokely Carmichael that had taken place after Martin Luther King Jr.'s assassination. Carmichael called on the Student Nonviolent Coordinating Committee to relinquish the path of nonviolence and demanded the liberation of H. Rap Brown, another leader of this organization who was imprisoned in Maryland at the time. Carmichael declared that a racial war was playing out in the United States in 1968 and that the nation's white politicians, whether Republican or Democratic—starting with Democratic presidential candidate Robert Kennedy—were accomplices of assassinations and abuses against blacks.[55] From the perspective of *Pensamiento Crítico*'s editors and that of the island's followers of the Black Panthers generally, Carmichael's analysis was correct insofar as the finality of revolutionary violence was none other than the destruction of the capitalist system.

The greatest difficulty encountered by this juxtaposition between the black Left and the Marxist Left was that the discourse of the Black Panthers was not always anticapitalist. In their issue devoted to the Black Panther intellectuals, *Pensamiento Crítico*'s editors sought to employ for their own purposes the famous interview between Malcolm X, Jack Barnes, and Barry Sheppard that had taken place in 1965 shortly after King's assassination; their translation of the interview was entitled, "It Is Impossible for Capitalism to Survive" (Para el capitalismo es imposible sobrevivir).[56] The interview had coincided with Malcolm X's rupture with the Black Muslims and his turn toward anticolonial Pan-Africanism. In the piece, the black leader criticized what he viewed as anti-Negro pacifism, denounced the war in Vietnam, condemned apartheid in South Africa, and sympathized with the guerrilla war in the Congo, but the tone of his discourse was more anticolonial than anticapitalist. The editors of *Pensamiento Crítico* were attempting to draw figures such as Stokely Carmichael, H. Rap Brown, and Malcolm X himself into the Marxist fold, yet for these black leaders, racial emancipation in the United States was not necessarily related to the socialist project. In a celebrated interview with Oriana Fallaci, Brown acknowledged his conviction that a war was waging in the United States between the black movement and the nation's white elites, but he insisted that this type of war should not be associated with the urban guerrilla movements then spreading in Latin America.[57]

In 1967 Brown had attended a UN-sponsored seminar in Zambia on apartheid and the struggle against African colonialism. The ideas he defended in that forum subscribed to the pacifist tradition of the Student Nonviolent Coordinating Committee, of which he served as chairman.[58] In fact, most of Brown's positions during the seminar were limited to backing the resolutions of the UN General Assembly against racial discrimination, ethnic segregation, and restrictions on the civil liberties of the black population in the United States, as well as South Africa, Angola, Mozambique, Rhodesia, and Bissau.[59] Although Brown declared that he was not a Christian and was ready to kill if necessary, and although he defended the right of American blacks to resist military recruitment as a rejection of the Vietnam War (appealing to the argumentations of Robert F. Williams in *Negroes with Guns*), nonetheless his argumentation was far from subscribing to the Marxist philosophy of the Guevarist guerrilla struggle. Even so, the editors of *Pensamiento Crítico* presented him as a supporter of the "guerrilla war" in the United States.[60]

The Cuban Marxist translation of the black nationalist or Pan-African anticolonialist ideas of African American civil rights leaders was an easier task with regard to the discourse of the highest levels of leadership in the Black Panthers, such as that of the group's defense minister, Huey P. Newton, who openly incorporated the socialist project in his discourse and put emphasis on the Cuban referent. In 1968, for example, Newton began to question aspects of the culturalist argument for the "return to Africa," maintaining that for the radical black leadership, revolutionary nationalism and Marxist socialism were conjoined.[61] The mixture of decolonizing nationalism and Marxist socialism that Newton encountered in Ben Bella's Algeria, Ho Chi Minh's Vietnam, and Castro's Cuba seemed to him ideal for the American black movement.[62] It was Newton, and not Brown, who explicitly bridged the American Black Panthers and the Latin American guerrillas:

> The guerrilla is a very unique man. This is in contrast to Marxist-Leninist orthodox theories where the party controls the military. The guerrilla is only the warrior, the military fighter; he is also the military commander as well as the political theoretician. Debray says "poor the pen without the guns, poor the gun without the pen." The pen being just an extension of the mind, a tool to write down concepts, ideas. The gun is only an extension of the body, the extension of our fanged teeth that we lost through evolution. It's the weapon, it's the claws that we lost, it's the body. The guerrilla is the military commander and the political theoretician all in one.[63]

The fusion of body and soul that Newton saw personified in Guevara or Mao implied a call to unify the roles of the intellectual and the politician within the Black Panther Party, a unity that preempted the necessity of separating the army from the party within the same organization. Newton's comments implicitly rejected a hierarchical relation with communist parties loyal to Moscow, which garnered a broadly sympathetic response from the European and American New Left, the theoretical vitality of which the editors of *Pensamiento Crítico* could verify in the Cultural Congress of Havana in 1968.[64] By sustaining the archetype of the warrior as both soldier and philosopher of guerrilla warfare, Newton, without citing Antonio Gramsci, levied a critique against the Leninist and Stalinist tradition that was highly problematic for Cuba in the 1960s, despite the distance between Moscow and Havana during that decade:

> In Bolivia Che said that he got very little help from the Communist Party there. The Communist Party wanted to be the mind, the Communist Party wanted to have full control of the guerrilla activity. But yet weren't taking part in the practical work of the guerrillas. The guerrilla on the other hand is not only united within himself, but he also attempts to spread this to the

> people by educating the villagers, giving them political perspective, pointing out things, educating them politically, and arming the people. Therefore the guerrilla is giving the peasants and workers a mind. Because they've already got the body you get a unity of the mind and the body. Black people here in America, who have long been the workers, have regained our minds and we now have a unity of mind and body.[65]

Newton's application of a heterodox vanguard idea drawn fundamentally from the Cuban experience to the Black Panther Party's theory and praxis also implied the need for greater flexibility in relations between the black movement and white revolutionaries.[66] Newton reproached other black leaders in the United States for maintaining an ethnic dogmatism that prevented them from dialoguing with radical Marxists outside of the African American context.[67] Newton's view in this sense dovetailed with the reading of the American black movement proposed by the editors of *Pensamiento Crítico* in the issue's introductory essay, insofar as Newton advocated subordinating the black cause to a larger socialist cause, the latter understood as resulting from a violent anticapitalist revolution that needed to exceed African American demands in order to involve other popular sectors in the United States as well. Certain black Marxist intellectuals, such as sociologist Robert L. Allen—also featured in this issue of *Pensamiento Crítico* and author of some of the first historicizations and theorizations of this thesis, including *Black Awakening in Capitalist America: An Analytical History* (1969) and *A Guide to Black Power in America: An Historical Analysis* (1970)—also helped give visibility to this current within the African American Left.[68]

Other black intellectuals of Newton's generation, including H. Rap Brown, Stokely Carmichael, and Eldridge Cleaver, had a different way of conceiving the relation between black nationalism, decolonizing Pan-Africanism, and Marxist socialism in both its old and new variants. These authors opened a volatile intellectual fault line in the ideological relations between the Black Panther Party and the Cuban Revolution that would reveal the clash between Cuban socialism's integrationist position and the racial politics of the African American New Left. Carmichael was the first of the African American intellectual leaders to place the black movement within a broad perspective on decolonization and African antiracism, yet one not necessarily associated with the socialist option, in his book *Black Power: The Politics of Liberation in America* (1967), written in collaboration with Charles V. Hamilton, professor of social sciences at the University of Chicago.

A Spanish translation of *Black Power* was published that same year, in 1967, by Siglo XXI in Mexico City, and the work's first chapter, "Poder blanco: Situación colonial" (White Power: The Colonial Situation) was also featured in the above-cited issue of *Pensamiento Crítico*. Carmichael's sources for his important book included, in particular, studies by African American sociologists, psychologists, economists, and historians (Kenneth B. Clark, E. Franklin Frazier, Andrew F. Brimmer, John Hope Franklin, and others) whose work had examined the transition from slavery to wage labor in the United States between the end of the nineteenth century and the middle of the twentieth, as well as the formation of urban ghettos as a consequence of restrictions on civil rights, income disparity, and ethnic segregation.[69] Although Carmichael also cited white social scientists—such as I. F. Stone, Robin M. Williams, James Q. Wilson, William C. Mitchell, and William A. Price, the majority of whom were functionalists rather than Marxists—it was clear that one of Carmichael's objectives in *Black Power* was to showcase the African American intellectual contribution to the civil rights struggle.

Carmichael had studied at Howard University in Washington DC under black professors—such as Sterling Brown, Nathan Hare, and Toni Morrison—who had introduced him to the field of African American activism and thought. Carmichael's research on the construction of white power in the United States grew out of his knowledge of this field to propose a conceptualization of the mechanisms of exclusion and marginalization of the black population as a continuation of eighteenth- and nineteenth-century structures of colonialism and slavery. In the process, *Black Power* notably established a connection between the American black experience and African decolonizing processes of the mid-1950s. The work's identification with Kwame Nkrumah, the Ghanian leader who had worked toward Pan-African decolonization at the end of the 1950s, along with Patrice Lumumba of the Congo, Tanzania's Julius Nyerere and Guinean leader Amílcar Cabral, was indicative of the nationalist thrust of Carmichael's discourse.[70]

Unlike Huey Newton, who prioritized dialogue with openly socialist African leaders such as Algeria's Ahmed Ben Bella, Carmichael urged the Black Panthers to support African decolonizing platforms that had either predated or evaded alliances with the Soviets, such as that of Nkrumah of Ghana or Ahmed Sekoú of Guinea. In 1967, when *Black Power* was published, Carmichael argued that the most effective path toward a massive project of decolonization and antiracism, inspired by the radical ideas of figures such as Frantz Fanon, was through the efforts of nonaligned governments that defended their sovereignty by maintaining open diplomatic relations with both the United States and the Soviet Union, as was the case with the Nkrumah administration. This viewpoint posed a doubly uncomfortable alternative within issue 17 of the journal *Pensamiento Crítico*, since it added to the subscription to the Fanonian decolonizing optic a call to confrontation with the United States from Africa that did not necessarily pass through Moscow.

Nonetheless, it was not in the "White Power" chapter excerpted in *Pensamiento Crítico* where Carmichael and Hamilton's book had most directly addressed the African American "colonial situation." Rather, it was in the book's preface, a tribute to Frederick Douglass and Frantz Fanon, where the authors' "politics of difference" was featured in both its most sophisticated intellectual legitimization and its boldest political translation.[71] According to the authors, Douglass's observation that "the limits of tyrants are prescribed by the endurance of those whom they oppress" had been reformulated in Fanon's *The Wretched of the Earth* and in Jean Paul Sartre's prologue to this work.[72] In Sartre's idea that the support of European intellectuals for African decolonization redeemed them as men and in Fanon's defense of anticolonial violence as a process of creation of "new men," Carmichael found the doctrinal basis of the black movement in the United States.[73]

This humanist interpretation of Sartre's existentialism and Fanon's Marxism, featured in the transcription of a long passage from the "Conclusion" to *The Wretched of the Earth*,[74] placed Carmichael on the wing of the New Left that *Pensamiento Crítico* had rejected, starting with its fifth issue, in which André Gorz and Jean-Paul Dollé (the latter a disciple of Louis Althusser) had criticized leftist humanism, such as that of Sartre or Schaff, based on readings of Marx's *Economic and Philosophic Manuscripts* (1844).[75] Carmichael, like Fanon—who considered the leadership of Nkrumah and Touré as fundamental—defended anticolonial violence without favoring alignment with the USSR or China. This position still predominated in the text in his second book, *Stokely Speaks: Black Power Back to Pan-Africanism* (1971), despite this work's dedication to a leader like Guinean Sékou Touré, who was now inscribed in the socialist camp.[76]

Carmichael's first formulation of a symbiosis between the antiracist and anticolonial struggles, on the one hand, and the anticapitalist struggle, on the other, was his 1970 essay "Pan-Africanism," which featured multiple citations of Marx and linked the cause of black nationalism to concrete socialist movements, such as that of Chairman Mao in China, Ho Chi Minh in Vietnam, and Castro in Cuba.[77] However, in the essay "From Black Power to Pan-Africanism," which would function as the conclusion to *Stokely Speaks* and inspire the book's title, Carmichael once again conceived the Pan-African project from the Fanonian anticolonialist liberation perspective, a framework that, although open to dialogue with Marxism, did not advocate alliances with the Cold War socialist bloc.[78] Carmichael, now living in Guinea with his wife, singer Miriam Makeba, continued to frame his Pan-Africanism following the example of the nonaligned socialism of former Ghanian president Kwame Nkrumah: as an antiracist and anticolonial movement that, while confronting the forces of NATO, refused to gravitate toward the Soviet orb.

In a work of somewhat less doctrinal weight, *Die Nigger Die!* (1969), the political autobiography of H. Rap Brown, it is possible to note the same point of disencounter with Cuban socialism. Brown profusely cites Mao and Fidel and demonstrates his familiarity with Latin American leftist debates in the wake of Guevara's death in Bolivia.[79] But as he makes clear in the final pages of his autobiography, although African American leftists mobilized against the unjust practices of racial segregation that upheld restrictions on civil rights, they were aware that "the elimination of segregation was the solution, not integration."[80] This certainty set up an unavoidable contradiction with the Cuban project, insofar as the social model unleashed on the island was one that explicitly aspired to black and white integration within a socialist community regulated by equality of rights and duties.[81]

Brown did not venture very far into this contradiction, but he seemed to make subtle reference to it in citing the line from Régis Debray's book *Revolution in the Revolution?* (1967, published by Paul Sweezy and Leo Huberman at Monthly Review Press), "Revolutions cannot be imported or exported."[82] In Cuba, he added, socialism had incorporated itself within a national ideological tradition and had thereby constructed itself as an alternative of social development. In the United States, however, the possibility of such a scenario was remote, in addition to the fact that the rhythm of capitalist development conspired against it. Brown concluded that socialism was not practicable for "certain oppressed peoples."[83] In the case of black oppression in the United States, however, what could be done was to struggle against racism, understanding it as part of a system of colonial exploitation and supplementing Marxist analysis with a study of the processes of decolonization in the Third World.[84]

Together with issue 17 of *Pensamiento Crítico*, another notable intervention in the debate opened by the Black Panthers within the Cuban intellectual field was the anthology *Now: El Movimiento Negro en Estados Unidos* (1967), edited with a prologue by Cuban writer Edmundo Desnoes. Desnoes was the author of the novel *Memorias del subdesarrollo* (1965), which he had adapted into a screenplay for the 1968 film by the same title (directed by Tomás Gutiérrez Alea). Desnoes's selection for his anthology was similar to that of the *Pensamiento Crítico* issue, but he introduced an important innovation in seeking to call attention to the cultural theory derived from the black political project in the United States.

The volume included stories by James Baldwin and LeRoi Jones, as well as essays by the former on the suppression of race in the work of William Faulkner and by the latter on the contribution of jazz to American culture, within a larger framework focused on exemplifying the strong critique of the discourse of white cultural identity in the United States.

None of the fictional works or essays by Baldwin and Jones favored abandoning ethnic integrationism, the position publically advocated by the Black Panther leaders.[85] Desnoes did not seek a balance between integrationists and anti-integrationists in his volume so much as to demonstrate the debate between the two positions while favoring the latter. In his prologue, he counterposed his portrait of Martin Luther King Jr. as a moderate reformer whose principle of nonviolence had produced results that Desnoes referred to as "vociferous yet sparse, much racket but little substance" (ruidosos pero escasos, mucha bulla pero pocas nueces) to a characterization of Malcolm X as a revolutionary who viewed whites as the personification of evil.[86] Desnoes's anthology also presented Black Panther leaders H. Rap Brown and Stokely Carmichael as natural heirs and transcenders of Malcolm X.[87] The Cuban writer was conscious that he was writing his prologue at a time when the Cuban Revolution was supporting Guevarist guerrilla initiatives and was heavily engaged with Third World decolonization.

Desnoes went beyond the editors of *Pensamiento Crítico* in his support for American black nationalism. His solution to the dilemma posed by this US cultural-political current to the Cuban Revolution's aim of ethnic integrationism was to argue that blacks in the United States did not constitute a minority but rather a nation, one that had experienced subalternization and colonization on the part of a white, capitalist, slavist, and racist bourgeoisie[88]—the same white capitalist bourgeoisie that had exploited the underdeveloped nations of Latin America and the Third World. The struggle of blacks against racial discrimination in the United States, Desnoes argued, was also a struggle for decolonization like that which had occurred in Algeria, Vietnam, the Congo, or Bolivia. The Cuban Revolution was at the vanguard of this struggle, according to Desnoes, since after having achieved decolonization and having ended racial discrimination on the island, it was now supporting efforts to decolonize and overcome racism for the rest of the Third World and for the US black nation itself.

Sustaining himself on the ideological prestige of Frantz Fanon—who was cited profusely by Carmichael in his texts for the volume—Desnoes avoided any reference to Marxist-Leninism or to the role of the Soviet Union in the Cuban socialist project. In fact, he openly criticized American communist leader Gus Hall, who in an article for *Political Affairs* in 1965 had called for an alliance between white and black workers.[89] Desnoes's silence on the Soviet Union was revelatory both of the ideological coordinates of the ideological dialogue between the US black movement and the Cuban leadership, as well as of the geopolitical precariousness of that dialogue. The silence in question was related to another equally significant reticence: Desnoes's prologue made no mention of the question of racism, miscegenation, or ethnic integration in Cuban socialism. His discourse portrayed Cuba as a postethnic, homogeneous, and unified nation, thanks to its revolutionary process, which now stood as an interlocutor and guide for the American black nation.

Whether or not they identified with Pan-Africanism, and whether they were hostile toward or in dialogue with racial integration, the Black Panther intellectuals converged on a support for decolonization that was difficult to reconcile with Cuba's rigid inscription within the Soviet bloc. Some of the Black Panthers were drawn toward Mao's China while others supported Nkrumah's Ghana; some of them backed the Latin American guerrilla movements while others defended the principle of nonalignment; but none of these black intellectual leaders and activists could assent to the absorption and dissolution of black nationalism within international communism. Many of them lamented that the legacy of Patrice Lumumba, who had rhetorically defended Moscow, was then being abandoned by the Kremlin through the politics of "peaceful coexistence" it was now promoting. Cuba's role in Moscow's shift of global strategy—starting with Castro's support for the 1968 Soviet invasion of Czechoslovakia and confirmed by the island's accelerated integration to the Eastern Bloc over the years following—met with great controversy, and US black intellectuals called for accepting that support yet refusing to cover over the conflicts that it unleashed.

If it wishes to avoid the repetition of commonplaces, any study of the ideological relation between the US black movement and the Cuban Revolution during the 1960s must avoid the paradigm of "solidarity" with its subordination of the intellectual process to concrete political alliances. In the relation in question—a dialogue that juxtaposed Marxist, nationalist, anticolonial, and socialist views and passions—it was impossible for consensus to predominate. During the brief 1962–68 period when the Cuban revolutionary government was at its greatest distance from orthodox Marxist-Leninism and Soviet geopolitics, coincidences between the Black Panthers and the Cuban Revolution were more frequent. But by the beginning of the 1970s, the points of agreement diminished as Havana aligned itself ever more with Moscow and shifted its ideology toward greater orthodoxy.

The question of race was one of the points of irreducible divergence between US black nationalism and Cuban socialism. While the Cuban government carried out an ambitious project of social equality that aspired to civil—and therefore cultural and moral—homogeneity between blacks and whites, the African American Left in the United States fully invested its efforts in strengthening racial identity: a project that was consonant, it should be observed, with the critique of ethnic integrationism articulated by black Cuban intellectuals prior to the revolution's turn toward Moscow, such as Juan René Betancourt in *El negro: Ciudadano del futuro* (1959), and Walterio Carbonell in *Cómo surgió la cultura nacional* (1961).[90] The relation between Cuban socialism and the African American civil rights discourse thus became fraught with contradictions, despite the universality that characterized the discourses and practices of the New Left. On the margins of this disencounter, however, it is possible to note certain assimilations of the Black Panther project of decolonization and antiracism by young, critical sectors of Cuban socialism in the 1960s, as can be read in the journal *Pensamiento Crítico*.

Socialist Cuba enabled many of these Black Panther intellectuals to articulate a critique of white power in the United States that fully acknowledged the connection between the positions of the white elite and the imperial mechanisms of US hegemonic power that manifested its domination through interventions in Third World civil wars and alliances with European metropolitan powers opposed to decolonization and socialism in Asia and Africa. Starting with the Cuban revolutionary government's decision to more fully align itself with the Soviet bloc from 1968 onward, the geopolitical differences in the global context only augmented the intellectual disconnections experienced by Cuban communists and American antiracists in their efforts to address topics such as nation, race, and socialism. In the following decade, the differences in question would become irredeemable.

7

THE LEAGUE OF MILITANT POETS

★

In May 1963, a subcommittee of the House of Representatives of the US Congress held public hearings on a group of American intellectuals who had allegedly conducted "anti-American activities" of "pro-Castro propaganda" in violation of State Department Regulations. Two of the individuals called on to testify in the hearings were Leo Huberman, editor of the important socialist publication *Monthly Review*, and Chicana journalist and translator Elizabeth Sutherland Martínez. Martínez had published in *Monthly Review*, was serving as editor of *Pa'Lante* magazine (published by the League of Militant Poets of New York), and also worked as a researcher for the United Nations on topics of colonialism and development in the Third World.[1]

The members of the congressional committee insistently questioned Martínez about young Americans who traveled regularly to Havana and who had expressed solidarity with the Cuban Revolution. The young socialist deftly eluded her interrogators, assuring them that in Cuba she only remembered seeing the young independent African American photographer Leroy McLucas, who had been working on a story about daily life in Cuba. McLucas was a fellow collaborator of *Pa'Lante* and had published his "Letters from Cuba" in the magazine. Since 1960 he had also worked with *Kulchur* magazine, a publication edited by beat writer Marc Schleifer and whose format had inspired *Pa'Lante.*

Kulchur and *Pa'Lante* constitute a useful archive for reading the identification with the Cuban Revolution that developed among young American leftist radicals between 1960 and 1962. The two magazines shared a common aesthetic and ideological program with certain publications in Cuba, particularly *Lunes de Revolución*, a program that articulated the aesthetic vanguards of the 1960s and the New Left's discourses of decolonization, pacifism, and libertarianism.[2] Some of *Kulchur* and *Pa'Lante*'s collaborators also published in *Lunes de Revolución*, including Allen Ginsberg, LeRoi Jones, Lawrence Ferlinghetti, and photographer Leroy McLucas himself. It was when the Castro government closed down the Havana magazine at the end of 1961 that these writers and artists first began to express their objections to Cuban socialism.

In the pages that follow, I will seek to reconstruct the view of the Cuban Revolution and Cuban socialism that was projected in *Kulchur* and *Pa'Lante.* I am interested in documenting the role of the Cuban topic in the New York New Left's own process of construction during the 1960s, as well as the relation between the design of alternative New York political-aesthetic projects and Havana's own intellectual field. By means of this exercise, it will be possible to subsequently describe the aesthetic and ideological divergence that opened between the two cities after their brief moment of convergence at the beginning of the 1960s. The disencounter between the leftist communities in New York and Havana was aggravated after 1962 as a consequence of the military and political confrontation between the United States and Cuba, but also because the extraordinary radicalization experienced by the New York Left failed to find interlocutors in Havana's growing ideological dogmatism.

KULCHUR, OR THE BLAND REVOLUTION

Although *Kulchur*'s first issue in the spring of 1960 featured no editorials or manifestos, its readers had no trouble recognizing the source of the magazine's title in the work of Ezra Pound. In 1938 the American poet had published a strange book entitled *Culture*, written during his moment of greatest adhesion to Italian fascism. In 1952, James Laughlin reissued the book under the title of one of its section headings, *Guide to Kulchur* (1952), through the important New York vanguard publisher, New Directions. Pound's book was a miscellany, or collage, of Chinese and Japanese ideograms, aphorisms, and notes, philosophical and political essays, philological treatises, lengthy citations from classical Greek sources, and even musical scores, such as that of his own opera, *Le Testament de François Villon*.

This mélange of texts was nonetheless crossed through with Pound's distinction between two notions of culture, one of which was elevated over the other.[3] In the face of what he viewed as a book culture based on petrified knowledge that had lost its prestige due to usury and commerce—and that he associated particularly with the Anglo-Saxon nations—Pound proposed another notion of culture linked to the incorporation of knowledge and its fusion within human minds and bodies: "knowledge is NOT culture. The domain of culture begins when one HAS 'forgotten-what-book.'"[4] According to Pound, the incorporation of knowledge proper to a true culture was like a process of melting and soldering of metals, intervening in a physical way in historical universal causality: "that is no more a 'culture' than the invention of a new smelting process is culture. It is, or may be, a link in a chain of causation."[5]

Pound's reaction against the lettered idea of culture promoted by Western humanism converged on the cult of action in fascist ideologies of the 1920s and 1930s. In a section of *Kulchur* precisely entitled "Totalitarian," the poet declares, "the history of a culture is the history of ideas going into action."[6] It was not surprising that Pound viewed Mussolini as a genius who had turned his back on the idea of culture held by British and American Puritanism and who had recuperated, from a modern perspective, the classical legacy of the Greco-Latin Mediterranean.[7] Pound saw in Mussolini an agent for the realization of *kulchur* in history, insofar as the Italian dictator aspired to modernize the legacy of ancient Rome.

The passages of fascist sympathy and anti-Semitism in *Guide to Kulchur* were brief and almost imperceptible within its vast and jumbled assembly of references and commentaries. What attracted young avant-garde New Yorkers to Pound during the 1950s and 1960s, more than his criticism of book culture or his calls to action, was his notion of commitment to personal liberty as a distinguishing characteristic for the modern poet.[8] Only starting from this irreducible dedication to personal liberty, Pound felt, was the poet's involvement in collective causes conceivable. It was not the first time that writers of the New York liberal vanguard had read Pound. Ernest Hemingway and William Carlos Williams, for example, had admired Pound since the 1920s. Allen Ginsberg and the poets of the Beat Generation held the author of the *Cantos* in a similar esteem, which led them to deliberately ignore his fascism.

The back cover of the first issue of *Kulchur* magazine, which was released in the spring of 1960, bore an announcement from two presses, Totem Press of New York and Auerhahn of San Francisco, thus exemplifying the coast-to-coast intellectual network that beat literature was attempting to create. This first issue featured writings by Diane di Prima and Michael McClure; issue two featured William S. Burroughs and John Wieners. Some members of *Kulchur*'s editorial board, such as LeRoi Jones and Charles Olson, were well known in beat circles and gave the magazine a vanguard profile. The magazine was distributed by Totem Press, which that same year had issued the poetry volumes *This Kind of Bird Flies Backward* (1960), by Diane di Prima, and *Projective Verse* (1960), by Charles Olson.

The issue contained more prose than poetry, starting with "The Conspiracy" by William S. Burroughs, a fragment from *The Naked Lunch* that had been censored in the work's first edition due to its explicit treatment of drug consumption.[9] The issue also featured the short story "Ketama-Taza" by another cult writer, Paul Bowles, who inscribed the *kulchur* aesthetic in frequent North African, and specifically Moroccan, representations that attracted the Beat Generation as much for their links to drug culture as for their association with the experience of decolonization.[10] Bowles's text was followed in the issue by Allen Ginsberg's poem "Paterson," a title that alluded both to Ginsberg's own hometown in New Jersey and to William Carlos Williams's famous poetry collection by the same title. Like Bowles's piece, Ginsberg's poem included numerous allusions to drug use, such as the reference to "heroin dripping in my veins," "eyes and ears full of marijuana," and "eating the god Peyote" in the mountains of Mexico.[11]

The covers of the two following issues of *Kulchur*—fall 1960 and spring 1961—featured photos by Leroy McLucas, an African American photographer born in Saint Louis, Missouri, whose work focused on the representation of poverty in Harlem and other working-class neighborhoods of Manhattan. McLucas's New York photos during this period, which appeared in *Negro Digest*, *Harper's Bazaar*, *Esquire*, and other publications, situated him on the vanguard of the visual representation of the material residues and social ills generated by consumer society. McLucas's cover images for *Kulchur* revealed the misery of predominantly black New York neighborhoods and emphasized the African roots of Harlem, serving as early photographic portents of the intellectual radicalization that would lead within a few years to the rise of the Black Panthers, the birth of black Islamism, and the inception of the civil rights movement.

McLucas's photographic technique bore the aesthetic and ideological imprint of the Photo League, a cooperative of Jewish photographers, largely from Manhattan and Brooklyn, who documented New York City life from the end of the 1930s to the beginning of the 1950s. The group's members—Sid Grossman, Jack Delano, Helen Hewitt, Richard Lyon, Max Yavno, Morris Engel, Lucy Ashjian, Aaron Siskind, Jack Manning, Sol Prom, and others—had created the *Harlem Document* project, whose images testified to the deterioration of living conditions in the city's largest black neighborhood.[12] The Photo League was put on McCarthy's blacklist and shut down during the anticommunist hunt of 1952.

Along with LeRoi Jones, Allen Ginsberg, Marc Schleifer, and Lawrence Ferlinghetti, McLucas served as a member of the Fair Play for Cuba Committee. In the summer of 1960 he traveled to Havana to attend the celebrations of the anniversary of Castro's 1953 Moncada offensive. During that visit, which was organized and financed by the Cuban government, McLucas came into contact with Guillermo Cabrera Infante and the *Lunes de Revolución* editorial group. From Havana, McLucas sent an image to the *Kulchur* offices in New York that would be used on the cover of the magazine's fall issue (which also featured Jones's piece, "Cuba Libre") and also began work on a series of photos of Havana. The images from the series bear a remarkable similarity to McLucas's New York photos, thus demonstrating a deliberate effort to analogize and contrast images of the two cities through the same lens. One of the photographs McLucas shot in Havana was his portrait of Black Panther leader Robert F. Williams and his wife Mabel at the Plaza de la Revolución, an image that was included in *Negroes with Guns* (1962). The photo was taken on March 13, 1962, although both Williams and McLucas had been in contact in Havana since 1960.[13]

Evidence of this encounter and collaboration—which constituted a sort of Havana-Harlem axis—is provided by the July 1960 issue of *Lunes de Revolución* magazine entitled "Los negros en USA" (Blacks in the USA). From both a political and a literary standpoint, *Lunes de Revolución* constituted one of the strongest intellectual interventions in the US black movement of the period. Articles by Richard Gibson and Robert F. Williams in the July 1960 issue linked the nascent black nationalist movement with Cuban socialism, while articles by James Baldwin on the "Harlem ghetto," Harold Cruse on African American art, and John Henrik Clarke on the narrative of Richard Wright described a black vanguard culture in which values of decolonization and antiracism were interlinked.[14]

Kulchur's editor Marc Schleifer, a Jewish New Yorker who would later convert to Islam and change his name to Abdullah Suleiman Schleifer, had written the prologue and epilogue of *Negroes with Guns* for Williams, whom he had interviewed in Havana in the summer of 1961. Notably, Schleifer did not publish any of his texts on Cuba in *Kulchur* magazine, but rather in other, more aggressively ideological, New York publications. His "Cuban Notebook," which Todd F. Tietchen reads as one of the central texts of the beat movement's engagement with the Cuban Revolution, was printed in the summer 1961 issue of *Monthly Review*, and some of his later articles referencing Cuba, including the interesting critique

"Art and Socialist Realism" and his "Letter from Havana," appeared in *Monthly Review* and the *Nation*.[15] The "Cuban Notebook" piece, which was flanked in the *Monthly Review* issue by Che Guevara's critique of Cuban exceptionalism and Paul Baran's denunciation of the Bay of Pigs invasion, shared Ginsberg's and Jones's support for vanguard culture within the American leftist imaginary, but also expressed a more open support for the Cuban Revolution's socialist ideological orientation.

However, the most noteworthy coverage of the Cuban theme in *Kulchur*'s early 1960s journalistic repertoire was LeRoi Jones's "Cuba Libre" piece, which was featured at the end of the magazine's second (fall 1960) issue.[16] The article was consistent with Jones's work during this period, when he was associated with the Beat Generation and was married to Jewish writer Hettie Cohen. In the middle of the decade, Jones would leave his wife and cease his affiliation with the beat movement in a shift toward black nationalism. After Malcolm X's assassination in 1965, he converted to Islam and changed his name to Amiri Baraka in a move to associate himself with a more aggressively Marxist and black nationalist ideology. In 1960, however, in keeping with Jones's own political-aesthetic mode and *Kulchur*'s editorial emphasis, "Cuba Libre" constituted not an ideological call for commitment to the Cuban Revolution but a reflection on the ambivalent political engagement of a beat poet who prioritized personal liberty over any social project.

Scholars of Jones's work, such as Werner Sollors, William J. Harris, and Todd F. Tietchen, have demonstrated the many complex facets of the sympathy held by African American beat writers and artists for the Cuban Revolution.[17] These individuals were strongly attracted by the decolonizing and egalitarian elements of the revolutionary project, but they found its integrationist and socialist model of community difficult to assimilate, both from their libertarian poetic perspective and its emphasis on drugs, sex, and jazz and from the positive view of racial alterities that they shared with New York's Jewish, black, and Hispanic Left. The simultaneous acceptance and rejection of the revolution on the part of black beat figures resulted in a testimony that clearly demonstrates a tension between the Sartrean mode of engagement and another such mode of engagement that might be referred to as "Ginsbergian."

In "Cuba Libre," as well as in the poem "Betancourt," written after his Havana sojourn, Jones posed this dilemma by means of a transcription of his debate with Yucatecan journalist Ruby Betancourt Moguel and poet Jaime Augusto Shelley, two young Mexican socialists who were also visiting Cuba at the time. The latter reproached Jones for his "bourgeois individualism" and confronted him with a highly critical view of American culture, challenging the very basis of the black beat writer's sense of identity.[18] In response, Jones accepted the interpellation insofar as he perceived it as voiced by Latin American subjects who had suffered the effects of US imperialism. At the same time, however, he could not repress his instinct to preserve those elements of American culture that constituted him:

> She (Betancourt) questioned me endlessly about American life, American politics, American youth—although I was jokingly cautioned against using the word American to mean the US or North America. "Everyone in this car is American," she said. "You from the North, we from the South." I explained as best I could about the Eisenhowers, the Nixons, the Du Ponts, but she made even my condemnations seem mild. "Everyone in the world," she said, with her finger, "has to be communist or anticommunist. And if they are anticommunist, no matter what kind of foul person they are, you people accept them as your allies. Do you really think that hopeless little island in the middle of the sea is China? That is irrational. You people are irrational."
>
> I tried to defend myself, "Look, why jump on me? I understand what you are saying. I'm in complete agreement with you. I'm a poet . . . what can I do? I write, that's all, I'm not even interested in politics."[19]

The text abounds in other, similar frictions, marking a clash of two modalities of intellectual engagement. At one point, Jones joins his voice to the cry, "Cuba sí, Yanquí no," but after a moment, overwhelmed by repeated shouts of "Long live . . ." from the revolutionaries ("Viva Fidel," "Viva la Revolución," "Viva

Cuba Libre"), he begins to voice his own version of the "vivas," referring to symbols of New York and American culture: "'Viva Calle Cuarenta y dos' (Forty-Second Street), 'Viva Symphony Sid,' 'Viva Cinco Punto' (Five Spot), 'Viva Turhan Bey.' I guess it was the heat."[20] Jones's description of Juan Almeida, the only black commander he met during his trip, and of Castro himself, is not particularly enthusiastic, despite the detailed transcription of his conversation with the latter. When Castro asks Jones what the US government thinks of his trip to Cuba, Jones deflects the question in what he subsequently describes as a "reflex action": "I shrugged my shoulders and asked him what did he intend to do with this revolution."[21]

Castro characterizes Jones's question as a "poet's question," and responds that he will attempt to "do what I think is right, what I think the people want." Shortly after, Jones formulates the central question of the New York debate on the Cuban Revolution: "What about communism?" Castro responds with some irritation, "I've said a hundred times that I'm not a communist. But I am certainly not an anti-communist. . . . I said also a hundred times that I consider myself a humanist. A radical humanist."[22] At the end of the text, Jones concludes that his visit to Cuba had reaffirmed his conviction that the United States should not interfere in the affairs of the new nations of Asia, Africa, and Latin America, and had convinced him of the low probability for a revolutionary rationality to take hold in American cultural politics. His final reflection seems to constitute his response to Ruby Betancourt's argument about Americans' "irrationality":

> The idea of "a revolution" had been foreign to me. It was one of those inconceivably "romantic" and/or hopeless ideas that we Norteamericanos have been taught since public school to hold up to cold light of "reason." The reason being whatever repugnant lie our usurious "ruling class" had paid their journalist to disseminate. The reason that allows that voting, in a country where the parties are exactly the same, can be made to assume the gravity of actual moral engagement. The reason that permits a young intellectual to believe he has said something profound

> when he says, "I don't trust men in uniforms." The *residue* had settled on all our lives, and no one can function comfortably in this country without it. That thin crust of lie we cannot even detect in our own thinking. That rotting of the mind which had enabled us to think about Hiroshima as if someone else had done it, or to believe vaguely that the "counter-revolution" in Guatemala was an "internal" affair.
>
> The rebels among us have become merely people like myself who grow beards and will not participate in politics. A bland revolt.[23]

In *The Autobiography of LeRoi Jones* (1984), Jones, then writing as Amiri Baraka, comments that the Cuba trip was a "turning point" in his life. The later evolution of his thinking confirms this observation.[24] The Cuban Revolution radicalized Jones intellectually and politically, opening him to the world of Afro-Caribbean literature through the poetry of Nicolás Guillén and Aimé Césaire. The latter's collection *Notebook of a Return to the Native Land* (*Cahier d'un retour au pays natal*, 1939) led Jones to read the work of Frantz Fanon and Amílcar Cabral.[25] This radicalization, of course, was a gradual and progressive process, since in Jones's poetic collections from the first half of the 1960s, such as *The Dead Lecturer* (1964)—printed by Grove Press with a cover by Leroy McLucas—and *The System of Dante's Hell* (1965), he maintained his poetic praxis within the limits of what he had referred to as "bland revolt."

Jones's poems in the first of these two collections, such as "A Poem for Neutrals" or "A Poem for Willie Best," moved toward a subtle politicization of art through their calls for historical consciousness and a practice of memory that went beyond the blue nights and luminous landscapes of Kyoto or Fanonian demands for the revelation of one's true face behind the black renegade mask.[26] Other compositions in the collection, including "War Poem" and "Political Poem," were more clearly oriented toward a criticism of the war in Vietnam or a defense of public intellectual intervention. However, the modality of engagement defended by Jones at the time was one that oscillated between his proposal for a "black-dada nihilism," which combined Mondrian's geometrism and Sartrean existentialism; his articulation of guerrilla poetry; and his calls for nonviolent protest against lettered culture, all expressed out of a longing for a radical world, as formulated in the poem "Valéry as Dictator."[27]

As Kimberly W. Benston notes, *The System of Dante's Hell* (1965), the last poetry collection LeRoi Jones would write prior to his conversion to Islam, already announces a rejection of any form of intellectual alienation.[28] Through an effective use of allegory, Jones announces America's destruction at the hands of capitalist modernity and repudiates the nation's dominant racial hypocrisy.[29] By this time, Jones had traced a sufficiently negative representation of US white culture so as to fuel his subsequent transition to black nationalism and, later, Marxist-Leninism. Playing a decisive role in this transition was the 1965 assassination of Malcolm X, who, like Jones, had closely followed the Cuban experience since 1960. In September 1960, a few months following Jones's return from his first trip to the island, Malcolm X and Castro held their celebrated meeting at the Theresa Hotel in Harlem, an event that further padded the FBI's file on the black leader.

Malcolm X's perception of Cuba in the early 1960s was quite similar to Jones's perspective in "Cuba Libre."[30] When FBI agents interrogated the black leader after his interview with Castro, Malcolm X stated that although he was not a communist—because he rejected communist atheism—he thought that when a country as small as Cuba defied a country as large as the United States, it was because it had accumulated a great many complaints against Washington's behavior in the Caribbean.[31] In LeRoi Jones and Malcolm X's view, Cuba, like China or Vietnam, had an anticolonial substrate that did not exist in the Soviet Union and the real socialisms of Eastern Europe, and its experience of socialism needed to be comprehended accordingly. It was precisely his drifting momentum from a radical anticolonialist notion of socialism that led to beat writer LeRoi Jones's change of name to Amiri Baraka and his repositioning, first in Islam and then in communism.

Jones/Baraka's evolution would not only distance him in the 1970s from other beat writers of his generation, such as Ginsberg and Ferlinghetti, but also put him in tension with certain intellectual leaders of the Black Panthers, such as Eldridge Cleaver, Stokely Carmichael, and Robert F. Williams, Jones's companion on that first trip to Cuba. Baraka's adoption of Marxist-Leninism significantly modified his view of the racial and colonial question in the Caribbean, as seen, for example, in his essays on Nicolás Guillén and Aimé Césaire from the 1970s. At that time, what interested Baraka about both of these poets was not their racial representation of Caribbean subjects—which connected them with Langston Hughes, W.E.B. Du Bois, and the Harlem Renaissance, as well as constituting them as forerunners of the struggle for civil rights—but instead their ideological surpassing of black nationalism in their own turn toward Marxist-Leninism.[32]

PA'LANTE AND THE SOCIALIST CONGA

The year 1961 was one of ideological disenchantment for the debate on the Cuban Revolution in New York. The Bay of Pigs invasion and the Marxist-Leninist positioning of the Cuban government aggravated the fissures in the New York Left, which had been evident since the previous year. The liberal wing of this leftist community, although opposing US interventionism and CIA-led efforts to overthrow the Cuban government under the Kennedy and Eisenhower administrations, began to publicize their disagreement with the Havana-Moscow alliance. By contrast, socialist and communist sectors of the New York Left celebrated the Cuban government's turn toward Marxism, although the most heterodox members of these groups began to express reservations about the dangers of Havana's adoption of Soviet-style bureaucratic elements.

The lesser known and short-lived New York publication *Pa'Lante* joined the *Monthly Review* in defending Cuban socialism in New York. *Pa'Lante*'s editors were Jewish Marxist Howard Schulman and two young Hispanic socialists: Chicana activist Elizabeth Sutherland Martínez and José Yglesias, a Cuban American from Tampa descended from a family of nineteenth-century tobacco producers. The first and only issue of *Pa'Lante* was released on May 19, 1962, the anniversary of José Martí's death. The editors announced that the publication would appear three times a year in spring, summer, and winter issues. Schulman, Martínez, and Yglesias presented themselves as members of an organization called the League of Militant Poets and summarized their ideological platform in their opening editorial:

> *Pa'Lante* is devoted to the American Renaissance and the writing of a new world. This new world is the world of the future whose image may be found in the fraternal socialist countries. . . . By publishing the guerilla writing of Latin America and new work from the socialist nations, it seeks to demolish the walls put up in fear between men's minds. By including the writing of Young Americans, it affirms the bloom of art in our country as an indication of radical economic and social change to come.[33]

Pa'Lante's ideological repertoire was already far from espousing liberal humanism, which accepted the democratic and nationalist elements of the Cuban Revolution while questioning its shift toward the socialist bloc. For the magazine's young New York editors, Cuba's push toward socialist radicalization was useful for helping to reinforce their own struggle against McCarthyism and anticommunism in the United States, and particularly in New York City, where periodic purges targeting leftist intellectuals accused of being accomplices or agents of Moscow had been carried out since the 1950s. *Pa'Lante*'s editors declared, "We militantly oppose the pseudo-ethic of anticommunism that has replaced our Jeffersonian tradition of moral revolution."[34] These subscriptions to Jeffersonian republicanism or Whitmanian democracy were merely a courteous strategy for presenting a communist intellectual project to the New York public, one that subscribed to a positive view of the Soviet Union, Eastern Europe, and Third World nations like Cuba, which had begun to join the socialist camp:

> America, we are Yankee poets who believe that socialism will make you more beautiful, hundreds of times richer, and sane. The form of communal society to which we aspire will revive

> your revolutionary tradition and enhance our creativity. Put your bombs away. Don't waste blood fighting history in Vietnam, Laos, Cuba. Turn with us to love, beauty, the dream of Whitman.[35]

Pa'Lante's format was quite similar to *Kulchur*'s, and most of the collaborators in its first issue were poets and artists of the Beat Generation circle. The issue's back cover featured lines from a well-known conga composition that had been heard in Havana since the declaration of the revolution's socialist character in April 1961: "somos socialistas / pa'lante y pa'lante / y al que no le guste / que tome purgante" (we are socialists, forward ever forward, and whoever doesn't like it can go take a laxative). The issue's front cover featured a photo by Leroy McLucas of a young bearded Cuban soldier drinking coffee in Havana, a pistol hanging prominently from his holster. On the cover's lower right-hand corner, three words were superimposed, as if in the form of a haiku:

> New Writing:
> CUBA
> IVAN
> USA

The middle word in the sequence, IVAN, was difficult to comprehend without examining the table of contents or reading the full issue. This Russian name referred to a fragment from the script of Sergei Eisenstein's film *Ivan the Terrible*, translated into English by Paul Blackburn, which suggested a subtle criticism of Stalinism, articulated during the Soviet Union's Khrushchev Thaw. On *Pa'Lante*'s cover, the name "Ivan" appeared without any direct allusion to Eisenstein's script, sandwiched between the words "Cuba" and "USA." It would not be forced to suggest that on the *Pa'Lante* cover, this name in fact signified the Soviet Union, the third angle of a Cold War triangle that was spreading to the Caribbean with Cuba's incorporation into the Soviet bloc.

The Cuban soldier portrayed by McLucas on the cover was not just any military figure. His well-groomed beard corresponded to the "look" favored by many Rebel Army officials at the time, and the style of his trousers and shirt drew him toward the beat style popular among Americans of the same generation. The position of the pistol hanging from a holster over the soldier's right thigh bore a striking similarity with the style associated with Cuban commander Camilo Cienfuegos—who had lived briefly in New York during the Batista years (and who disappeared over the ocean during a night flight from Camagüey to Havana)—and also recalled the poses of certain heroes of Hollywood westerns, such as Gary Cooper in *High Noon* (1952) or that of *Double Elvis* in Andy Warhol's famous painting. The soldier's figure also projected a certain "cool" demeanor in his gesture of drawing the coffee to his lips, a certain calmness in the midst of the violence and war that would have been familiar to young American leftists at the time, thanks to their modeling, as LeRoi Jones recalls in "Cuba Libre," by the Hollywood imaginary.

Photographer McLucas was himself a defender of the "cool" style within African American culture. A number of his images—such as those featured in Robert F. Williams and LeRoi Jones's books published at the beginning of the 1960s, his shot of a child in Harlem precisely entitled "Cool," or his numerous portraits of Malcolm X—endeavored to transmit the same sense of calm in the midst of the storm. The Cuban Revolution, in addition to representing a decolonizing cause with which one could express solidarity, offered New York's New Left a spectacle of beautiful young people, both black and white, that was closer to that Left's aesthetic style than images from the Soviet Union, Eastern Europe, China, or even Vietnam. For the Hispanic editors of *Pa'Lante*, and for McLucas himself, this aesthetic solidarity was fundamental.

In addition to these seductive images, *Pa'Lante* offered its New York readers what constituted perhaps the first collected translation project of the work of poets and narrators of the Cuban Revolution in English. The repertoire included poems by Nicolás Guillén, Rolando Escardó, and Pablo Armando Fernández, translated by José Yglesias; the first version in English of Guillermo Cabrera Infante's story "Ella cantaba boleros" (She Sang Boleros), translated by Chamberlain and Sam Hilanan; and an article by Marxist critic José Antonio Portuondo, entitled "A New Art from Cuba," which defended socialist realism and questioned poetic surrealism and artistic abstractionism as the work of bourgeois decadents (the last work represented another turn of the screw of Juan Marinello's essay *Conversación con nuestros pintores abstractos* (Conversations with Our Abstract Painters), which had just been published in Cuba.[36]

The sample of Cuban literature in *Pa'Lante* revealed a transaction between two aesthetic, ideological, and generational currents then in conflict on the island: that of the young writers of *Lunes de Revolución* magazine (Cabrera Infante, Baragaño, Fernández, Escardó, and others) and that of the older communist writers affiliated with the old Popular Socialist Party (Marinello, Guillén, Portuondo, Aguirre, and others). When the first issue of *Pa'Lante* appeared, *Lunes* had already been shut down, and the New York magazine's sample of Cuban writing—whoever its collaborators in Havana may have been—reflected an attempt to avoid the appearance of sectarian favoritism. The *Pa'Lante* issue united established and emerging writers, prerevolutionary communists and anti-Stalinist socialists, and both Marxist-Leninists and liberals, who dialogued with Trotskyism and existentialism.

Pa'Lante was conceived as a venue for dialogue among literary voices on the left—the socialist Left in the Cuban case and the vanguard or pro-socialist Left in the American case—for which reason the sample of Havana writers in the issue was paired with a selection of New York writing that consisted primarily of the work of beat poets. One such piece was "Monday (in the Jungle)," a work of lyrical prose fiction by John Wieners, author of *The Hotel Wentley Poems* and a writer Allen Ginsberg described as a poet of "Keatsian eloquence" and "substantial passion."[37] Wiener's piece made no direct references to the guerrilla movements that were then beginning to form in many Latin American countries, but the allusion to these movements in *Pa'Lante*'s editorial and the author's own aesthetic invited readers to traverse as a single forest both the "jungle" of the beat travelers and the jungle of the South American guerrillas.

The *Pa'Lante* issue also included a poem by Joel Oppenheimer, a figure who, together with poet and translator Paul Blackburn, was an important member of the New York intellectual Left in the

1960s as a cultural promoter for socialist bohemian circles associated with both the *Village Voice* and the Poetry Project at the New School for Social Research. Also featured in the issue's sample of New York writing was one of the most anticapitalist fragments of LeRoi Jones's poetry collection *The System of Dante's Hell* (1965).[38] None of these texts alluded directly to the Cuban Revolution or the debate over its ideology in the New York public sphere, but they served as a sounding board for a cultural atmosphere in which the bohemian beat movement was beginning to engage in concrete political causes, such as radical equality and opposition to the war in Vietnam and Laos, in a clear movement beyond the moderate positions of the Democratic Party and the Kennedy administration.

The two texts of *Pa'Lante* that directly treated the topic of Cuba were "Prose Contribution to the Cuban Revolution" by Allen Ginsberg and the poem "Fidelio" by Michael McClure. Both writers established the twin poles of the New York Left's relation to nascent Cuban socialism. Ginsberg's piece did not call for supporting the Cuban revolutionary process but expounded on beat aesthetics and ideology with the goal of exploring the possibility that the Cuban revolutionaries might advance toward some of the beat's political positions, such as sexual liberation or the legalization of drugs.[39] By contrast, McClure's poem expressed a more direct solidarity with Cuba, casting that solidarity as an affective strategy oriented toward protecting the Cuban revolutionary experience and the life of the revolutionary leaders themselves in the face of US government aggressions.

McClure was a young poet from San Francisco, a key figure in that city's hippie counterculture, a character in several fictional works of Jack Kerouac, and a friend of Bob Dylan. He had joined his own writing to a number of that generation's cultural currents, such as rock and roll, Buddhism, ecology, and pacifism. In a letter of recommendation sent to the Guggenheim Foundation on McClure's behalf, Allen Ginsberg emphasized the quality of the San Francisco writer's poetry collections, such as *Dark Brown* and *A Book of Torture*, both of which appeared in 1961, published by the venerable vanguard venue Grove Press. In his poem "Fidelio," however, McClure adopted a direct tone of warning to Castro regarding the dangers against his life posed by agents of US military and economic power. The poem presented Castro as Fidelio, the character from Beethoven's opera of the same title. In that opera, Fidelio is the name of the false prison guard identity adopted by Leonor in order to liberate her lover Florestan, who has been condemned to death for treason. Hence the allusion in McClure's poem to the "charming bearded singer":

> Charming bearded singer! Make the beast's tune
> that precedes the triumphal ending of mankind's symphony.
> We hold our breath & listen to the roar.
> Your tongue is ruby meat and vibrates a new melody
> of new virtue to the starving and the poor
> Eyes are mild within your lion's face.
> A finish will come for the old lore;
> and with your clean arm and paw,
> the clotted massy dishes will be swept
> and the world
> left as pure as an old dark table
> covered by a gleaming linen cloth
> so stark and warm
> it may reflect the high points of your song.
> But beware the eagle with white head!
> Watch it closely with your dark starred
> mammal eyes.
> The hopes of freedom are with you . . .
> and opposed are the lies.[40]

McClure's poem, particularly in its placement in the *Pa'Lante* issue immediately following Portuondo's article—in which the latter called for art and literature in a socialist realist style—seemed to shake off the ambivalences of beat political engagement. The composition constituted a transparent song of praise and warning to Castro and the revolution. "Fidelio" was closer to Lawrence Ferlinghetti's poem "One Thousand Fearful Words for Fidel Castro" (1961) than to the prose writings of Ginsberg or Jones.

Pa'Lante, however, was not a publication that favored socialist realism, however much it sympathized with the real socialisms of Eastern Europe. In the text placed after McClure's poem, "Letters from Cuba" by photographer Leroy McLucas, the magazine affirmed a more clearly beat or Ginsbergian engagement with the Cuban Revolution. McLucas's letter was addressed to *Pa'Lante* editors Howard Schulman and Elizabeth Sutherland Martínez from Havana and Santiago, narrating the writer's vicissitudes as a black and American photographer in revolutionary Cuba. He informed the editors that Minister of Education Armando Hart had arranged a tour of the island for him with the goal of documenting the Literacy and Agrarian Reform Campaign in rural regions of the island. One of the difficulties McLucas encountered during his tour was that the Cubans he wished to photograph would pose for the camera, and he wanted to capture their spontaneous expressions and gestures. "That is not so good, cause one could easily have a book of pictures of everyone looking at you."[41] McLucas commented that he would spend the entire day telling his subjects (in Spanish): "no meter en la cámara, por favor" (Don't get in the camera, please).[42]

The photographer observes in his letter that despite the advanced state of photography in Cuba, the mentality of nearly every photographic professional that he had met on the island was quite conservative. Some of the professionals in question, he commented, were jealous of the opportunities offered to him as an American photographer. On one occasion, he met a well-established Cuban photographer who lived in a nice apartment and listened to Thelonius Monk. McLucas assumed that the man would be a vanguardist sympathizer, but soon discovered that he was quite "square," despite his appreciation for jazz: "I thought he was a sort of hip, in the long run I come to find out that he was extremely very square, like the rest of the arty crowd here."[43] McClure's conclusion was resolutely unfavorable to the island's intellectual elite: while the American artists were trying to conduct a revolution, the Cubans were not at the level of Castro's project and did not wish to participate in it.[44]

McClure's highly critical view of the island's writers and artists not only coincided with Guevara's own criticisms as expressed a few years later in the latter's essay *El Socialismo y el hombre en Cuba* (1965), but also represented a view already being formulated at the time in the opinions of Carlos Franqui, Guillermo Cabrera Infante, and other writers who wrote for *Lunes de Revolución*. The "absence of soul," the "wandering on the moon," the "living on another planet" that McLucas observed in the island's intellectual elites seemed a consequence of dogmatic ideas from Cuban society itself, as a legacy of old Catholicism, of the bourgeois liberalism of the ancien régime, and of the orthodox Marxist-Leninism that had already begun to predominate in the cultural politics of the revolution. In his letter, McLucas reported unenthusiastically on Cuba's revolutionary press—*Bohemia* magazine, the newspapers *El Mundo* and *Revolución*—and lamented the closing of *Lunes de Revolución*, in the October 6 issue of which he had managed to publish some photos of New York.[45]

McLucas warns in his letter about the growing dogmatism that he saw invading Cuban culture, in commenting on reactions from the orthodox faction of the elites against Néstor Almendros's free-cinema experiment, *Gente en la playa*. He describes the work of Almendros as a breath of fresh air in an ever more asphyxiating atmosphere, and he criticizes a note that appeared in *Bohemia* that cataloged film as a decadent and bourgeois medium.[46] McLucas does not refer in his letter to *PM*, the short film by Orlando Jiménez Leal and Sabá Cabrera Infante, whose censorship led to the closing of *Lunes de Revolución*, but the cultural-ideological intolerance he describes is the same. McLucas was impassioned about the Cuban Revolution and the vertigo of social transformation that it propelled and that he sought to document, but he felt that Cuban intellectuals were not at the level of the transformations that were surpassing them.

McLucas further illustrates his sense of disenchantment with the Cuban social project in a story he recounts in his letter to *Pa'Lante*'s editors. One afternoon, after walking down Virtudes de La Habana Street, he engaged in a tryst with a prostitute. The young woman was ill at ease during the encounter and explained to McClure that although she was sympathetic to some elements of the revolution, she did not support socialism.[47] McLucas felt he understood the girl's disquiet, equating it with the melancholy that he, too, was feeling and that made him long for the struggle for freedom and peace on the streets of New York. In the midst of the great social change that was taking place on the island, he could feel only sadness and loneliness, and did not desire to "infect" the image of the revolution with this melancholy.[48] McLucas reveals the affective disencounter between the New York Left and the Cuban Revolution when he comments that as the Cuban project affirmed itself in socialism, he felt more alone or less enthusiastic.[49] In this state, his greatest satisfaction, which led him to find the "soul" he could not identify in the culture itself, was the sense of rhythm he observed among Cuban children.[50]

This letter from Havana by the African American black photographer opens a dissonant note within the beat movement's relation to the Cuban Revolution. McLucas's letter goes beyond the ambivalence expressed by Ginsberg or Jones in their writings about the Cuban experience during the period by levying a harsh judgment on the empty soul of Cuban socialism itself. In words penned by a photographer, the judgment in question was as sobering as it was free of any hint of exaggeration. The subsequent history of *Pa'Lante* magazine's demise would itself reflect the affective disencounter between the New York Left and the Cuban Revolution that was announced in McLucas's testimony. After the magazine closed, two of its editors, José Yglesias and Elizabeth Sutherland Martínez, would return to the Cuban topic with a growing skepticism toward the discourses and practices of Cuban socialism.

Yglesias, who had been born in Tampa in 1919, in a family of Cuban and Gallegan ancestry, authored a pair of books that evoked his Cuban background: the novel *Ybor City* (1963) and the memoir *The Goodbye Land* (1967). In the latter work, he wove together the two sides of his family tree and voiced criticisms against Spanish dictator Francisco Franco and the dictatorships of Machado and Batista in Cuba.[51] After the success of his memoirs, Penguin Books of New York contracted Yglesias to write a long report on a rural town in revolutionary Cuba. The writer selected Mayarí, a small urban center located off the Bay of Nipe on the north shore of the eastern part of the island, and resided there during the first few months of 1967.

Cover of magazine *Pa'Lante*, edited by the League of Militant Poets, an association of the Hispanic Left in New York.

The product of Yglesia's Cuban trip, *In the Fist of the Revolution: Life in Castro's Cuba* (1968), could be characterized as part travel journal and part anthropological study. The work begins with an account of Yglesias's arrival in Cuba and in particular his description of the concerns expressed to him by the Cuban Ministry of Foreign Relations officials who met with him prior to his journey to Mayarí. If these officials were hoping that Yglesias's book would constitute an apology for the revolution, they were certainly deeply disappointed. Yglesias recounts the enthusiastic description one of his informants, a Dr. Morales, gave of the impressive modernization of rural life initiated by the revolutionary government's Agrarian Reform, Literacy Campaign, Urban Reform, and public health programs.[52] From the first pages of the book, however, Yglesias denounces the UMAP work camps where thousands of gay and vanguardist youth were forced to labor. The social profiles of these youth were quite similar to those of members of the New York Left, but in Cuba they were diagnosed by official socialist psychology as practitioners and carriers of morally "deviant" behavior.[53] Yglesias devotes a whole chapter of his book, entitled "La enfermedad," to a short anthropological study of the "enfermitos" (literally "the little sick ones"), youth who in other circumstances might have been members of a Cuban hippie culture but who had suffered repression during the Revolutionary Offensive and been characterized as "extranjerizantes," subjects demonstrating excessive foreign influence.[54]

In the course of his book, the Cuban American writer reports on the many complaints and demands he heard from people who claimed they had been harmed by the revolution due to lower salaries, food shortages, and transportation difficulties. Yglesias also objects to the spread of machista and racist attitudes—particularly against young mulatto and black youth from the town of Bitirí near Mayarí, religious intolerance, the invasion of private life, and the climate of vigilance and denunciation generated by the Committees for the Defense of the Revolution (CDR).[55]

Without going as far as Yglesias's critique of Cuban socialism, *Pa'Lante*'s other (now former) editor Elizabeth Sutherland Martínez likewise conducted a research project in Cuba around the same time, and her work shared with that of Yglesias a profile of anthropological interventionism and reportage on the ideological dramas of Cuban socialism. Following various visits to the island in the middle of the 1960s, Martínez published her study, *The Youngest Revolution: A Personal Report on Cuba*, in 1969.

The publication of Martínez's work coincided with the period following Guevara's death in Bolivia and the Western New Left's moment of greatest ascendance following the student movements of 1968. In her book, Martínez describes the ideological polemic between the Guevarist and pro-Soviet currents within the Cuban revolutionary political class and clearly expresses her support for the former of the two positions.[56] Whereas Aníbal Escalante and other prerevolutionary communist leaders personified the shift toward a bureaucratic model of real socialism, younger revolutionaries associated with the literary magazine of the Communist Youth Union, *El Caimán Barbudo* (published in 1966), and with the social sciences journal *Pensamiento Crítico* (1967–71) represented the Havana variant of the New Left.[57] In these two youth-oriented projects, which were integrated within Cuban revolutionary culture but were at the same time critical of the growing Stalinist tendency, Martínez saw the incarnation of Guevara's ideas in *El socialismo y el hombre en Cuba* (1965).

Like Yglesias, Martínez observed with alarm the rise of machismo, homophobia, and racism in revolutionary Cuba, refusing to view these tendencies as mere remnants of the bourgeois past.[58] She felt there were elements of revolutionary culture, particularly those legitimized by the bureaucratic orthodoxy, which had facilitated the reproduction of these values within socialist Cuba. She argued that a critique of these discourses and practices of exclusion and intolerance was necessary from the Left, particularly from a Left such as that of New York, which was confronting similar problems in the United States. Martínez justified her critique with citations of Castro's own speeches in which he had called on the friends of the revolution not to merely point out the good in the revolution but to also signal the movement's errors in order to learn from them and avoid repeating them.

Although on balance Martínez's view of Cuba in *The Youngest Revolution* is positive, her critical narration of utopia is marked by a note of melancholy. In her description of a visit to the Isla de a Juventud (then named the Isla de los Pinos), an island located south of the island's western region, the melancholy tone increases.[59] Her passion in recounting the birth of a completely new community on the small island is always accompanied by her observations of what she considers morally reprehensible customs and the sense of strangeness these customs produce in her. Not surprisingly, the book, which is splendidly illustrated with photos by Martínez's former *Pa'Lante* colleague Leroy McLucas, concludes with the texts of letters sent by McLucas from Havana in the summer of 1961.[60] To Martínez, these letters seemed the ineluctable complement of the ambivalent images of socialist utopia captured by McLucas's camera.

The socialist conga dance that these intellectuals of the New York Left joined in 1961 ended like the congas of the Havana carnival always end: in dissolution and complaints. The Cuban Revolution had given the New York Left an opportunity to openly question the imperial policies of the United States toward the Caribbean, Central America, and the Third World. But the island's alignment with the Soviet Union and its adoption—particularly after 1968—of institutions and concepts from the real socialisms of Eastern Europe severely complicated the praxis of critical solidarity. As the editors of *Kulchur* and *Pa'Lante* would attest, that praxis could be as risky as it was exciting. In the exercise of ideological agreement, the gaze's complicity too often gave way to the melancholy of estrangement.

8

THE SKIN OF SOCIALISM

★

ALONG WITH WALDO FRANK, ANOTHER PROMINENT FIGURE who lent his support and reputation to the Fair Play for Cuba Committee (FPCC) in the early 1960s was veteran journalist and Latin American scholar Carleton Beals (1893–1979). The FPCC was an association of intellectuals and activists who sought to promote respectful relations with Cuban socialism in American public opinion from 1960 to 1962. Despite Beals's support for the FPCC, during a Senate hearing into the FPCC's activities, presided over by James O. Eastland in 1961, it was revealed that CBS correspondent Robert B. Taber, one of the Cuban government's main interlocutors in New York, had offered Beals the coleadership of the FPCC together with Frank but that Beals had declined the offer, objecting to the presence of communists in the association and its financial support from the Cuban government. As Beals stated during the hearing, "It would be as bad, in my eyes, to twist any part of the record in favor of the Cuban government, as to falsify the record against Castro and his government."[1]

Born in Kansas at the end of the nineteenth century, Beals had forged a long and distinguished intellectual career in the American Left prior to the 1960s.[2] From the time of his early years growing up in California, he had become keenly interested in the Mexican Revolution and its impact on Central America and the Caribbean. Between 1920 and 1940, he traveled frequently throughout these regions, and at the start of the Cold War, his interest in Latin America had extended to the history, society, and politics of the Andean nations and the rest of the South American continent. By the time of the Cuban Revolution, Beals had published more than forty books and was considered one of the leading authorities on Latin America in US academia and public opinion, and served as an important mentor for young New Left socialists.

In 1957 Beals wrote a series of articles on the Cuban Revolution that testified to a rapid evolution in his initially negative view of the phenomenon. In two articles that appeared in 1957, "Rebels without a Cause" and "A New Crime of Cuba," the veteran journalist had questioned the Cuban revolutionaries' extremism and lack of ideological program and had also made some disrespectful allusions to Castro's father.[3] Mario Llerena, president of the 26th of July Committee in exile, responded with letters of protest to the *Nation*'s editor Carey McWilliams and to Beals, to which he attached the program he had written, *Nuestra Razón*, which subscribed to social democracy, or to the leftist or democratic noncommunist nationalism predominant in Latin America. In a subsequent article, Beals corrected his perception of the Cuban revolutionaries.[4]

At the time of the Cuban Revolution's triumph, Beals was residing in Deep River, Connecticut, where he enjoyed easy access to New York City and his friends at Columbia University, where he had studied in the 1920s. It was to be expected that Beals, as an established Latin Americanist, would become one of the key referents of the Cuban debate in Manhattan at the beginning of the 1960s. But Beals's position in that debate was a singular one: while defending Cuba's right to socialist radicalization, he also did not hold back from criticizing the Cuban political system's adoption of autocratic elements and the island's alliance with the Soviet Union and the socialist bloc. Beals's criticisms in this sense were more defined than those of Waldo Frank, C. Wright Mills, and the collaborators of *Monthly Review*, *Kulchur*, or *Pa'Lante*.

Beals's critique of Cuban socialism had its origin in his familiarity with the Mexican Revolution, which he conceptualized as the mother of all Latin American revolutions in the twentieth century. In the process of his engagement with the Mexican Revolution and its effects in Central America and the Caribbean, Beals came to create his own notion of the face of revolutionaries in countrysides and cities throughout the region, featuring that face in his texts and in the celebrated images that accompanied them, such as Walker Evans's photographs of Havana under dictator Gerardo Machado that illustrated Beals's *The Crime of Cuba* (1933).

In the pages that follow, I would like to propose a rearticulation of this face of the revolution that Beals promoted in his books on Mexico, Nicaragua, and Cuba, and to suggest some keys for understanding its influence on the young generation of the New York Left, which identified with Cuban socialism. For example, the way in which certain writers and artists of the *Pa'Lante* group discussed in chapter 7 (José Yglesias, Elizabeth Sutherland Martínez, and photographer Leroy McLucas) approached the Cuban experience and sought to represent its voices and faces demonstrates a tangible debt to the author of *The Crime of Cuba*. The 1960s mark a convergence between Carleton Beals's effort to adapt his historical idea of twentieth-century revolutions for the New Left, on the one hand, and the approach of young New York socialists toward Cuba and its revolution, on the other.

THE REVOLUTIONARY ZEITGEIST

Beals was always as much interested in the images of Latin American revolutions as in their ideas. A number of his books featured illustrations by artists such as Mexican Diego Rivera, Guatemalan Carlos Mérida, Peruvian José Sabogal, and American photographer Walker Evans. *Mexican Maze* (1931) was illustrated by Rivera, *Banana Gold* (1932) by Mérida, *The Crime of Cuba* (1933) by Evans, and *Fire in the Andes* (1934) by Sabogal. Significantly, these artists and photographers were all accomplished portraitists. All four of the works in question were published by the J. B. Lippincott

Company of Philadelphia, which had started in the early nineteenth century as a publisher of Protestant Bibles and prayer books, and by the middle of the twentieth century had assumed a clear antifascist profile.

During the 1930s, Lippincott promoted Beals as a versatile and productive writer, a specialist in Latin America, and a critic of European fascism. The press's editors classified Beals's prose in curious categories: "Contemporary chronicles" (such as *Rome or Death* [1923], *Mexico: An Interpretation* [1923], and *The Crime of Cuba* [933]); "Travel and Description" (*Mexican Maze* [1931], *Banana Gold* [1932], and *Fire in the Andes* [1934]); "Personal Experience" (*Glass Houses: Ten Years of Free-Lancing* [1938], *Brimstone and Chili* [1927], and others); "Biography" (*Porfirio Díaz: Dictator of Mexico* [1932] and *The Story of Huey P. Long* [1935], among others); and "Novels" (including such works as *The Stones Awake* [1936], *Black River* [1934], and *Destroying Victor* [1929]).

The first two of these genres were at times indistinguishable in their application to Beals's books, since his "chronicles" originated as travel notebooks documenting the author's journeys through Mexico, Central America, the Andes, and the Caribbean. Some of his novels and biographies, such as *Stones Awake* or *Porfirio Díaz*, also shared a Mexican thematic, a topic Beals had begun to devote himself to following his first trip to Mexico in 1918.[5] His journey on foot, horseback, and train through what Mexican revolutionaries Emiliano Zapata, Francisco Villa, Venustiano Carranza, and Álvaro Obregón referred to as "reinos" (kingdoms) would forever mark Beals's vision of Latin America as a region in which twentieth-century history manifested itself in a revolutionary way.

From that point onward, Beals demonstrated a photographic interest in his efforts to reconstruct the face of revolution. In his view, Mexico's "indigenous heritage" and "Spanish heritage" defined some factions of this face but not the face in its entirety,[6] since revolutions could not be explained by ethnic lineages alone. He argued that the revolution begun by white criollo Francisco I. Madero in the twentieth century was a continuation of the "revolution of Benito Juárez," an indigenous and liberal president in the latter half of the nineteenth century.[7] Beals did not repeat the common error of associating Juarismo with Zapatismo based on the indigenous origins the leaders of the two movements shared.

Beals believed that the face of the revolution did not remit only to race but also reflected the social class of the political subjects involved. The agrarian question and the labor question were interwoven in the revolutionary process by means of the politicization of the popular masses, he asserted.[8] The reaction of the clergy and the oligarchy against the revolutionary movement socially radicalized the struggle against the accumulated grievances of the old Porfirian regime.[9] In turn, the "penetration" of American capital in the Mexican economy caused the agrarian and labor revindications promoted by the revolution to acquire a nationalist and anti-imperialist meaning that was lacking in European and American socialism.[10]

It was in this symbiosis of socialism and nationalism where Beals saw the face of the Mexican and Latin American Revolution reveal itself. "The Mexican as he is" was the phrase he chose to illustrate the emergence of a revolutionary identity within the Mexican citizenry.[11] Fifteen years later, after exploring revolutionary struggles in Central America, Beals would repeat the phrase as "the Cuban as he is" in order to signal the projection of an analogous revolutionary subject in the Caribbean, in the context of popular struggle against the dictatorship of Gerardo Machado y Morales in 1933.[12]

Mexico absorbed Beals's attention throughout the decade of the 1920s. *Mexican Maze* (1931), the book illustrated by Diego Rivera, was in some ways a sequel to *Mexico: An Interpretation* (1923), in which the historian's project in the former is replaced by the gaze of the traveler-anthropologist in the latter. *Mexico: An Interpretation* documents Beal's journeys throughout the Mexican nation: in the state of Yucatán he is captivated with the socialist project of Felipe Carrillo Puerto; he travels through "magical" agrarian villages such as Guadalupe-Hidalgo, Tlaxcala, Amecameca, Milpa Alta, and Tepoztlán in search of local physiognomies;[13] he lingers with muleteers in the Sierra Madre mountain range, with Yaqui indigenous peoples in the northern state of Sonora, with the traveling theater performers of Las Carpas, and with a group of Mexican avant-garde poets known as the Estridentistas. Out of his immersion in revolutionary Mexico emerged Beals's certainty that the great nation to the south had found its "new idols" in revolutionary figures such as Zapata, Villa, and Carrillo Puerto.[14]

The revolution was creating a new society and a new culture in a nation of spiritual traditions dating back millennia, Beals believed. He considered it of the utmost importance that the new Mexican social imaginary was being produced on the southern border of the United States, a nation serving as the conduit of an extreme mode of industrial capitalism. The Mexican Revolution, by contrast, was constructing a society that would offer communitarian alternatives to the capitalist life of the "machine age."[15] Echoing the ideas of José Martí, José Enrique Rodó, and José Vasconcelos, Beals presented the Mexican revolutionary experience as a forward-looking movement for Latin America, one that staged the cultural contradiction between the two halves of the Americas in the middle of the twentieth century:

> Today the American and Latin-American cultures also represent two poles of the human spirit. Neither is complete in itself. In general our genius is practical, Roman, legal, mechanistic, materialistic. Theirs is romantic, spiritual, song-making, beauty-loving, idealistic, adventurous.[16]

However, closer to Martí than to Rodó or Vasconcelos, Beals believed that a confrontation between these two civilizing modes was not inevitable and that what both "poles" needed was a mutually compensatory relation. The North required the spiritualism of the South and the South required the North's materialism. Any advance in this dialectic of civilizing interchange, Beals argued, had to start with a recognition of the American continent as a space held in common by its two cultural currents. For the United States, accepting this premise would require its abandonment of all policies of aggression or intervention against the national sovereignties of Latin America: "any aggression against Latin America is a profanation of the human spirit of which we are but a part."[17]

From Mexico under the presidential administrations of Plutarco Elías Calles and Lázaro Cárdenas at the end of the 1920s and the beginning of the 1930s, Carleton Beals perceived that the revolutionary winds were extending to bordering regions such as Central America and the Caribbean. His books *Banana Gold* (1932) and *The Crime of Cuba* (1933) constituted an effort to demonstrate that the impact of the Mexican Revolution was being felt in Guatemala, Nicaragua, Cuba, and the Dominican Republic. Beals began his route to Central America and the Caribbean from the state of Chiapas, crossing through the "Quetzal kingdom."[18] As he approached the Panama Canal, the American journalist noted the assertion of Washington's continental hegemony in the region in the signs of US military and economic expansion.[19]

If Beals perceived the Mesoamerican world as made up of "kingdoms"—the "kingdom" of Zapata or the Quetzal "kingdom"—the Central American isthmus seemed to him to be ruled by an "empire": the United Fruit Company.[20] This company, along with similar operations like the Cuyamel Fruit Company or the Standard Fruit Company, was forging a microcosm of power in the region through the *latifundio* (land tenure) system, the business class, clubs, schools, hospitals, the Catholic church, and even radio and the press, all of which were in the service of the oligarchies, the army, and Washington's embassies.[21] In Central America, even more so than in Mexico, the causes of agrarian reform and national sovereignty were interwoven.

According to Beals, the figure who personified the Central American Revolution was Nicaraguan general Augusto César Sandino. After numerous obstacles, Beals managed to interview Sandino before his assassination in 1934. The American journalist did not fail to note the significant differences between Sandino's leadership in Central America and Zapata's in Mexico. For the Nicaraguan leader, agrarian reform was not tied to the goal of communal property as it was in Mexico, and resistance against American occupation and interventionism was a more vital priority.[22] The revolutionary tide was spreading from Mexico, Beals concluded, yet it was adopting its own form and accent in every region it touched.

Cuba, the next destination in Carleton Beals's trajectory, presented a scenario similar to that of Central America, but under a more sophisticated dictator, Gerardo Machado, veteran of the nation's war of independence. Beals noted the affinity between

Machado's reelection strategy—as established through the "extension of powers" act of 1928—and the prerevolutionary regime of Porfirio Díaz in Mexico, which he had just described in his biography of the Mexican dictator one year before his journey to Cuba.[23] But in Cuba, as John A. Britton has argued, Beals encountered greater economic, political, and military dependence on the United States and consequently a greater degree of anti-imperialist and nationalist sentiment on the part of the leftist opposition to Machado's dictatorship.[24]

Just as he had done in his travels through Mexico and Central America, Beals focused his gaze on the faces of revolutionary actors in Cuba. He was equally interested in "white" Cuba and "black" Cuba, seeking to identify under these antithetical colors the "Cuban just as he is."[25] Although his book on Cuba opened with a phrase that was difficult to reconcile with the very anti-Machado leftism that Beals sympathized with—"we liberated Cuba from Spain, but established a quasi-protectorate by forcing the Cubans to accept the Platt Amendment as part of their Constitution"—the book's central argument constituted a strong repudiation of the island's limited sovereignty as established under the "Plattist" regime, and a clear denunciation of Washington's complicity with the Machado dictatorship.[26]

Beals's Cuba trip took place prior to Machado's fall from power, during a period when repression against the country's liberals, nationalists, and communists was reaching its climax. But before *The Crime of Cuba* was published, Beals managed to add an appendix that narrated the dictator's ousting in August 1933 and the rise to power of Ramón Grau San Martín's revolutionary movement. The final pages of the book give evidence of the paradoxes that underlie the formula, defended by Beals and other US leftist intellectuals such as Waldo Frank, regarding the harmonization of the two halves of America. Beals argued for the legitimacy of Grau's government and praised Washington's change of attitude toward the Machado dictatorship. However, he warned that the new US ambassador, Benjamin Sumner Welles, and Department of State official Adolf A. Berle Jr. had begun to conspire with a military faction led by Fulgencio Batista against Grau, the latter's minister of the interior, Antonio Guiteras, and the revolutionary movement itself.[27]

Beals concluded that Welles and Berle were betraying the Good Neighbor Policy introduced by President Roosevelt and were heading toward an imminent annulment of the Platt Amendment. Roosevelt's policy required US diplomacy to involve itself in Latin American matters to the point where it could investigate and sue not only Machado for his crimes but also the American government itself for complicity with those crimes from Washington.[28] In this way, Beals reinforced the arguments of voices representing authoritarian Cuban and Latin American nationalism, such as prominent Machadist intellectual Alberto Lamar Schweyer, who accused the United States of having conspired in favor of the dictator's fall.[29]

The paradox of the leftist Americanism that public intellectuals such as Carleton Beals and Waldo Frank subscribed to was that it based its call for respecting the self-determination of Latin American nations not on a principle of ideological neutrality but on a support for political interventionism targeting the oligarchies and military and ecclesiastical power on the right. Beals's interventionist stance strengthened, starting in the middle of the 1930s, supported by the New Deal and opposition to European fascisms. In books such as *America South* (1937), *The Coming Struggle for Latin America* (1938), and, above all, *Pan America* (1940), Beals argued for the necessity of an alliance between the United States and Latin American governments against fascism and Nazism.

The reformulation of Pan-Americanism that Beals and Frank supported was one that repudiated all vestiges of imperialism from the era of James G. Blaine and Theodore Roosevelt and endorsed both the liberal and socialist goals of the New Deal. However, neither US liberalism nor US socialism always looked favorably on the Soviet Union's growing influence over the Marxist or communist Left in Latin America. In *The Coming Struggle for Latin America*, Beals warns of "red star" influence in South America, after providing a panoramic description of the specter of fascist influence in the region that frequently incurs exaggeration, such as references to "Japanese battleships in the Pacific," the "swastika over the Andes," "black shirt marches in Buenos Aires," a "Francoist invasion of México," and so on.[30] Although he considered the communist threat a lesser risk than fascism, Beals also did not believe that communist persuasion would be sufficient for stemming the tide of the greater danger of fascism.[31]

In his book, Beals observed that the rise of fascism in Latin America operated not only on the level of ideology but also in political styles: the massive popular mobilization that characterized both the Nazi and the Soviet regimes fascinated Latin American leaders. And although Beals did not underestimate the gravitation toward fascism on the part of popular leaders such as Getulio Vargas of Brazil or Juan Domingo Perón of Argentina, he recognized that these figures, together with Mexican president Lázaro Cárdenas, represented an inevitable evolution toward nationalism in Latin American politics that the United States, in order to counter the Soviets, needed to encourage rather than combat.[32]

A number of Beals's public assertions in the American public sphere during the 1930s identified him with a populist socialism that was growing in the shadow of the New Deal at the time. This socialist identification led Beals to express sympathy for Huey P. Long, the populist governor of Louisiana assassinated in 1935, and to join in the defense of Leon Trotsky—together with John Dewey, Otto Rühle, Benjamin Stolberg, and Suzanne La Follette—in opposition to Stalin's accusations against the Bolshevik leader during the Moscow Trials.[33] Beals's expressions of support for liberal or socialist leftism rather than for communist or pro-Soviet leftism increasingly profiled him as an interlocutor for revolutionary nationalism in Latin America, which sought to maintain a distance from communist parties.

When the Cold War reoriented US domestic and international policies toward anticommunism and McCarthyism, Beals situated himself against this trend, advocating good relations with socialist governments and movements independent of the Soviet Union. His support for Víctor Raúl Haya de la Torre and the American Popular Revolutionary Alliance (APRA) in Peru, Jorge Eliécer Gaitán in Colombia, Grau San Martín and Prío Socarrás in Cuba, Víctor Paz Estenssoro in Bolivia, Juan José Arévalo and

Jacobo Arbenz in Guatemala, José Figueres in Costa Rica, and Rómulo Betancourt and Rómulo Gallegos in Venezuela was consistent with his conviction favoring a revolutionary structure for Latin American nationalism constructed out of the Mexican matrix. Beals read the Cuban Revolution's triumph as one more example of the stability of this structure and the misguided nature of US policy opposing it, as verified in the military coup against Arbenz in Guatemala in 1954.[34]

Beals, who even translated a book by Arévalo on anticommunism in Latin America, became a champion of the thesis claiming that US backing of noncommunist nationalist revolutionary leftist factions would make it more difficult for the Soviet Union to garner support in the region.[35] From 1957 onward, Beals began to publish articles for a number of publications, such as his piece "Terror under Neon Lights" for the *Nation*, in which he denounced the Batista dictatorship's repression of Cuban revolutionary youth and called on Washington to break with authoritarian regimes, such as Batista's in Cuba, Pérez Jiménez's in Venezuela, Rojas Pinilla's in Colombia, Trujillo's in the Dominican Republic, and Somoza's in Nicaragua.[36] When the United States began to express its first objections to the Cuban Revolution at the end of 1959 and the beginning of 1960, the elderly Beals joined forces with the Fair Play for Cuba Committee and other American voices that called for not repeating the "crime against Guatemala" on the island.[37]

In the aforementioned article for the *Nation*, Beals observed that the clash between Havana's neon lights, vibrant nightlife culture, casinos, and hotels on the one hand and the Castro-led youth rebellion on the eastern side of the island on the other was largely a historical consequence of US policies toward the island. Washington, in his view, had accommodated itself to an authoritarian, demagogical, and corrupt political class originated in the 1933 Revolution. Even politicians who expressed civil opposition to the dictatorship, such as former president Grau San Martín or congressman Carlos Márquez Sterling, were but "old names. Old faces."[38] Nonetheless, Beals seemed to support a peaceful solution that would renew the legacy of the 1933 Revolution, which he had defended at the time as consistent with his views on the Latin

American revolutionary tradition that started in Mexico at the beginning of the twentieth century.

Beals's articles for the *Nation* did not idealize Castro and the young revolutionaries, although—or perhaps because—they were written several months after Herbert Matthews's series of articles on the Sierra Maestra guerrillas for the *New York Times*. Beals rejected the label of "criminals" that the Batista government had applied to the young Revolutionary Council members who had assaulted the Presidential Palace on March 13, 1957, but his use of the terms "terror" or "terrorism" seemed to apply both to the repressive measures carried out by Salas Cañizares and other Batista henchmen and to the actions of the young revolutionaries themselves. Beals's insistent interrogation into the possibility of a "peaceful solution that will bring justice to the Cuban people" was a demonstration of the mistrust he felt in the face of the new revolutionary violence.[39]

At the beginning of January 1959, Beals was sent to Cuba by the *Nation* in order to cover the triumph of the revolution and Castro's arrival in Havana. Beals's old concerns about the heavy toll of militarism in Cuban history reappeared in his article, "Cuba: The Revolution without Generals," which was published in the *Nation* in mid-January 1959. The article was also translated several months later for the Cuba-themed March 1959 issue of the *Revista de la Universidad de México*. In the article in question, Beals emphasized the fact that the young Sierra Maestra rebels entering Havana with their beards and crucifixes looked like biblical prophets approaching a new Mecca of justice and liberty.[40] What most enthused the veteran journalist was Castro's declaration, delivered during one of his first speeches at Camp Columbia (Ciudad Libertad), that the old military caste had been eliminated and that the Cuban Revolution was "the only revolution that no single general had emerged from nor would ever emerge from."[41]

Just as in his June 1957 article for the *Nation*, Beals once again ascribed responsibility to the United States for having backed the Batista regime militarily and diplomatically, although he acknowledged the impact of the arms embargo recently imposed by the Eisenhower administration. In keeping with his customary fidelity to New Deal strategy, Beals called on the United States to divest itself of its old ideological prejudices and narrow interests and back the Cuban Revolution through the adoption of a constructive Latin Americanist policy that would forestall another militarization of the island's government, such as the one that had occurred under Batista after the fall of Machado. As he had done three years earlier, Beals appealed to the analogy of Cuba as a Hungary ninety miles off the US coast that required assistance in throwing off caudillismo and underdevelopment and consequently the influence of international communism.

During the Bay of Pigs invasion barely two years later, Beals became convinced that the United States had repeated its error and that its aggression against Cuba was opening doors for the Soviet Union on the island. The distinguishing factor of Beals's reaction to the Cuban situation in the early 1960s was that his ingenuous belief in the possibility that US policies toward Cuba might be corrected was accompanied by his clear frustration with the pro-Soviet shift that he saw Cuban socialism making. Unlike many of his contemporaries on the American Left, Beals did not regard Castro with great sympathy. His friendship with Cuban political figures such as Grau, Prío, and other Latin American leaders, such as Betancourt and Figueres, who would soon pass over to the anti-Castro opposition, perhaps influenced his distance from the young Cuban revolutionaries.

Starting already in 1963, Beals observed certain authoritarian gestures in Castro that disquieted him.[42] The image of the bearded young commander with doves perched on his shoulders during a memorable speech at the Columbia barracks reminded Beals of nineteenth-century dictators or annexationists, such as Antonio López de Santa Anna or Sam Houston. But beyond his sense of personal antipathy toward Castro, what concerned Beals the most was that Cuban socialism seemed to be abandoning what he called Latin America's "revolutionary zeitgeist":[43] a historical structure of the nationalist Left with a precise genealogy stemming from Zapata and Sandino, and a common spiritual language based on sovereignty and justice rather than on the materialist or scientific concepts of Marxist-Leninism.

By the end of the 1960s, these reservations about the Cuban Revolution and its leaders appeared to have grown more intense in the aging Beals. In a book conceived as a synthesis of his ideas about the Latin American revolutionary tradition, philosophically entitled *The Nature of Revolution* (1970), Beals reiterated his notion of Latin America's "revolutionary zeitgeist," but this time he placed that zeitgeist within a universal history of modern revolutions, starting in the United States, France, and Hispanic America at the end of the eighteenth century and the beginning of the nineteenth, passing through Lenin and Trotsky's Russia, Villa and Zapata's Mexico, and leading finally to 1960s Cuba.[44] Beals's condensed encyclopedic historical trajectory was sufficiently exhaustive to include the revolutions of Republican Spain, the Maoist Revolution, and the Mau Mau uprising in Kenya.[45]

Although not excluding communism from his universalist view of revolution, Beals continued to understand Latin America within the framework of the "zeitgeist" of nationalism and anti-imperialism established in Mexico in 1910. His growing distance from Cuban socialism was evident in the book's chapter "The New Cuba," which was written after the 1968 student movement and Che Guevara's death in Bolivia. "In short," he asserted emphatically, "Cuba technically is a one-man, one-party dictatorship."[46] However, Beals placed the greatest blame for the authoritarian degeneration of Cuba's originally Martí-inspired revolution on the United States, whose hostile policies he felt had strengthened the island's communist minority. In any case, Beals's characterization of the Cuban system as totalitarian continued to be a nuanced one:

> [Cuba] has acquired a somewhat amiable totalitarian system, largely directed by a single outstanding leader who has shown more interest in the welfare of his subject than any previous ruler. It is a system not without its own peculiar brand of democracy; despite the general regimentation, there are notable pockets of freedom.[47]

Beals's view of the Cuban Revolution was shared by Waldo Frank, above all, although the latter's involvement with socialism and Trotskyism had been greater. There were differences between them, as Beals himself recognized in the above-cited letter to Taber in which he declined the coleadership of the Fair Play for Cuba Committee: "we do not see eye to eye on a great many things, particularly in the political field."[48] But the two figures coincided in their leftist Americanism, in their repugnance for McCarthyism, and in their shared belief that American policies should recognize and respect the existence of a revolutionary and nationalist tradition in Latin America that was leading to governments, leaders, and institutions different from those that characterized democracy in the United States or Europe.

THE SKIN OF SOCIALISM

At the end of the 1960s, Beals set about updating his knowledge of Latin America and opening that knowledge to a dialogue with the Western New Left. In addition to extensively reading analyses favorable to the Cuban Revolution, which had been produced during that decade in New York (the work of Waldo Frank and C. Wright Mills, Paul Sweezy and Leo Huberman, and Herbert Matthews and Tad Szulc, among others), Beals joined in the theoretical debates of 1968 in his reviews of *Obsolete Communism: The Left-Wing Alternative*, by Daniel Cohn Bendit; *The Unperfect Society*, by Milovan Djilas; the well-known essays of Jean Paul Sartre; and Régis Debray's book on Cuba and Latin American guerrilla movements.[49]

Beals's dialogue with the New Left was reciprocated in the engagement of certain young New York intellectuals with the ideas of the *Mexican Maze* author. One of those intellectuals was young Chicana socialist Elizabeth Sutherland Martínez, whose anthropological study, *The Youngest Revolution* (1969), bears the perceptible imprint of Beals's work. Like Beals, Martínez was a traveler. She had sought to open her eyes to the realities of Cuban socialism and avoid the tropical stereotypes that so frequently surrounded the American perception of the Cuban experience in the 1960s. She recalled reading a tourism advertisement at Rockefeller Plaza in the 1950s that later came to define her mission: "Discover the real

Cuba by yourself. You'll love the difference."[50] Conscious of her Mexican ancestry, the young anthropologist appropriated for her own purposes Beals's idea of a Latin American "revolutionary zeitgeist" set in motion with the overthrow of Mexican dictator Porfirio Díaz, and she likewise conceived the Cuban Revolution as the youngest revolution in a continental saga.

Like Beals, Martínez also sought to discover the face of Cuban revolutionary youth in her work. Where Beals had chosen to illustrate his 1933 book on Cuba with photographs by Walker Evans, Martínez accompanied the text of *The Youngest Revolution* with photographs by African American photographer Leroy McLucas, who had spent periods in revolutionary Havana since the years of the Fair Play for Cuba Committee. Like those of Evans before him, McLucas's images were an obligatory complement for a quest to capture the faces and gestures of a Latin American epic—not those of the revolution's leaders and heroes but of the ordinary subjects, men and women, young and old, workers and peasants, soldiers and beggars, who experienced the dramas and conflicts of social change from below.

McLucas's portrayal of the skin of Cuban socialism in the 1960s largely followed the example of Walker Evans's photos of the 1933 Revolution. Neither Evans nor McLucas featured revolutionary leaders in their images. Against the grain of conventional Cuban revolutionary photography (the work of Raúl Corrales, Osvaldo Salas, Liborio Noval, Alberto Korda, and others), which was largely focused on images of revolutionary commanders such as Fidel, Che, Camilo, Raúl, and Almeida, McLucas turned his lens toward nurses and militiamen, soldiers and literacy workers, vagabonds and *santeras*. In the letters McLucas sent from Havana to Martínez, which are included in her book, the artist complains that revolutionary photographers were apprehending the revolution with the mentality of the bourgeois ancien régime.[51]

Thirty years earlier, Evans had likewise avoided capturing images of Havana's symbolic political protagonists. As evident in his correspondence with Carleton Beals, Evans became familiar with the upper strata of Cuban society, the island's intellectual and political elites, and, naturally, some of the principal leaders of the

1933 Revolution.[52] However, his Havana photos did not explore this world of the elite but the world of Havana's lower classes and street life. Of the more than sixty photos that Evans took in Cuba, about half—thirty-one in total—were included in Beals's book *The Crime of Cuba*.[53] Of these images only a handful—"A Document of the Terror," "Gonzalez Rubiera," "Terrorist Students in Jail," and "Wall Writing"—served as direct political testimony of the revolution that was being carried out against the Machado dictatorship.

Nor did all of Evans's photos seek to reflect a society in crisis. His images of sleeping vagabonds on park benches, beggars at mansion doors, crowds of famished people in rags hoping for a piece of bread, marginal neighborhoods, and run-down *bohíos* (mansions turned tenement houses) coexisted with portrayals of a nation in peace and harmony: images of trains, fruit carts, lottery venders, and architectural monuments like the magnificent facade of the Gallego Center in Havana's Central Park. In his selection from Evans's photos, Beals carefully excluded portrayals of Havana's glamour and cosmopolitanism, such as images of movie houses, elegantly dressed mulattos and mulattas, newspaper stands, cafés, food stands selling *lechón asado* (suckling pig), modern factories, or Havana's picturesque esplanade, the Malecón.[54]

A few of Evans's Cuban images that later became emblematic of his photography—such as the black Cuban dandy featured in *Citizen in Downtown Havana*, the woman in *Woman in Café*, or the mulatta woman with a scarred upper arm in *Woman on the Street*—were not included in Beals's book because they did not conform to a denunciation of the Machado dictatorship's crimes. Evans's photos of crowds, such as his images of men in hats gathered in front of the Asturian Center or the Capitolio building, did not project social tension or a sense of expectation for the national political story. In Evans's photograph of delivery boys awaiting the arrival of their newspapers—the image featured on the cover of *The Crime of Cuba*—close observation shows that the boys are openly posing for the photographer, who portrays them from above. In another photo taken of the same Havana street, an image not included in Beals's book, the boys laugh and call out directly to Evans, showing him the front page of their newspapers.

A similar contact between the photographer and the photographed is evident in the photos taken by Leroy McLucas in socialist Havana thirty years later. In his letters to Martínez, McLucas complains that it was virtually impossible to do his work on the streets without people attempting to pose for his shots.[55] One even notes different modes of posing for the camera on the part of the revolutionary subjects portrayed by McLucas. In one photo, several Cubans of different ages, genders, and races smile at the camera. However, one member of the group, a black woman, inserts herself into the frame, elevating her head above the shoulder of the individual in front of her. In a photo of a group of nurses, the two subjects in the foreground focus on McLucas's lens with different expressions as the two figures behind them look away, smiling, in another direction. The photo's *punctum*, to borrow a term from Roland Barthes's *Camera Lucida*, is constituted by the gaze of the young woman at the center, whose seriousness does not seem to respond to any effort of posing or to a gesture of intersection with the photographer's perspective, as was the case of the black woman in the photo just discussed.[56] The young woman's face in the latter photo does not express curiosity or estrangement but merely the natural dignity of one who reveals a "we" rather than an "I"—in short, the face of the revolution.

It is clear that in this young woman's face, McLucas was seeking to capture an expression similar to what he had achieved with his images of New York City children in his two series *Cool* and *Harlem: Roots of Revolt*, which he also partially exhibited at the Casa de las Américas in Havana. The faces of the subjects of both the New York and Havana photos show a seriousness and a resoluteness that affirms children as civil subjects of their respective cities. The shared aesthetic commonalities of the New York and Havana photographs diverge into geopolitical differences: the expressions of black children in McLucas's New York photos reflect the social neglect of an indigent subaltern population, whereas the expression on the face of the young black Cuban woman described above signals the protection of the socialist state. However, to draw once again on a Barthesian terminology, the expressions of the New York children constitute a *studium*, or the photographic image's central signification, whereas the expression of the Cuban girl constitutes the image's *punctum*, its lateral or peripheral signification.

Certain concepts on photography from theorists Walter Benjamin, Susan Sontag, and Roland Barthes are helpful for assessing the face of the Cuban Revolution captured by Leroy McLucas. These three writers' essays on photography are characterized by an interesting genealogical linkage: Benjamin's studies of photographic art in the 1930s served as a key point of departure for Sontag's study of the history of photography in the United States in the 1960s and 1970s, and while Barthes's *Camera Lucida* (1980) does not cite Benjamin, it reformulates numerous concepts from Sontag's work.[57]

As Sontag notes, the symbolic operation through which a scene from the past is visually encapsulated is melancholic:[58] hence, photographers' taste for buildings in ruins or abandoned spaces and installations. McLucas's photographs often focus on the vestiges of Cuba's former capitalist regime: an image portraying the old industry of street cleaning juxtaposed with a modern building that displays a sign reading "Venceremos" (We will overcome); another image showing the Christ of Havana statue next to a pile of tires; one of the Los Pinos studio featuring a pulley that bears a similarity to a gallows; or images of the same ruined mansions that Evans had portrayed in the 1930s. Barthes would translate this melancholy as an indistinction between the photograph and its referent ("the photograph is never distinguished from its referent") or as a "return of the dead."[59] Photography, he writes, "always carries its referent with itself, both affected by the same amorous or funereal immobility."[60]

Barthes distinguishes between the face that poses—the self-constitution of the image prior to its capture by the lens—and the face that does not pose but nonetheless looks directly at the camera.[61] He also observes that a face, whether it poses or not, can at times become a "likeness," or "an uncertain, amythic subject."[62] McLucas's photos of socialist Cuba demonstrate a search for these likenesses and subjects. A shopkeeper who smiles, not at the client but in a direction somewhere outside of his shop; an alert soldier; toothless peasants; a dancer with her back to the mirror; a literacy worker teaching a country woman who struggles against her ignorance; poorly clothed children in the new socialist urbanization—all possess that quality that Barthes calls "likeness," a quality of the effigy or the mask, of emblematic subjects of social change propelled by the revolution.

In McLucas's photos the images melancholically project a state of mutation or metamorphosis, as if the change of skin effected by the revolution inflicted pain on its protagonists or caused them to tremble. Melancholy is particularly notable in McLucas's photos that represent musical scenes. A conga drummer's face, his mouth resting on the surface of his drum during a pause in the rumba performance; a clarinetist and a child; the grimace on the face of a rumba player as he improvises a *guaguancó* with what he has at hand; and black dancers dressed in white, which produces a curious stylization of their bodies—all testify to a melancholy related to the drama of change. In McLucas's photos the music is not a frenetic or Dionysian experience but a solitary, taciturn art that opens the subject's heart to his or her past.

But these photos do not allude only to melancholy; they also portray the heroism and evangelism that Sontag identifies with modern photography.[63] If the photograph, according to Barthes, is not merely "the absence of the object [but] also, by one and the same movement, on equal terms, the fact that this object has indeed existed and that it has been there where I see it," then how are we to understand McLucas's interest in photographing religious and political altars?[64] His photographs showing walls adorned with portraits of the heroes of the revolution or bearing graffiti representing "the three kings" (Fidel, Che, and Almeida) with the image of Camilo Cienfuegos inside the star of Bethlehem represent a belief that cannot be taken as something that occurred in a prior time, as an event of the past. In another photo, a portrait of Conrado Benítez, martyr and black literacy worker of the revolution, the subject looks at the camera while a soldier furrows his brow in a gesture of boredom or weariness. Photography's "flat death," in Barthes's formulation, here acquires a religious and perhaps a political dimension.

It is not surprising that McLucas, like Walker Evans before him, was interested in the rituals and practices of Afro-Cuban Santeria during a period of social revolution. Evans portrayed an image of Saint Lazarus as a "patron saint" syncretically identified in

Afro-Cuban religion with Babalú Ayé, the orisha charged with the cure of venereal diseases, skin disorders, leprosy, smallpox, and the plague, and who gives shelter to the poor and the defenseless. The revolutionary subject, under McLucas's lens, was alien to Marxist atheism or laicism, which considered Afro-Cuban religions mere superstitions of the capitalist and bourgeois past that needed to be eradicated through socialist education.

The skin of socialism also took a yearly beating during the December 17 pilgrimages to El Rincón, the Havana neighborhood where the church of San Lázaro is located. Several avant-garde cinematographic projects of the early 1960s showed their clear affinity with this popular expression of revolutionary subjectivity, such as the documentaries *PM* (1961) by Orlando Jiménez Leal and Sabá Cabrera Infante and *Gente en la playa* (1961) by Néstor Almendros, both of which McLucas defended in his letters to Elizabeth Sutherland Martínez.[65] According to the photographer, the orthodox communist attacks on Almendros's film in *Bohemia* magazine and other official publications only confirmed the fact that the two conceptions of socialism, one dogmatic and the other libertarian, were contending for socialism's soul.

McLucas greatly admired the free-cinema style of Almendros's film, which was produced with a handheld camera on the beaches of Eastern Havana. *Gente en la playa*, a twelve-minute film, narrates a Sunday at the beach enjoyed by several dozen Cubans, from the time they board the bus in Havana to sunset on the coast. The film's context was the revolution's nationalization of Cuba's beaches, and Almendros chose to focus particularly on families of blacks, mulattos, and poor whites. The truck tires the swimmers use as floats and their criolla food denote humble social origins. The music they listen and dance to—*pasodoble*, *punto guajiro*, cha-cha-chá, and a bolero at the end—remits to a universe of popular culture. The Cubans portrayed in Almendros's film were of the same social group that was depicted in Jiménez Leal y Sabá Cabrera Infante's *PM* (1961), in Leroy McLucas's own photographs, and in later short cinematic films by Nicolás Guillén Landrián, particularly in *Los del baile* (1965) and *Retornar a Baracoa* (1966).

What McLucas admired about *Gente en la playa* was its mode of testimonial determination. As Almendros argued in *PM*, he and his fellow young film directors sought to turn a "hidden, non-intrusive" camera into an experiential testimony of popular culture of the neighborhoods of Regla, Cuatro Caminos, and Marianao.[66] What Almendros, Cabrera Infante, Jiménez, and, later, Guillén Landrián achieved in their films was precisely what McLucas was aspiring toward when he cried to the curious Habaneros: "no meter en la cámara, por favor." These artists' conception of photographic or filmic testimony was therefore divergent from the expectations of literary testimony, the latter of which was treated with great favor by Cuba's official political culture. The subjectivity of literary *testimonio*—for example, that of narrator Lisandro Otero in *Cuba, Z.D.A.* (1960) or poet José Álvarez Baragaño in *Himno a las milicias* (1961)—sought to make itself fully manifest through an explicit engagement with the revolution's social project.

The films of Almendros and his colleagues stage a poetics of race divested of any broader allusions, whether to the revolution, to the Playa Girón invasion, to the Literacy Campaign, or to the Committees for the Defense of the Revolution. Socialism seems a phenomenon distant from the beach scenes filmed in *Gente en la playa*, but the bathers are nevertheless carrying out an act of public occupation of hitherto privately owned spaces. In his photographs, McLucas attempted to show that the subjects who danced in the congas of Havana parks were the same subjects who were promoting literacy in the mountains, conducting agrarian reform, or enrolling in the militias. The face of the revolution that he filmed with his camera reflected a diversity of race, gender, culture, and religion that represented the island's social heterogeneity in the middle of the twentieth century. According to McLucas's camera, the "new man" was not a genetic construction of the future but the totality of Cuban citizens involved in the socialist experiment.

For this African American photographer, and for Chicana anthropologist Martínez, the youthfulness of the Cuban Revolution did not so much reflect the youthful ages of its leaders and followers but rather the fact that it was the most recent of the Latin American revolutions of the twentieth century. For McLucas and Martínez, as readers and disciples of Carleton Beals, the Cuban phenomenon was not an isolated and exceptional phenomenon. What was taking place in Cuba had tangible roots in the Mexican Revolution and the latter's Central American echoes during the first decades of the twentieth century. For these young American activists, the revolutionary experience of 1959 was likewise incomprehensible without the earlier Cuban Revolution, the one Walker Evans had portrayed in 1933 and in which a very similar heterogeneity had unfolded before the photographer's lens.

In the minds of these young intellectuals, the mission of the New York Left was to transmit this face of the revolution to the US public. In their view, the iconic image of Cuban revolutionary leaders projected by the liberal mass media and the often satanizing anticommunism projected by the same media for the consumption of right-wing public opinion were equally deceitful. The task, these young intellectuals believed, was to make visible the skin of a decolonizing and egalitarian process that was taking place in a Caribbean country historically subordinated to US hegemony, with the goal of helping to profile the American Left's revolutionary will. The message of socialist Cuba in the United States was one that worked to strengthen the youthful political movements that called for racial equality and social justice in the urban centers on the East and West Coasts.

In the most radical sectors of those movements, such as those of Martínez and McLucas, whose conception of Latin America was formed through their readings of the work of Carleton Beals and Waldo Frank, it was not enough to merely promote respect for the sovereignty of Latin American nations or to reject Cold War anticommunism; it was necessary to go beyond this New Deal leftism personified by Beals and Frank in order to work toward reincorporating the United States within the "revolutionary zeitgeist." Leftism, for these young intellectuals, was not merely a matter of solidarity with Third World nations that confronted US hegemony. Socialism and revolution were also necessary in New York, Washington, Chicago, and Los Angeles. Martínez and McLucas were themselves proof that new political subjects were taking shape in the American sphere as well.

In their response to the old Rooseveltian Left, of which they considered themselves heirs, these young activists articulated a subtle call for abandoning the colonialist elements of the US populist

Cover of anthropologist Elizabeth Sutherland Martínez's book on the Cuban Revolution, *The Youngest Revolution* (1969), illustrated by African American photographer Leroy McLucas.

tradition itself. That tradition identified with Latin American revolutionary movements as a way to assert a difference between Southern and Northern political forms, identifying the latter as democratic and liberal and the former as nationalist and revolutionary (and not authoritarian and totalitarian, as argued by the anticommunist Right or the anti-Stalinist Left). But this difference asserted by the older New Deal generation cast the United States as a nation whose foundational revolution had already taken place at the end of the eighteenth century and that did not require another radical change in its history.

The youth of New York City in 1968 did not agree. On the contrary, they believed that the revolution once again needed to touch the gates of the great cities of the United States, where racial and social inequality, poverty, unemployment, and Vietnam military recruitment was harming American citizens. This need for a revolution—and according to some voices, for a socialist transformation as well—made this great nation of the North similar to, rather than different from, the small countries of the South. The difference between the two Americas was not ontological, and the political dynamics of the two regions were approaching a spiritual homologation or ideological contact in which a popular epic in Mexico or Guatemala, Buenos Aires or Havana, could produce echoes in San Francisco or New York.

The American New Left, or at least a recognizable current within it, and one that Martínez and McLucas identified with, supported the Cuban Revolution without ideological paternalism or colonial overtones. It is not surprising that this fusion of the two cultural scenarios—the United States and Cuba, Manhattan and Havana—led Martínez and McLucas to openly critique the orthodox and dogmatic political elements that they saw being reproduced in Cuban socialism. Their close identification with the Cuban process gave these young New Yorkers a sense of free passage within the drama of the island. Much like the Havana youth they portrayed in their work, they, too, began to look directly at the camera and constitute themselves under the skin of socialism as one more of the revolution's faces.

EPILOGUE

★

Hannah Arendt, theorist of totalitarianism and the human condition, at least partially glimpsed the revolutionary spirit that disseminated in the West during the 1960s. In her essay *On Revolution* (1963), written in New York during the fall of 1962—and coinciding with the Cuban Missile Crisis in October—Arendt compared the French and American Revolutions based on their different ways of confronting the social question and the pursuit of happiness. Her objective in this work was to explore how these two great Atlantic revolutionary traditions weighed on the global experience of the Cold War.[1] Arendt's essay was a further development of work she had delivered at the April 1959 seminar at Princeton, "The United States and the Revolutionary Spirit," the same event where then prime minister of Cuba, Castro, had delivered the keynote address.[2]

Arendt's book does not mention the Cuban Revolution or its leader—a bit like Hegel's *Phenomenology of Spirit* likewise ignores the Haitian Revolution, which nonetheless served as the historical backdrop for the master-slave dialectic, as Susan Buck-Morss argues.[3] It is likely that by the fall of 1962, Arendt believed the Cuban Revolution's ideological and geopolitical inscription in the Soviet bloc situated the island within the bureaucratic socialisms of Eastern Europe and therefore within a totalitarian model that she viewed as part of the Stalinist legacy. In any event, her relative disinterest both in the colonial question and the experience of Latin America and the Third World—regions she nonetheless viewed as more propitious to the legacy of the French Revolution than to the American Revolution due to the inequality that predominated in their societies—led to her erasure of the Cuban referent and to her failure to note the effect of the Cuban Revolution on the propagation of the "revolutionary spirit" that accompanied the New Left's articulation.[4]

Although the concepts of Arendt's political philosophy were rapidly incorporated into the ideological archive of anticommunism, some intellectuals and journalists of the New York Left also came to rely on these concepts as a way of marking their distance from the Cuban government—as public opinion in the city demanded, particularly after October 1962. As we have seen, Latin Americanist journalist and historian Carleton Beals came to use terms such as "one-party dictatorship" or "totalitarianism" to characterize the Cuban political regime in the 1960s, although he often did so with willful nuances reflecting his conviction that the introduction of socialism on a Hispanic Caribbean island during the Cold War would ultimately result in a social order different from that of Eastern Europe, even if it involved the reproduction of Soviet-style institutions and practices.[5]

All the movements, publications, and intellectual figures of the New York Left that expressed critical solidarity with the Cuban Revolution (Waldo Frank and C. Wright Mills, *Monthly Review* and *Dissent*, Norman Mailer and Susan Sontag, the *New York Times* and the *Village Voice*, the Black Panthers and the beats) shared the conviction—as formulated by Castro in his Princeton address—that the United States bore responsibility for Latin American and Caribbean deprivation and underdevelopment. As an intervening, colonizing, and modernizing power in the region, Washington was responsible—guilty, according to some—for both the Batista dictatorship and Cuba's deficient social indicators. The best way to address this error, according to the viewpoint in question, was for the United States to enact respectful and honest policies that would encourage the young leaders of the revolution in their originally nationalist and democratic project.

This objective was shared by the intellectuals studied in this book, although, as we have seen, not all of them did so out of the same ideological suppositions or—subsequently—out of the same expectations with regard to the political evolution the revolutionary government would follow. Waldo Frank and Carleton Beals rejected the socialist radicalization of the Cuban revolutionaries, while C. Wright Mills, Paul Sweezy, Leo Huberman, and Paul Baran critically assimilated that radicalization. Likewise, young members of the Beat Generation, members of the African American and Hispanic Left, and Susan Sontag and Norman Mailer, likewise did not object to the Marxist-Leninist reorientation of the Cuban Revolution's ideology, although they clashed with the island's adoption of authoritarian and repressive practices and values proper to Marxist-Leninist dogmatism or Western conservatism, such as homophobia, racism, machismo, and censorship.

It could be argued that just as these leftist or liberal New York groups sympathized with the decolonizing promise that the revolution represented for Cuba, the Caribbean, and Latin America in general, they were not all ready to accept that the assertion of sovereignty on an island so close to US shores would involve the establishment of a communist system like that of the Soviet Union or the countries of Eastern Europe. Of course, as we have seen in this book, Cuba's Sovietization did not occur all at once, such as with the April 1961 declaration of Marxist-Leninism as the ideology of the revolutionary leaders, with the military alliance of October 1962, or even with the creation of the new Communist Party in 1965. Sovietization took hold of the island only gradually, and the process was not without moments of tension and distance between Havana and Moscow. Cuba's adoption of the Soviet model occurred by degrees through the 1960s, accelerated between 1968 and 1971, and culminated in the definitive institutionalization of the state and society during the first half of the 1970s.

Republican and liberal traditions weighed heavily in the American Left's rejection of this Soviet transformation of Cuban socialism. These traditions were still very much alive among members of a generation that was otherwise strongly critical of the imperialist and authoritarian aspects of American democracy. Also weighing heavily in this rejection of Cuba's Sovietization were the limitations and ambivalences inherent in the imagined configuration of Cuba, the Caribbean, and Latin America as the American "other." For example, Beals, despite his strong anthropological sensibility, always thought of that "other" as a civilization culturally, ethically, and religiously different from America.

Conversely, Frank, Mills, the Marxists of *Monthly Review*, the African American leaders of the Black Power movement, Elizabeth Sutherland Martínez, José Yglesias on the Hispanic Left, members of the Beat Generation, and writers and editors associated with the *Village Voice* all believed, in line with Castro's April 1959 Princeton address, that Cuba's decolonization was part of a necessary process of regeneration for American political life as well. These figures saw no essential differences between the two Americas that might impede the revolution's projected social development or fatally condemn it to the adoption of an authoritarian or totalitarian order.

Even the Marxists of *Monthly Review* (Paul Sweezy, Leo Huberman, Paul Baran, J. P. Morray, and others) who backed the island's integration to the Soviet bloc—albeit with pointed objections, particularly in matters of political economy—while recognizing the structural specificities of the Latin American economies, societies, and cultures nonetheless argued for a socialist modernization that they sought for the United States as well. The socialist ideology of these Marxists, like the humanism of Waldo Frank or the discordant liberal socialism of Michael Walzer or C. Wright Mills, was universalist, applicable to the historical conditions of any nation of Europe or America, Africa, or Asia. These New York Marxists, humanists, and liberals believed that Cuba's development would obtain the island's sovereignty without risking its adoption of an anti-Western or specifically anti-American cultural identity.

The narratives of development followed and promoted by these intellectuals and by the leaders of the Cuban Revolution itself is a topic that exceeds the scope of this study. But it would not be excessive to observe that during the first stage of the revolution, the Cuban leaders most closely aligned with New Left positions (such as Che Guevara) shared an idea of Latin American development based on agrarian reform, industrialization, and scientific and technical innovation, whose echoes were also found in authors such as Albert O. Hirschman or in Latin American economists such as Raul Prebisch and the founders of ECLAC (the United Nations Economic Commission for Latin America and the Caribbean).[6] The critique of instrumentalist rationality that underlay these notions of development—and hence of underdevelopment—and that were also articulated in New York countercultural circles in the 1960s and 1970s had a limited impact on Cuba, given the shift of the island's public sphere toward a Marxist-Leninist ideology, but it is not impossible to identify certain countercultural traces in Cuban art and society during those decades.[7]

The countercultural ideas manifested among members of the Beat Generation, the African American and Hispanic Left, and bohemian circles associated with the *Village Voice*, even when they reinforced solidarity with decolonization struggles, also did not abandon the leftist transnational or universalist perspective that demanded a moral or political questioning of the authoritarian modes of nationalist and popular movements in the Third World. There was an internationalism operant on the left in 1960s New York—akin to the phenomenon studied by Claudio Lomnitz among Mexican American anarchists in Los Angeles during the 1920s—that could act in favor of solidarity with Cuban socialism but could just as easily voice criticisms of that socialism.[8] This double propensity for solidarity with and critique of the Cuban Revolution was evident in other Western cultural capitals as well, whether in London, Paris, Mexico City, or Buenos Aires, but nowhere with as much intensity as in New York City.

The journey this debate took on its way to the Cuban public sphere suffered accidents and was incomplete, but something of that critical repertoire can be read in publications, writings, artworks, and even forms of life of minority sectors of Cuban youth during the 1960s and 1970s. The ideological hegemony of other more rigid ways of understanding socialism, whether framed by

Soviet-style Marxist-Leninism or by a narrow, Manichean revolutionary nationalism, prevented political and poetic expressions fully inscribed in the New Leftist imaginary to make headway on the island and provide continuity for libertarian traditions stemming from the end of the nineteenth century and the first half of the twentieth. Today, a significant part of contemporary Cuban culture, both within and outside of the island, is undergoing a process of recovery of the legacy of these currents and traditions of the Left in order to promote a democratization of society and the state in Cuba.

NOTES

INTRODUCTION

1. Christa Cleeton, "Fidel Castro Visits Princeton University," *Mudd Manuscript Library Blog*, Princeton University, October 5, 2012, https://blogs.princeton.edu/mudd/2012/10/fidel-castro-visits-princeton-university/.

2. Hannah Arendt, *On Revolution* (New York: Viking Press, 1963), 12.

3. "Excerpts from a speech given by Dr. Fidel Castro, Premier of Cuba"; from Cleeton blog page, "Fidel Castro Visits Princeton University." Castro's remarks are drawn from notes on the speech written by Paul D. Taylor, who decades later would serve as ambassador to the Dominican Republic.

4. Ibid.

5. Ibid.

6. Louis A. Pérez Jr., *On Becoming Cuban: Identity, Nationality, and Culture* (Chapel Hill: University of North Carolina Press, 2007) and *Cuba in the American Imagination: Metaphor and the Imperial Ethos* (Chapel Hill: University of North Carolina Press, 2011). See also Christine Skwiot, *The Purposes of Paradise: US Tourism and Empire in Cuba and Hawaii* (Philadelphia: University of Pennsylvania Press, 2010), 189–202.

7. Russell Jacoby, *The Last Intellectuals: American Culture in the Age of Academe* (New York: Basic Books, 2000), 3–26.

8. Paul Hollander, *Political Pilgrims: Western Intellectuals in Search of the Good Society* (New Brunswick: Transaction, 1998), 223–67; Kepa Artaraz, *Cuba and Western Intellectuals since 1959* (New York: Palgrave, 2009), 3–18.

9. Paul Buhle, *Marxism in the United States: A History of the American Left* (New York: Verso, 2013), 226.

10. Ibid., 223–42.

11. Razmig Keucheyan, *The Left Hemisphere: Mapping Critical Theory Today* (New York: Verso, 2013), 8–9, 18, 39, 71, and 94.

12. Mary Louise Pratt, *Imperial Eyes: Travel Writing and Transculturation* (London: Routledge, 1992), 1–12; Laura Lomas, *Translating Empire: José Martí, Migrant Latino Subjects, and American Modernities* (Durham, NC: Duke University Press, 2008), 216–77; Douglas Robinson, *Translation and Empire: Postcolonial Theories Explained* (New York: Routledge, 2011), 8–30; Robert Stam and Ella Shohat, *Race in Translation: Culture Wars around the Postcolonial Atlantic* (New York: New York University Press, 2012), 1–25.

13. Claudio Lomnitz, *The Return of Comrade Ricardo Flores Magón* (New York: Zone Books, 2014), 165–78.

14. Jorge Mañach, *Teoría de la frontera* (San Juan, Puerto Rico: Editorial Universitaria de Puerto Rico, 1970), 21–48.

15. Lynn Hunt, *Inventing Human Rights: A History* (New York: W. W. Norton, 2007), 27–32; Samuel Moyn, *The Last Utopia: Human Rights in History* (Cambridge, MA: Harvard University Press, 2012), 176–211; David Priestland, *The Red Flag: A History of Communism* (New York: Grove Press, 2009), 273–314; Archie Brown, *The Rise and Fall of Communism* (New York: HarperCollins, 2009), 9–25.

16. Arendt, *On Revolution*, 247–48; Frantz Fanon, *Toward the African Revolution* (New York: Monthly Review Press, 1964), 99–105.

17. Samuel Moyn and Andrew Sartori, "Approaches to Global Intellectual History," in *Global Intellectual History*, ed. Moyn and Sartori (New York: Columbia University Press, 2013).

18. Thomas Bender, *New York Intellect: A History of Intellectual Life in New York, from 1750 to the Beginnings of Our Times* (Baltimore: Johns Hopkins University Press, 1987), 3–7.

19. Nick Salvatore, *Eugene V. Debs: Citizen and Socialist* (Chicago: University of Illinois Press, 2007), 129–31.

20. Werner Sombart, *Why Is There No Socialism in the United States?* (New York: M. E. Sharpe, 1976), 15–24.

21. Moshik Temkin, *The Sacco-Vanzetti Affair: America on Trial* (New Haven, CT: Yale University Press, 2009), 9–57.

22. Alan M. Wald, *The New York Intellectuals: The Rise and Decline of the Anti-Stalinist Left from the 1930s to the 1980s* (Chapel Hill: University of North Carolina Press, 1987), 27–30, 46–49, and 74–81.

23. Alexander Bloom, *Prodigal Sons: The New York Intellectuals and Their World* (Oxford: Oxford University Press, 1986), 209–73; Terry A. Cooney, *The Rise of the New York Intellectuals: Partisan Review and Its Circle: 1934–1945* (Madison: University of Wisconsin Press, 1986), 120–45.

24. Neil Jumonville, *Critical Crossings: The New York Intellectuals in Postwar America* (Berkeley: University of California Press, 1991), 17–34, 134–43, and 194–202.

25. Cooney, *The Rise of the New York Intellectuals*, 38–66; Jumonville, *Critical Crossings*, 186–93 and 221–26.

26. Wald, *The New York Intellectuals*, 311–20 and 334–37.

27. Irving Howe, *Politics and the Novel* (New York: Horizon Press Books, 1957), 15–24.

28. Ibid., 159–200.

29. Ibid., 235–50.

30. Irving Howe, *The Decline of the New* (New York: Harcourt, Brace, 1970), 66–74 and 211–68.

31. Irving Howe, ed., *The Radical Papers* (New York: Anchor Books, Doubleday, 1966), 13–33, 57–74, 148–89, and 307–26; Irving Howe, ed., *A Dissenter's Guide to Foreign Policy* (New York: Frederick A. Praeger, 1968), 173–94, 208–23, 241–59 and 303–13; Jeremy Larner and Irving Howe, *Poverty: Views from the Left* (New York: William Morrow, 1968), 13–38.

32. Walter Laqueur, "Reflections on the Third World," in Irving Howe, ed., *A Dissenter's Guide to Foreign Policy*, 173–94; Richard Lowenthal, "The Prospect for a Maoist International," in Irving Howe, ed., *A Dissenter's Guide to Foreign Policy*, 208–23; Robert L. Heilbroner, "Counter-Revolutionary America," in Irving Howe, ed., *A Dissenter's Guide to Foreign Policy*, 241–59.

33. Irving Howe, ed., *The Radical Imagination* (New York: New American Library, 1967), 1–6, 921, and 20–63.

34. Ibid., 247–86.

35. Ibid., 287–303.

36. Ibid., 87–88.

37. Ibid., 89.

38. Ibid., 86.

39. Wald, *The New York Intellectuals*, 338–43.

40. Ibid., 326.

41. Ibid.

42. Harvey Swados, "C. Wright Mills: A Personal Memoir," in Irving Howe, ed., *The Radical Imagination*, 408–16.

43. Wald, *The New York Intellectuals*, 338–43.

44. Stanley Aronowitz, *Taking It Big: C. Wright Mills and the Making of Political Intellectuals* (New York: Columbia University Press, 2012), 167–86.

45. For a portrait of Max Shachtman, see Wald, *The New York Intellectuals*, 172–75.

46. *Socialist International Information*, Firestone Library, Princeton University, vol. 11, no. 17, April 29, 1961, 256.

47. Ibid., 258–59.

48. Ibid., vol. 11, no. 19, 302.

49. Ibid., 302.

50. Ibid., vol. 11, no. 22, 329–31.

51. Ibid., vol. 12, no. 45, 640–42.

52. Ibid., vol. 12, no. 46, 658–60.

53. Arthur M. Schlesinger Jr., *Journals: 1952–2000* (New York: Penguin Books, 2000), 106–18.

54. J. P. Morray, *The Second Revolution in Cuba* (New York: Monthly Review Press, 1962), 117–32.

55. Michael Reynolds, *Hemingway: The 1930s through the Final Years* (New York: W. W. Norton, 2012), 636.

56. Carlos Granés, *El puño invisible* (Madrid: Taurus, 2011). On the decadence of New York bohemian culture, see Russell Jacoby, *The Last Intellectuals*, 27–53.

57. Norman Mailer, "Open Letter to JFK and Fidel Castro," *Village Voice*, April 27, 1961, 14.

58. Hillary Mills, *Mailer: A Biography* (New York: Empire Books, 1982), 219, 235, and 239.

59. Norman Mailer, *Advertisements for Myself* (New York: G. P. Putman's Sons, 1959), 337–58, 372–403, and 423–30; Norman Mailer, *The Armies of the Night: History as a Novel, The Novel as History* (New York: New American Library, 1968), 28–42 and 219–36; Norman Mailer, *Why Are We in Vietnam?* (New York: G. P. Putnam's Sons, 1967), 15–18.

60. Norman Mailer, *Harlot's Ghost* (New York: Random House, 1991), 929–80; Norman Mailer, *An American Dream* (New York: Dial Press, 1965), 20–32; Carl Rollyson, *The Lives of Norman Mailer: A Biography* (New York: Paragon House, 1991), 150–52; Robert Merrill, *Norman Mailer* (Boston: Twayne, 1978), 92, 97, and 125.

61. Norman Mailer, *Miami and the Siege of Chicago: An Informal History of the Republican and Democratic Conventions of the 1968* (New York: World, 1968), 133.

62. Susan Sontag, "Some Thoughts on the Right Way (for Us) to Love the Cuban Revolution," *Ramparts*, April 1969, 10.

63. Susan Sontag, *Reborn: Journals and Notebooks, 1947–1963* (New York: Picador, 2009), 228 and 313.

64. Susan Sontag, *Against Interpretation and Other Essays* (New York: Macmillan, 1966), 8 and 10.

65. Citation translated from Robert Taber, "Playa Girón: Réquien al imperialismo," in *Playa Girón: Derrota del imperialismo* (Havana: Ediciones R, 1962), 1:305–16; see also Robert Taber, *War of Flea: The Classic Study of Guerrilla Warfare* (Washington, DC: Brassey's, 2002), 25–38.

66. Elizabeth Sutherland [Martínez], *The Youngest Revolution: A Personal Report on Cuba* (New York: Dial Press, 1969), 169–90.

1: HIPSTERS AND APPARATCHIKS

1. Arthur M. Schlesinger Jr., *A Thousand Days: John F. Kennedy in the White House* (Boston: Houghton Mifflin, 1965), 215.

2. Ibid., 224.

3. Ibid., 220.

4. Ibid., 265–85.

5. Ibid., 286.

6. Robert A. Rutland, *The Newsmongers: Journalism in the Life of the Nation, 1690–1972* (New York: Dial Press, 1973), 374.

7. Christopher B. Daly, *Covering America: A Narrative History of a Nation* (Boston: University of Massachusetts Press, 2012), 287–321.

8. Ibid., 340–51.

9. G. Calvin Mackenzie and Robert Weisbrot, *The Liberal Hour: Washington and the Politics of Change in the 1960s* (New York: Penguin Press, 2008), 38–83.

10. Ruby Hart Phillips, *Cuba: Island of Paradox* (New York: McDowell, Obolensky, 1959), 298–302. Herbert L. Matthews confirmed this version in his book, *The Cuban Story* (New York: George Braziller, 1961), 19–23.

11. Ruby Hart Phillips, *Cuban Sideshow* (Havana: Cuban Press, 1935), 315–17.

12. Anthony De Palma, *The Man Who Invented Fidel: Cuba, Castro, and Herbert Matthews of the "New York Times"* (New York: Public Affairs, 2006), 9–24.

13. Herbert L. Matthews, "Cuban Rebel Is Visited in Hideout," *New York Times*, February 24, 1957, 1 and 34; Herbert L. Matthews, "Rebel Strength Gaining in Cuba, but Batista Has the Upper Hand," *New York Times*, February 25, 1957, 1 and 11; Herbert L. Matthews, "Old Order in Cuba in Threatened by Forces of Internal Revolt," *New York Times*, February 26, 1957, 13.

14. Matthews, *The Cuban Story*, 28.

15. Herbert L. Matthews, "Old Order in Cuba Is Threatened by Forces of Internal Revolt," *New York Times*, February 26, 1957, 13.

16. Ruby Hart Phillips, "Censorship Ends Today, Cuba Says," *New York Times*, February 26, 1957, 12.

17. Herbert L. Matthews, "Castro's Rebels Gain in Face of Offensive by the Cuban Army," *New York Times*, June 9, 1957, 1 and 13; Herbert L. Matthews, "Populace in Revolt in Santiago de Cuba," *New York Times*, June 10, 1957, 1 and 10; Herbert L. Matthews, "Power Transfer Pondered in Cuba," *New York Times*, June 17, 1957, 3.

18. "Communist Threat to the United States through the Caribbean," http://www.latinamericanstudies.org/us-cuba/gardner-smith.htm.

19. Matthews, *The Cuban Story*, 67–71.

20. Ruby Hart Phillips, *The Cuban Dilemma* (New York: Ivan Obolensky, 1962), 347–53.

21. Mario Llerena, *La revolución insospechada: Origen y desarrollo del castrismo* (Buenos Aires: Universidad de Buenos Aires, 1981), 121–34.

22. Homer Bigart, "Castro's Failure Bolsters Batista," *New York Times*, April 15, 1958, 3.

23. "Havana Quitter; Regime and Union Say Strike Failed," *New York Times*, April 11, 1958, 1 and 8; "Raiders in Cuba: Blast Arms Dump," *New York Times*, April 12, 1958, 1 and 9; "Havana Failure Dismays Rebels," *New York Times*, April 13, 1958, 1 and 14.

24. Herbert L. Matthews, "Batista and Regime Flee Cuba; Castro Moving to Take Power; Mobs Riot and Loot in Havana," *New York Times*, January 2, 1959, 1 and 3; Ruby Hart Phillips, "Army Halts Fire: Rebels Seize Santiago and Santa Clara; March on Capital," *New York Times*, January 2, 1959, 1 and 3; Peter Kihss, "Castro Superior in Arms, Batista Declares in Exile," *New York Times*, January 2, 1959, 1 and 7; Dana Adams Schmidt, "US Aids Wary of Cuba's Future," *New York Times*, January 2, 1959, 1 and 6; Ruby

Hart Phillips, "Castro Names President as Rebels Enter Havana," *New York Times*, January 3, 1959, 1–2; Herbert L. Matthews, "Havana Swarms with Rebel Units," *New York Times*, January 3, 1959, 1 and 3; Gay Talese, "Cuba's Consul Surrenders Office in a Peaceful Shift," *New York Times*, January 3, 1959, 1 and 3; "US Foresees No Obstacle to Early Recognition of the Castro Regime," *New York Times*, January 3, 1959, 3; Ruby Hart Phillips, "Castro Heads Cuba's Armed Forces; Regime Is Sworn In," *New York Times*, January 4, 1959, 1 and 3; Herbert L. Matthews, "Castro Decrees a Halt in Strike Paralyzing Cuba," *New York Times*, January 5, 1959, 1 and 3.

25. Ruby Hart Phillips, "Havana Welcomes Castro at End of Triumphal Trip," *New York Times*, January 9, 1959, 1 and 9.

26. Phillips, *Cuba: Island of Paradox*, 277–85.

27. "Fidel Castro: A Symbol of Rebellion," *New York Times*, January 2, 1959, 3; "Urrutia: An Idealistic Cuban," *New York Times*, January 3, 1959, 2; "Raúl Chibás," *New York Times*, January 5, 1959, 3.

28. Frank Kelly, "Purge Is Started in Cuba," *New York Herald Tribune*, January 5, 1959, 1–3; Frank Kelly, "Batista's Congress Dissolved," *New York Herald Tribune*, January 5, 1959, 1 and 8; Frank Kelly, "Castro in Havana at Last, with a Gun and Pop Bottle," *New York Herald Tribune*, January 9, 1959, 1 and 2; Frank Kelly, "Reds Get Right to Form Party," *New York Herald Tribune*, January 10, 1959, 3.

29. Joe Seldin, "How Castro Began: Story of His 5-Year Fight," *New York Herald Tribune*, January 2, 1959, 2.

30. "Castro to Visit US Next Month," *New York Times*, March 4, 1959, 1 and 11.

31. E. W. Kenworthy, "Castro Will Meet Nixon on US Trip," *New York Times*, April 11, 1959, 1 and 6.

32. E. W. Kenworthy, "Castro Declares Regime Is Free of Red Influence," *New York Times*, April 18, 1959, 1 and 10.

33. Ibid.

34. Dana Adams, Schmidt, "Castro Rules Out Role as Neutral; Opposes the Red," *New York Times*, April 20, 1959, 1 and 5.

35. Ruby Hart Phillips, "Nye Goes on Trial as Plotter in Cuba," *New York Times*, April 12, 1959, 1 and 14.

36. Ruby Hart Phillips, "Cuba Sentences Nye to Death as Plotter but Lets Him Leave," *New York Times*, April 13, 1959, 1 and 13.

37. Phillips, *Cuba: Island of Paradox*, 406 and 414.

38. Ibid., 417.

39. Ibid., 419–22.

40. Phillips, *The Cuban Dilemma*, 206–28.

41. Ibid., 265–84.

42. Arthur Krock, "The New Sugar Daddy from Moscow," *New York Times*, February 14, 1960, 8E.

43. Max Frankel, "Castro Can't Find Lodging Here," *New York Times*, September 16, 1960, 1 and 12; Max Frankel, "Hotel Will Admit Castro and Aides," *New York Times*, September 18, 1960, 1 and 39; Max Frankel, "Cubans in Harlem," *New York Times*, September 20, 1960, 1 and 16.

44. Harrison E. Salisbury, "Russian Goes to Harlem, Then Hugs Cuban at UN," *New York Times*, September 21, 1960, 1 and 16.

45. Max Frankel, "Nasser Asks Cuba to Join Neutrals," *New York Times*, September 24, 1960, 1 and 16.

46. Tad Szulc and Karl E. Meyer, *The Cuban Invasion: The Chronicle of a Disaster* (New York: Ballantine Books, 1962), 65–71.

47. Ibid., 77–84.

48. "Text of US Note to Cuba," *New York Times*, November 13, 1960, 5; "Justice under Castro," *New York Times*, November 14, 1960, 30.

49. Max Frankel, "Cuba Doubts Kennedy Will Try to Alter Policy to Ease Crisis," *New York Times*, November 25, 1960, 1 and 18; Max Frankel, "Extent of Red Grip in Cuba Is Related by Party Chief," *New York Times*, November 27, 1960, 1 and 35.

50. Tad Szulc, "Pilot Describes Strafing Raids," *New York Times*, April 16, 1961, 1 and 4; Tad Szulc, "Asylum Granted to Three Airmen," *New York Times*, April 17, 1961, 1 and 3; Tad Szulc, "Rear Guard Is Hit," *New York Times*, April 20, 1961, 1 and 10.

51. Arthur M. Schlesinger Jr., *A Thousand Days*, 245–47.

52. "Landing in Cuba," *New York Times*, April 18, 1961, 36.

53. Ibid.

54. "Cuba and the Cold War," *New York Times*, April 20, 1961, 32.

55. Arthur Krock, "Hazards of Presidential Absolute Pledges," *New York Times*, April 19, 1961, 32; Arthur Krock, "Khrushchev's Unintended Aid to Cuban Freedom," *New York Times*, April 20, 1961, 32.

56. Phillips, *The Cuban Dilemma*, 338–46; Matthews, *The Cuban Story*, 231–79; Szulc, *The Cuban Invasion*, 146–56.

57. Juan de Onis, "Latin Sympathy for US Rises in Castro Dispute," *New York Times*, October 22, 1962, 1 and 16; Paul Kennedy, "Region Maintains Watch on Castro," *New York Times*, October 22, 1962, 17; Kathleen Teltsch, "Crisis over Cuba Preoccupies UN," *New York Times*, October 23, 1962, 25; Juan de Onis, "Cuba Compromise Urged in Brazil," *New York Times*, October 27, 1962, 39; James Reston, "To Deal or Not to Deal: That's the Question," *New York Times*, October 28, 1962, 10E; Arthur Krock, "After the Crisis," *New York Times*, October 28, 1962, 11E; Tad Szulc, "Castro Asks Guantanamo; Strives to Repair Prestige," *New York Times*, October 29, 1962, 1 and 19, James Reston, "The President's View," *New York Times*, October 29, 1962, 1 and 17; "Europeans Hail Kennedy as Hero," *New York Times*, October 30, 1962, 1; Tad Szulc, "Diplomats Expect Castro to Seek Inspection Delay," *New York Times*, October 31, 1962, 1.

58. Gay Talese, *The Kingdom and the Power* (New York: World, 1966), 4–5.

59. Michael Schudson, *Discovering the News: A Social History of American Newspapers* (New York: Basic Books, 1978), 172; Richard F. Shepard, *The Paper's Papers* (New York: Random House / Times Books, 1996), 187–95.

60. Tad Szulc and Karl E. Mayer, *The Cuban Invasion*, 157. Recent studies still appeal to the same terms, such as Jim Rasenberger's, *The Brilliant Disaster: JFK, Castro, and America's Doomed Invasion of Cuba's Bay of Pigs* (New York: Scribner, 2011).

61. "The Watch on the Caribbean," *New York Times*, October 28, 1962, 32.
62. Michael Walzer, *Cuba: The Invasion and the Consequences* (New York: Dissent Publishing Association, 1961), 8.
63. Ibid.
64. Ibid., 1.
65. Ibid., 3.
66. Ibid., 12.
67. Ibid., 7.
68. Ibid., 3–4.
69. Ibid., 14.
70. Ibid., 15.
71. Michael Walzer, *The Revolution of the Saints: A Study in the Origins of Radical Politics* (Cambridge, MA: Harvard University Press, 1965), 1–21.
72. Ibid., 230.
73. Ibid., 300–320.
74. Ibid., 148–98.
75. Ibid., 176–77.
76. Jerry Hopkins, "The Beat Generation: There Is Only Faith in Search," *Village Voice*, January 21, 1959, 1 and 3; David McReynolds, "Politics and the Beat Generation," *Village Voice*, March 11, 1959, 3 and 4; David McReynolds, "The Hipster General Strike," *Village Voice*, December 11, 1959, 4 and 12.
77. Louise Tallmer, "Voice Feminine," *Village Voice*, March 2, 1960, 11; "Open Forum on Disarmament," *Village Voice*, March 4, 1960, 3; J. R. Goddard, "The Green Revolution and the Search for a New Order," *Village Voice*, June 1, 1960, 3; Ken Sobol, "The Race Is to the Rich and the Rugged," *Village Voice*, August 11, 1960, 1 and 12.
78. Ken Sobol, "Beatnik, Stay Home!," *Village Voice*, July 14, 1960, 7 and 11; [Howard] R. Moody, "On the Liberalism of Impure Intentions," *Village Voice*, August 11, 1960, 3.
79. Mary Perot Nichols, "Calls Nixon a Believer in Fatalism Conspiracy," *Village Voice*, October 6, 1960, 2 and 3; Norman Mailer, "Open Poem to John Fitzgerald Kennedy," *Village Voice*, November 23, 1961, 4.
80. Nat Hentoff, "The Soft Decay of the *New York Times*," *Village Voice*, June 1, 1960, 7 and 11.
81. David McReynolds, "I Still Say No," *Village Voice*, November 2, 1961, 9.
82. Martin Kenner, "Cuba: Myths and Debacles," *Village Voice*, June 28, 1962, 10 and 12.
83. Ibid., 12.
84. Stephanie Gervis, "Ole Miss: The View from the UN," *Village Voice*, October 25, 1962, 4 and 5; Stephanie Gervis, "UN: A Drink at the Edge of the Abyss," *Village Voice*, November 1, 1962, 1.
85. Norman Mailer, "An Open Letter to JFK," *Village Voice*, December 20, 1961, 1 and 7.
86. Nat Hentoff, "The Peace Movement and Cuba," *Village Voice*, December 27, 1961, 4 and 5.
87. Stephanie Gervis, "Stevenson and Zorin," *Village Voice*, December 27, 1962, 317; Stephanie Gervis, "A Good Time Was Had by One," *Village Voice*, December 27, 1962, 17.

88. "Soviet Line Wavers on Art," *Village Voice*, January 3, 1963, 3; "Is Architecture Totalitarian?" *Village Voice*, April 16, 1964, 1.

89. David McReynolds, "The Negro Riots: The Issue Isn't Color," *Village Voice*, October 1, 1964, 1 and 6; Jack Newfield, "View from the Far Left: The Enemy Is the Liberal," *Village Voice*, December 17, 1964, 3 and 11; Jack Newfield, "LeRoi Jones at Army Blues for Mr. Whitey," *Village Voice*, December 17, 1964, 1 and 12.

90. David McReynolds, "Vietnam Is Our Hungary," *Village Voice*, December 17, 1964, 7 and 23.

91. Ibid., 23.

92. Stephanie Harrington, "Quiet Evening in a Revolutionary Life," *Village Voice*, October 19, 1967, 35.

93. Ibid., 36.

94. Marlene Nadle, "Debray in Bolivia," *Village Voice*, October 5, 1967, 3; Marlene Nadle, "The End of Guevara and the Change in Debray," *Village Voice*, October 19, 1967, 1 and 36.

95. Marlene Nadle, "The Power of Flowers vs. the Power of Politics," *Village Voice*, June 15, 1967, 1 and 16.

96. Marlene Nadle, "The Coming of King: A Charismatic Moment," *Village Voice*, June 22, 1967, 1 and 9.

97. Leticia Kent, "High on Life and Deader than Dead," *Village Voice*, October 12, 1967, 1 and 3.

98. "Slain Guerrilla Shown by La Paz," *New York Times*, October 11, 1967, 1; "Bolivia Confirms Guevara Death: Body Displayed," *New York Times*, October 11, 1967, 18; Juan de Onis, "Setback to Castro," *New York Times*, October 11, 1967, 18; Paul Hofmann, "Che Guevara: Latin American Political Adventurer," *New York Times*, October 11, 1967, 18; "Guevara: Man and Myth," *New York Times*, October 12, 1967, 37.

99. John Kifner, "The East Village: A Changing Scene for Hippies," *New York Times*, October 11, 1967, 32.

100. Jack Newfield, "Kennedy and the Bombings: Crossing of the Rubicon," *Village Voice*, March 2, 1967, 1 and 26.

101. Joe Flaherty, "The Fifth Avenue Parade," *Village Voice*, May 18, 1967, 1 and 9.

102. Tad Szulc, *Fidel: A Critical Portrait* (New York: William Morrow, 1986), 614–20.

103. Leticia Kent, "A Message to Moscow; Via an Unhappy Medium," *Village Voice*, August 29, 1968, 3; David McReynolds, "Report from Prague; Viewing a Disaster," *Village Voice*, August 29, 1968, 1, 12 and 13.

2: NAMING THE HURRICANE

1. Citations translated from Waldo Frank, "Carta a Fidel Castro" (October 10, 1959), originally available at http://europa.cubaminrex.cu/Patrimonio/Artículos/2009/Waldo.html but recently removed.

2. Ibid.

3. Ibid.

4. Ibid.

5. Heberto Padilla, "Habla Waldo Frank," *Lunes de Revolución*, October 12, 1959, 3; Alcides Iznaga, "Rahab: Una novela de Waldo Frank," *Lunes de Revolución*, October 12, 1959, 4–5.

6. For an exhaustive list of these books, see Sergio Guerra and Alejandro Maldonado, *Historia de la revolución cubana* (Navarra, Spain: Editorial Txalaparta, 2009), 154–55.

7. Waldo Frank, *Cuba, isla profética*, trans. Luis Echávarri (Buenos Aires: Editorial Losada, 1961), 7. English original published as *Cuba: Prophetic Island* (New York: Marzani and Munsell, 1961). Both the Marzani edition and the Losada translation will be cited in this chapter (as indicated), in reflection of content differences between the two editions.

8. Letter from Armando Hart, Minister of Education, to Raúl Cepero Bonilla, President of Banco Nacional, July 5, 1961 (National Archives and Record Administration [NARA], Washington, DC, Department of State, Lot Files, Record Group 59, Papers of Arturo Morales Carrión, box 9, folder 5). See also Paul J. Carter, *Waldo Frank* (New Haven, CT: United Printing Services, 1967), 164; Michael A. Ogarzaly, *Waldo Frank: Prophet of Hispanic Regeneration* (London: Associated University Presses, 1994), 151.

9. Frank, *Cuba, isla profética*, 7.

10. Carter, *Waldo Frank*, 165; Oleg Kalugin, *The First Directorate: My 32 Years in Intelligence and Espionage against the West* (New York: St. Martin's Press, 1994), 45, 50–52.

11. Citation translated from Frank, *Cuba, isla profética*, 7: "No necesito decir que mi obligación era hallar la verdad, tal como la entendía, y decirla. Ciertos aspectos de lo que vi y pensé pueden no agradar a algunos amigos de Cuba. Pero ellos estarán de acuerdo con que decir toda la verdad de lo que encontré, nada menos, era mi solo deber, mi obligación única."

12. C. Wright Mills, "Listen, Yankee: The Cuban Case against the United States," *Harper's Magazine*, December 1960, 31–37; Herminio Portell Vilá, Charles O. Porter, Ira B. Joralemon, Charles S. Grant, Stan Weisberger, Rafael Lecuona, John W. Dalton, "Letters," *Harper's Magazine*, February 1961, 6–12.

13. Maurice Isserman, *If I Had a Hammer: The Death of the Old Left and the Birth of the New Left* (New York: Basic Books, 1987); Maurice Isserman, *America Divided: The Civil War of the 1960s* (Oxford: Oxford University Press, 2000); Howard Brick, *Age of Contradictions: American Thought and Culture in the 1960s* (Ithaca, NY: Cornell University Press, 1998), 1–22.

14. Stefan Zweig, *Brasil: País del Futuro* (Madrid: Espasa Calpe, 1942); Gustavo Guerrero, *Historia de un encargo: "La catira" de Camilo José Cela* (Barcelona: Anagrama, 2008); Emil Ludwig, *Biografía de una isla* (Mexico City: Editorial Centauro, 1948).

15. Ludwig, *Biografía de una isla*, 343.

16. Ibid. Citations from Ludwig's work are translated from the Spanish-language original.

17. Ibid., 336.

18. Ibid., 7.

19. Frank, *Cuba, isla profética*, 178–79.
20. Frank, *Cuba: Prophetic Island*, 89.
21. Ibid., 33–38.
22. Ibid., 83–108.
23. Ibid., 108–24; "un apoderamiento de Cuba por parte de los cubanos."
24. Ibid., 132.
25. Ibid., 1–11.
26. Ibid., 14; "un indicio de indiferencia del hombre por los dictadores de América Latina, Europa y Asia—los soldados cautivos de los valores del ejército, los hombres en el poder, encadenados al poder"; "grupito que en la Asamblea escucha a su jefe."
27. Ibid., 15; "Simplificación falsa."
28. Ibid., 45; "un acontecimiento que tiene su peligro"; "el abrazo íntimo e inmediato podría hacerse necesario para Fidel, podría enviciarle."
29. Ibid., 17 and 40.
30. Ibid., 51–52; "poca sofisticación," "immadurez," and "inocencia"; "barroco chabacano"; "horrendo peligro que existe bajo la superficie de la revolución más benemérita."
31. Ibid., 43.
32. Frank, *Cuba: Prophetic Island*, 14
33. Carter, *Waldo Frank*, 165. See Jean Paul Sartre, *Sartre visita Cuba* (Havana: Ediciones R, 1961), 1–17.
34. Frank, *Cuba: Prophetic Island*, 149.
35. Waldo Frank, *Dawn in Russia: The Record of a Journey* (New York: Charles Scribner's Sons, 1932), 232–72.
36. Frank A. Ninkovich, *The Diplomacy of Ideas: US Foreign Policy and Cultural Relations, 1938–50* (New York: Cambridge University Press, 1981), 30–45; Michael A. Ogorzaly, *Waldo Frank*; Ricardo Fernández Borchardt, *Waldo Frank: Un puente entre las dos Américas* (La Coruña, Spain: Universidade da Coruña, 1997).
37. Heberto Padilla, "Habla Waldo Frank," *Lunes de Revolución*, October 12, 1959, 2–3.
38. Ibid., 3; "Los escritores deben trabajar por sus países. Si hay que darles conferencias a los campesinos, dénselas, pero que no se pierda la independencia, que el compromiso no vele la función crítica que le corresponde al escritor. Su deber es reflejar artísticamente la realidad, sea Cuba o Islandia. Un arte de propaganda es un arte de traidores. ¡Cuidado con eso!"
39. Frank, *Cuba, isla profética*, 98–99; "Independencia y libertad."
40. Ibid., 99; "derecho del Negocio Norteamericano—la anatomía y los órganos vivos del país—a hacer lo que quería hacer con Cuba."
41. Ibid., 149; "visión democrática judeo-cristiana del hombre total."
42. Frank, *Cuba: Prophetic Island*, 64.
43. Ibid., 64–65.
44. William Bittner, *The Novels of Waldo Frank* (Philadelphia: University of Pennsylvania Press, 1955), 20–32.
45. Waldo Frank, *The Unwelcome Man* (Boston: Little, Brown, 1917), 264–66.

46. Waldo Frank, *City Block* (New York: Waldo Frank and Darren Conn, 1922), 169, 177, and 179; Waldo Frank, *Holiday* (New York: Boni and Liveright, 1923), 31–38.

47. Waldo Frank, *The Dark Mother* (New York: Boni and Liveright, 1920), 63–64, 84, 108–10.

48. Ibid., 234–35.

49. Alan Trachtenberg, ed., *Memoirs of Waldo Frank* (Amherst: University of Massachusetts Press, 1973), 3–4.

50. Ibid., 236.

51. See Irene Rostagno, "Waldo Frank's Crusade for Latin American Literature," *Americas* 46.1 (1989): 41–69; and Ilán Stavans, ed., *Mutual Impressions: Writers from the Americas Reading One Another* (Durham, NC: Duke University Press, 1999), 250–52.

52. Ernest Hemingway, *A Moveable Feast* (New York: Scribner, 2009), 57–64.

53. Ernest Hemingway, *Complete Poems* (Lincoln: University of Nebraska Press, 1992), 278.

54. F. Scott Fitzgerald, *A Short Autobiography* (New York: Scribner, 2011), 88.

55. Edward Abrahams, *The Lyrical Left: Randolph Bourne, Alfred Stieglitz, and the Origins of Cultural Radicalism in America* (Charlottesville: University of Virginia Press, 1986); Christopher Lasch, *The New Radicalism in America, 1899–1963: The Intellectual as Social Type* (New York: Norton, 1965).

56. Frank, *The Dark Mother*, 34.

57. "Fair Play for Cuba Committee Hearings Before the Subcommittee to Investigate the Administration of the Internal Security Act and Other Internal Security Laws of the Committee on Judiciary, United States Senate," April 1960–January 1961, http://www.archive.org/stream/fairplayforcubac0102unit/fairplayforcubac0102unit_djvu.txt.

58. Christopher Neal, "Carleton Beals: Disidente solitario," *Letras Libres*, May 2007.

59. George Sokolsky, "Fair Play for Cuba Committee Is Headed by Waldo Frank," *Evening Independent*, April 13, 1960, 15.

60. James L. Brewer, *The Anticommunist Peril of Waldo Frank* (Halifax: New Christian Books, 1955), 1–12.

61. J. P. Morray, "Cuba and Communism."

62. Sam Dolgoff, *The Cuban Revolution: A Critical Perspective* (Montreal: Black Rose Books, 1976), 5–6.

63. Theodore Draper, *Castro's Revolution: Myths and Realities* (New York: Frederick A. Praeger, 1962), 3–11.

64. Ibid., 115–36.

65. Ibid., 173–92.

66. Ibid., 166.

67. Citation translated from Frank, *Cuba, isla profética*, 176.

68. Ibid.

69. Ibid.

70. Trachtenberg, *Memoirs of Waldo Frank*, 234.

71. Julio Cortázar, *Último round* (Buenos Aires: Siglo XXI, 1986), 2:273–74.

72. Theodore Draper, *Castroism: Theory and Practice* (New York: Frederik A. Praeger, 1965), 214–15.

3: SOCIALISTS IN MANHATTAN

1. Albert Einstein, "Why Socialism?" *Monthly Review*, May 1949, 55–61.
2. Paul M. Sweezy, *The Present as History: Essays and Reviews on Capitalism and Socialism* (New York: Monthly Review Press, 1953), 295–301.
3. Ibid.
4. Paul M. Sweezy, *Socialism* (New York: McGraw-Hill, 1949), 12–32.
5. Paul M. Sweezy, *The Theory of Capitalist Development: Principles of Marxian Political Economy* (New York: Oxford University Press, 1942), 51–52.
6. Paul M. Sweezy and Leo Huberman, eds., *F. O. Matthiessen: A Collective Portrait (1902–1950)* (New York: Henry Schuman, 1950), 3–20.
7. Sweezy, *The Present as History*, 253–90.
8. Sweezy, *The Theory of Capitalist Development*, 192–206.
9. Ibid., 47; and Paul M. Sweezy, *Modern Capitalism and Other Essays* (New York: Monthly Review Press, 1972), 92–109.
10. Sweezy, *Modern Capitalism*, 375–78 and 15–24.
11. Paul A. Baran, "On Soviet Themes," *Monthly Review*, July 1956, 84–91; Anna Louise Strong, "Critique of Stalin Era," *Monthly Review*, July 1956; Joshua Kunitz, "Khrushchev and the Jews," *Monthly Review*, July 1956.
12. Paul M. Sweezy, "Marxian Socialism," *Monthly Review*, November 1956.
13. D. D. Kosambi, "China's Communes," *Monthly Review*, March 1959, 369–78; Charles Bettelheim, "China's Economic Growth," *Monthly Review*, March 1959, 429–58; Keith M. Buchanan, "The Many Faces of China," *Monthly Review*, May 1959, 8–18; Paolo Sylos Labini, "Chinese Economy and Economics," *Monthly Review*, July–August 1959; Keith M. Buchanan, "South from China," *Monthly Review*, September 1959, 149–54.
14. Ralph Miliband, "The New Capitalism: A View from Abroad," *Monthly Review*, July–August 1959; William Appleman Williams, "Empire, New Style," *Monthly Review*, July–August 1959.
15. Hobert P. Sturm and Francis D. Wormuth, "The International Power Elite," *Monthly Review*, December 1959.
16. Joseph Starobin, Stanley Moore, and Paul Baran, "Marxism," *Monthly Review*, September 1959, 136–38; Paul Baran, "Marxism and Psychoanalysis," *Monthly Review*, October 1959, 186–200.
17. Manuel Pedro González, "Why Cubans Resent the US," *Monthly Review*, May 1960, 18–23.
18. Ibid., 19 and 21.
19. Leo Huberman and Paul Sweezy, *Cuba: Anatomy of a Revolution* (New York: Monthly Review Press, 1961), 25–55.
20. Ibid., 3–16.
21. Ibid., 145.

22. Ibid., 146.
23. Ibid., 107–33.
24. Ibid., 149–57.
25. Theodore Draper, *Castro's Revolution*, 3–11. See also Theodore Draper, "Cuba," *New Left Review*, September–October 1961, 49–61.
26. Draper, *Castro's Revolution*, 115–36.
27. Fidel Castro, "A Real Democracy," *Monthly Review*, September 1960, 305–10.
28. Nancy Reeves, "Women of the New Cubans," *Monthly Review*, November 1960.
29. "The Siege of Cuba," *New Left Review*, January–February, 1961, 2–3.
30. Carl Marzani, "Reflections on American Foreign Policy," *Monthly Review*, January 1961.
31. Paul A. Baran, "Reflections on the Cuban Revolution," *Monthly Review*, January 1961, and "Reflections on the Cuban Revolution II," *Monthly Review*, February 1961.
32. J. P. Morray, "Cuba and Communism," 236–42. See also J. P. Morray, *The Second Revolution in Cuba*, 163–73.
33. Ernesto Che Guevara, "Cuba, Exceptional Case," *Monthly Review*, July–August, 1961, 222–24. See also Ernesto Che Guevara, *Obras* (Havana: Casa de las Américas, 1970), 2:403–19.
34. Baran died of a heart attack in 1964, and Paul Sweezy completed the edition of his work, which was entitled *Monopoly Capital: An Essay on the American Economic and Social Order* (New York: Monthly Review Press, 1966).
35. Richard Pipes, "The Public Mood," *Harper's Magazine*, May 1961, 107–12.
36. Robert B. Silvers, "The Voice of a Dissenter," *Harper's Magazine*, May 1961, 121–31.
37. Patricia Blake, "We Don't Breathe Easily," *Harper's Magazine*, May 1961, 118–21.
38. Alfred Kazin, "Among Russia's Jews," *Harper's Magazine*, May 1961, 135–39.
39. Peter Ferdinand Drucker, "A Plan for Revolution in Latin America," *Harper's Magazine*, July 1961, 31–38.
40. Paul A. Baran, "The Commitment of the Intellectual," *Monthly Review*, May 1961, 32; italics in the original.
41. Adolfo Gilly, *Inside the Cuban Revolution* (New York: Monthly Review Press, 1964).
42. Ibid., 1.
43. Ibid., 2–13.
44. Ibid., 26–33 and 83–88. On the economic debates between the Guevara camp and the old communists, see Carmelo Mesa Lago, *Breve historia económica de la Cuba socialista* (Madrid: Alianza Editorial, 1994), 43–81.
45. Régis Debray, *Revolution in the Revolution? Armed Struggle and Political Struggle in Latin America* (New York: Monthly Review Press, 1967), 7–12.
46. Ibid., 7.
47. Ibid., 104–16.

48. Régis Debray, "The Long March," *New Left Review*, September–October, 1965, 17–58; Régis Debray, "Problems of Revolutionary Strategy in Latin America," September–October, 1967, 13–41.

49. "The Marxism of Régis Debray," *New Left Review* 1, September–October, 1967, 8–12; Robin Blackburn and Perry Anderson, "The Marxism of Régis Debray," in Leo Huberman and Paul Sweezy, eds., *Régis Debray and the Latin American Revolution* (New York: Monthly Review Press, 1968), 63–69.

50. Andre Gunder Frank, "Class, Politics, and Debray," in Huberman and Sweezy, *Régis Debray and the Latin American Revolution*, 12–17.

51. Cléa Silva, "The Errors of the Foco Theory," in Huberman and Sweezy, *Régis Debray and the Latin American Revolution*, 18–35; Peter Worsley, "Revolutionary Theory: Che Guevara and Régis Debray," in Huberman and Sweezy, *Régis Debray and the Latin American Revolution*, 119–38.

52. Juan Bosch, "An Anti-Communist Manifesto," in Huberman and Sweezy, *Régis Debray and the Latin American Revolution*, 96–105.

53. William Appleman Williams, "Black Power and Student Power," in Huberman and Sweezy, *Régis Debray and the Latin American Revolution*, 84–87.

54. Simón Torres and Julio Aronde, "Debray and the Cuban Experience," in Huberman and Sweezy, *Régis Debray and the Latin American Revolution*, 44, 62; Nestor Kohan, *De Ingenieros al Che: Ensayos sobre el marxismo argentino y latinoamericano* (Buenos Aires: Biblos, 2000), 273.

55. Leo Huberman and Paul Sweezy, *Socialism in Cuba* (New York: Monthly Review Press, 1969), 22.

56. Ibid., 89 and 99.

57. Ibid., 102–3.

58. Ibid., 162–66.

59. Ernesto Che Guevara et al., *El gran debate: Sobre la economía en Cuba, 1963–1964* (Mexico City: Ocean Sur, 2005), 17–36, 154–89, 273–90, and 309–46.

60. Ibid., 219.

61. Ibid., 204.

62. Mesa Lago, *Breve historia económica de la Cuba socialista*, 43–59.

4: THE CULTURAL APPARATUS OF THE EMPIRE

1. C. Wright Mills, *White Collar: The American Middle Class* (New York: Oxford University Press, 1951), 324–27.

2. Walter Lippmann, *Public Opinion* (New York: Harcourt, Brace, 1922), 79–158 and 379–418.

3. Mills, *White Collar*, 77–141 and 324–54.

4. C. Wright Mills, *The Power Elite* (New York: Oxford University Press, 2000), 71–93.

5. Ibid., 321–61.

6. C. Wright Mills, *The Sociological Imagination* (New York: Oxford University Press, 2000), 165–76.

7. Stanley Aronowitz, *Taking It Big*, 187–213. See also Russell Jacoby, *The Last Intellectuals*, 112–39.

8. Mills, *Sociological Imagination*, 195–226.

9. C. Wright Mills, *The Politics of Truth: Collected Writings* (New York: Oxford University Press, 2008), 203–12.

10. Jürgen Habermas, *The Structural Transformation of the Public Sphere: An Inquiry into a Category of Bourgeois Society* (Boston: MIT Press, 1989); Louis Althusser, "Ideology and State Ideological Apparatuses (Notes towards an Investigation)," trans. Ben Brewster, in *Lenin and Philosophy and Other Essays* (New York: Monthly Review Press, 1971); Daniel Geary, *Radical Ambition: C. Wright Mills, the Left, and American Social Thought* (Berkeley: University of California Press, 2009), 189–97.

11. C. Wright Mills, *The Causes of World War Three* (New York: Simon and Schuster, 1958), 168–72; C. Wright Mills, "Letter to the New Left," *New Left Review*, September–October 1960, available at http://www.marxists.org/subject/humanism/mills-c-wright/letter-new-left.htm.

12. Giampaolo Catelli and Anna Solling, *Charles Wright Mills: Lupo solitario* (Rome: Bonnano Editore, 2005), 60–64 and 93–134; Daniel Geary, *Radical Ambition*, 1–13; Stanley Aronowitz, *Taking It Big*, 214–39.

13. Swados, "C. Wright Mills: A Personal Memoir," 408–16.

14. C. Wright Mills, Clarence Senior, and Rose Kihn Goldsen, *The Puerto Rican Journey: New York's Newest Migrants* (New York: Harper & Brothers, 1950), 139–70.

15. Ibid., 157–59.

16. Ibid., 165.

17. Ibid., 125–38.

18. Ibid., 3–4.

19. Ibid., 3.

20. Ibid., 5–6.

21. Ibid., 7.

22. Ibid., 8–10.

23. Ibid., 18–19.

24. Ibid., 22.

25. C. Wright Mills, *Listen, Yankee: The Revolution in Cuba* (New York: Ballantine Books, 1960), 190–91.

26. Ibid., 191.

27. Michael Walzer, *Cuba: The Invasion and the Consequences*, 2 and 3.

28. On the Cuban Revolution and the American press, see Enrique Camacho Navarro, "Fidel Castro en la perspectiva estadounidense: El primer año de la Revolución," in *Desde el Sur: Visiones de Estados Unidos y Canadá desde América Latina*, ed. Paz Consuelo Márquez-Padilla, Germán Pérez Fernández del Castillo, and Remedios Gómez Arrau (Mexico City: UNAM, 2003), 45–63.

29. Mills, *Listen, Yankee*, 7.

30. Ibid., 11–12.

31. Ibid., 13, 54, 71, 91 and 151.

32. Ibid., 13.

33. Ibid., 91–112.

34. Ibid., 104.
35. Ibid., 12.
36. Ibid., 180.
37. Mills, *The Marxists* (New York: Dell, 1962), 12–22.
38. H. H. Gerthe and C. Wright Mills, eds., *From Max Weber: Essays in Sociology* (New York: Oxford University Press, 1946), 7–15.
39. Mills, *The Causes of World War Three*, 81–90.
40. Originally translated as *Cuban Counterpoint: Tobacco and Sugar*, trans. Harriet de Onís (New York: Knopf, 1947).
41. Mills, *Listen, Yankee*, 160.
42. Ibid., 7.
43. Ibid., 191.
44. J. P. Morray, "Questions and Answers on Cuba," *Monthly Review* , September 1962, 236–42; J. P. Morray, *The Second Revolution in Cuba*, 5
45. Morray, *The Second Revolution*, 153–73.
46. Ibid., 4.
47. C. Wright Mills, *Escucha, Yanqui: La Revolución en Cuba* (Mexico City: Fondo de Cultura Económica, 1961), 200.
48. Ibid., 205.
49. C. Wright Mills, *Letters and Autobiographical Writings* (Berkeley: University of California Press, 2000), 312.
50. Mills, *Escucha, Yanqui*, 230.
51. See, for example, Theodore Draper, *Castro's Revolution*, 115–36.
52. Mills, *Letters and Autobiographical Writings*, 318 and 322.
53. Mills, *Escucha, Yanqui*, 238.
54. Ibid., 237.
55. *Harper's Magazine*, February 1961, 6–12.
56. Mills, *Listen, Yankee*, 179.
57. Mills, *Letters and Autobiographical Writings*, 324.
58. Ibid., 315.
59. Brian D. Palmer, *E. P. Thompson: Objections and Oppositions* (New York: Verso, 1994), 52–86.
60. E. P. Thompson, *William Morris: Romantic to Revolutionary* (Stanford: Stanford University Press, 1988), 512–51 and 597–604.
61. Carlos Illades, *Breve introducción al pensamiento de E. P. Thompson* (Mexico City: Universidad Autónoma Metropolitana, 2008), 59–76.
62. E. P. Thompson, *The Making of the English Working Class* (New York: Vintage Books, 1966), 102–88, 350–74, and 711–45. On Thompson's Marxist heterodoxy, see Gerard McCann, *Theory and History: The Political Thought of E. P. Thompson* (Aldershot, UK: Ashgate, 1997), 111–44; Robert Gray, "History, Marxism, and Theory," in *E. P. Thompson: Critical Perspectives*, ed. Harvey J. Kaye and Keith McVlelland (Oxford: Polity Press, 1990), 153–82.
63. Perry Anderson, "Limitaciones y posibilidades de la acción sindical," *Pensamiento Crítico* 13 (1968): 113–30; Perry Anderson, "Componentes de la cultura nacional," *Pensamiento Crítico* 34/35 (1969): 53–121; Robin Blackburn, "Introducción a la cultura burguesa," *Pensamiento Crítico* 34/35 (1969): 3–52; Eric Hobsbawm, "Los campesinos, las migraciones y la política," *Pensamiento*

Crítico 24 (1969): 75–107. See also Michael Newman, *Ralph Miliband and the Politics of the New Left* (London: Merlin Press, 2002), 139–41.

64. *Pensamiento Crítico*'s issue number 5 (June 1967) was devoted to Althusser. In addition to an article by André Gorz on Sartre and Marx, taken from the *New Left Review*, the issue also included a critique of Althusserian Jean-Paul Dolle's European "leftism" and "socialist humanism," which, although primarily directed against Polish Marxist Adam Schaff, endorsed the terms of orthodox Marxism's attack on Thompson's historiographical proposals. *Pensamiento Crítico* 5 (1967): 49–75. See also Illades, *Breve introducción al pensamiento de E. P. Thompson*, 29–42 and 43–58.

65. Gerard McCann, *Theory and History: The Political Thought of E. P. Thompson*, 8–32; Brian D. Palmer, *Thompson: Objections and Oppositions*, 107–25 and 137; Scott Hamilton, *The Crisis of Theory: E. P. Thompson, the New Left and Postwar British Politics* (New York: Manchester University Press, 2011), 103; Kate Soper, "Socialist Humanism," in *E. P. Thompson: Critical Perspectives*, ed. Harvey J. Kaye and Keith McClelland, 203–32.

66. Geary, *Radical Ambition*, 213; Aronowitz, *Taking It Big*, 207–13. In a televised speech given on December 2, 1961, Castro had declared, "I am a Marxist-Leninist, and I shall be a Marxist-Leninist to the end of my life" (citation taken from the translation of Castro's speech printed in a Fair Play for Cuba pamphlet published in 1962, available at http://www.walterlippmann.com/fc-12-02-1961.html).

67. See, for example, Artaraz, *Cuba and Western Intellectuals*, 21–46.

68. Holger Nehring, "Out of Apathy: Genealogies of the British New Left in a Transnational Context (1956–62)," in *Between Prague Spring and French May: Opposition and Revolt in Europe, 1960–1980*, ed. Martin Klimke, Jacco Pekelder, and Joachim Scharloth (New York: Berghahn Books, 2011), 15–31; Wade Matthews, "The Poverty of Strategy: E. P. Thompson, Perry Anderson, and the Transition to Socialism," *Labour/Le Travail* 50 (Fall 2002): 217–41.

69. "The Siege of Cuba," *New Left Review*, January–February 1961, 2–3.

70. Mills, "Letter to the New Left," 18–23.

71. Ibid., 18–20.

72. Archivo Histórico del Fondo de Cultura Económica (AHFCE), C. Wright Mills, 1957–63, box 7, file 367, folios 40–44.

73. Ibid., folio 50.

74. Ibid., C. Wright Mills, box 7, file 367, folio 56.

75. Ibid., folio 50.

76. Ibid., folio 61.

77. Ibid., folio 62.

5: MOONS OF THE REVOLUTION

1. Todd F. Tietchen, *The Cubalogues: Beat Writers in Revolutionary Havana* (Gainesville: University Press of Florida, 2010), 1–21. For an analysis of the leftist beat, see Jacoby, *The Last Intellectuals*, 54–71.

2. Tietchen, *The Cubalogues*, 1–21.

3. Richard E. Welch, *Response to Revolution: The United States and the Cuban Revolution* (Chapel Hill: University of North Carolina Press, 1985), 157–58; Van Gosse, *The New Left: An Interpretative History* (New York: Palgrave Macmillan, 2005), 53–62.

4. Lawrence Ferlinghetti, *Starting from San Francisco* (New York: New Directions, 1967), 48–49.

5. Ogorzaly, *Waldo Frank*, 151.

6. Germán Labrador Méndez, *Letras arrebatadas: Poesía y química en la transición española* (Madrid: Devenir Ensayo, 2009), 15–19.

7. William S. Burroughs, *Rub Out the Words* (New York: HarperCollins, 2012), 207–8.

8. Allen Ginsberg, *Reality Sandwiches, 1953–60* (San Francisco: City Lights Books, 1963), 17.

9. Allen Ginsberg, *Journals: Early Fifties, Early Sixties* (New York: Grove Press, 1977), 158.

10. Allen Ginsberg, *Collected Poems, 1947–1980* (New York: Harper and Row, 1984), 265.

11. Ibid., 275.

12. Ginsberg, *Journals*, 274.

13. Ibid., 275.

14. Allen Ginsberg, *Deliberate Prose: Selected Essays, 1952–1995* (New York: HarperCollins, 2000), 136.

15. Ibid.

16. Ibid., 137–42.

17. Ibid., 143.

18. Ibid., 143–44.

19. Ibid., 144.

20. Ibid.

21. Ibid.

22. Ibid., 144–45.

23. Ibid., 136.

24. Ibid., 145.

25. Ibid.

26. *Pa'Lante*, May 19, 1962, 5.

27. Ibid., 122–165 and 165–90.

28. On Ginsberg's trip to Havana and his expulsion from the island, see Michael Schumacher, *Dharma Lion: Biography of Allen Ginsberg* (New York: St. Martin's Press, 1984), 422–31; Barry Miles, *Ginsberg: A Biography* (New York: Viking Press, 1989), 351–52 and 367–68.

29. William Luis, *Lunes de Revolución: Literatura y cultura en los primeros años de la Revolución Cubana* (Madrid: Verbum, 2003), 85.

30. Ibid., 86–87.

31. Ginsberg, *Collected Poems, 1947–1980*, 323.

32. Guillermo Cabrera Infante, "Los escritores versus USA," *Lunes de Revolución*, April 18, 1960, 3–4; Oscar Hurtado, "¿Una generación derrotada?" *Lunes de Revolución*, April 18, 1960, 15–19.

33. Ibid., 19.

34. Ibid., 37.

35. Silvia Cezar Miskulin, *Os intelectuais cubanos: Política cultural da Revolucao, 1961–1975* (Sao Paulo: Alameda Casa Editorial, 2009), 89–138.
36. Jesús J. Barquet, ed., *Ediciones El Puente en La Habana de los años 60* (Chihuahua, Mexico: Ediciones del Azar, 2011), 183.
37. All poetry translations in this chapter have been prepared by the translator for this volume.
38. Ibid., 218–19.
39. José Mario, "Allen Ginsberg en La Habana," *Mundo Nuevo* (Paris), April 1969, 48–54.
40. Ibid.
41. Ibid.
42. Allen Ginsberg, *Spontaneous Mind: Selected Interviews, 1958–1996* (New York: HarperCollins, 2001), xvii, 17, 328.
43. Ibid., 328.
44. Ibid.
45. Ibid.
46. Ibid.
47. Ibid., 329.
48. Ibid.
49. Theodore Roszak, *The Making of a Counter Culture* (New York: Doubleday, 1969), 8–9.
50. Ibid., 124–54.
51. Ginsberg, *Spontaneous Mind*, 330.
52. Edward Sanders, *The Poetry and Life of Allen Ginsberg* (New York: Overlook Press, 2000), 61.
53. Ibid., 59.
54. Ginsberg, *Deliberate Prose*, 30.
55. Ibid., 210–11. On the legal and psychiatric categories employed by the Cuban government, see Pedro Marqués de Armas, "Psiquiatría para el Nuevo Estado: Algunos documentos," *La Habana Elegante* (Winter 2006), http://www.habanaelegante.com/Winter2006/Panoptico.html.
56. Ginsberg, *Collected Poems, 1947–1980*, 691.
57. Ibid., 743.
58. Ginsberg, *Collected Poems, 1947–1980*, 484–85.
59. Ibid., 485.
60. Ibid.
61. Robert Anton Wilson, "The Poet as Radar System," in *On the Poetry of Allen Ginsberg*, ed. Lewis Hyde (Ann Arbor: University of Michigan Press, 1984), 94–96.

6: NEGROES WITH GUNS

1. Van Gosse, *Rethinking the New Left: An Interpretative History* (New York: Palgrave, 2005), 31–52 and 111–30; Van Gosse, *The Movements of the New Left, 1950–1975: A Brief History with Documents* (New York: Palgrave,

2005), 55–56; Mark Q. Sawyer, *Racial Politics in Post-Revolutionary Cuba* (New York: Cambridge University Press, 2006), 79–101.

2. Ruth Reitan, *The Rise and Decline of an Alliance: Cuba and African American Leaders in the 1960s* (East Lansing: Michigan State University Press, 1999), 117–32.

3. Robert F. Williams, "El cielo guarda silencio," *Lunes de Revolución*, July 4, 1960, 15.

4. Clayborne Carson, *Malcolm X: The FBI File* (New York: Skyhorse, 2012), 63, 93 and 197–99.

5. Gosse, *The Movements of the New Left*, 55–56.

6. Robert F. Williams, *Negroes with Guns*, ed. Marc Schleifer (New York: Marzani and Munsell, 1962), 7–8.

7. *Crusader-in-Exile* 3, no. 8 (April 1962), 1.

8. Williams, *Negroes with Guns*, 9–16.

9. Ibid., 13.

10. William J. Schafer, *The Truman Nelson Reader* (Washington, DC: Thompson Shore, 1989), 3–5, 101–2, 95–200 and 215–16; Truman Nelson, *The Old Man: John Brown at Harper's Ferry* (Chicago: Haymarket Books, 2009).

11. Henry David Thoreau, *Walden and Civil Disobedience* (New York: Penguin Books, 1986), 389.

12. Ibid., 390–92.

13. Ibid., 412–13.

14. Williams, *Negroes with Guns*, 27–31.

15. Ibid., 32–33.

16. Ibid., 34–36.

17. Ibid., 40.

18. Ibid., 117.

19. Ibid., 118.

20. Ibid.

21. Ibid., 69–72. The *Crusader-in-Exile* was a continuation of the *Crusader*, the newsletter Williams had produced in North Carolina starting in 1959.

22. Ibid., 71.

23. Ibid., 126.

24. Ibid.

25. Ibid.

26. Ibid.

27. Ibid., 127.

28. Ibid.

29. Georges Sorel, *Reflections on Violence* (Cambridge: Cambridge University Press, 2002), 7–15.

30. Ibid., 27–39.

31. Ibid., 70 and 52.

32. Frantz Fanon, *The Wretched of the Earth*, trans. Richard Philcox (New York: Grove Press, 2004), 44.

33. Sorel, *Reflections on Violence*, 78.

34. Ibid., 85.

35. Ibid., 280.
36. Sawyer, *Racial Politics in Post-Revolutionary Cuba*, 70–101.
37. Bettelheim, "China's Economic Growth," 429–58; Buchanan, "The Many Faces of China"; Buchanan, "The Sino-Soviet Dispute," *Monthly Review*, December 1961, 337–46; Leo Huberman and Paul Sweezy, "Algeria, Vietnam and Punta del Este," *Monthly Review*, March 1962, 497–504.
38. Eldridge Cleaver, *Soul on Ice* (New York: Dell, 1999), 111.
39. Ibid., 117.
40. Ibid., 70–71.
41. Ibid., 38.
42. Ibid., 31.
43. John Clytus, *Black Man in Red Cuba* (Miami, FL: University of Miami Press, 1970), 15–20 and 57–64.
44. Skip [Henry Louis] Gates, "Cuban Experience: Eldridge Cleaver on Ice," *Transition* 49 (1975): 39.
45. Ibid., 33.
46. Ibid., 41–42. For a reconstruction of the debate between Moore and Depestre, see Linda S. Howe, *Transgression and Conformity: Cuban Writers and Artists after the Revolution* (Madison: University of Wisconsin Press, 2004), 80–82.
47. Carlos Moore, *Pichón: Race and Revolution in Castro's Cuba, a Memoir* (Chicago: Lawrence Hill Books, 2008), 282–88.
48. Reitan, *The Rise and Decline of an Alliance*, 9–17.
49. Ibid., 19–25 and 30–33.
50. The issue featured an opening a piece by Althusser, "Materialismo dialéctico e histórico" (3–26), followed by numerous articles that referenced the French Marxist's work, including Jean-Paul Dollé, "Sobre el izquierdismo y el humanismo socialista" (49–75); André Gorz, "Sobre Sartre y Marx" (77–108); and Jacques Goldberg, "Antropología e ideología" (27–47).
51. Maurice Godelier, "La noción de modo de producción asiático y los esquemas marxistas de evolución de las sociedades," *Pensamiento Crítico* 15 (1968): 169–214; K. S. Karol, "China: El otro comunismo," *Pensamiento Crítico* 16 (1968): 144–80.
52. Citation translated from "Presentación," *Pensamiento Crítico* 17 (July 1968): 4.
53. Ibid.
54. Ibid.
55. Stokely Carmichael, "Después de la muerte de Luther King," *Pensamiento Crítico* 17 (July 1968): 93–97.
56. Malcolm X, "Para el capitalismo es imposible sobrevivir," *Pensamiento Crítico* 17 (July 1968): 5–12.
57. H. Rap Brown, "La guerra de guerrillas es la solución que se impone," *Pensamiento Crítico* 17 (July 1968): 67–68.
58. Ibid., 78.
59. Ibid., 85.
60. Ibid., 67.

61. Huey P. Newton, "Para ser un nacionalista revolucionario se debe ser necesariamente un socialista," *Pensamiento Crítico* 17 (July 1968): 108–9.

62. Ibid., 109–11.

63. Passage from the interview translated into Spanish for *Pensamiento Crítico* (ibid., 118), here reproduced as the passage originally appeared in English, as cited in Philip Sheldon Foner, ed., *The Black Panthers Speak* (New York: Da Capo Press, 1970), 60.

64. Artaraz, *Cuba and Western Intellectuals*, 42–43.

65. Huey P. Newton, *Pensamiento Crítico* interview, 118; Foner, *The Black Panthers Speak*, 60.

66. Ibid., 122.

67. Ibid., 119.

68. Robert L. Allen, "La estrategia del gran capital," *Pensamiento Crítico* 17 (July 1968): 98–107.

69. Ibid., 24–47.

70. Ibid., 31–32.

71. Stokely Carmichael and Charles V. Hamilton, *Black Power: The Politics of Liberation in America* (New York: Random House, 1967), vii–xii and 164–77.

72. Ibid., x.

73. Ibid., xi–xii; Fanon, *The Wretched of the Earth*, 2.

74. Fanon, *The Wretched of the Earth*, 235–40.

75. Jean Paul Dolle, "Crítica del izquierdismo y el humanismo socialista," *Pensamiento Crítico* 5 (June 1967): 49–75; André Gorz, "Sobre Sartre y Marx," *Pensamiento Crítico*, 77–108.

76. Stokely Carmichael, *Stokely Speaks: From Black Power to Pan-Africanism* (New York: Vintage Books, 1971).

77. Ibid., 192–95.

78. Ibid., 221–27.

79. H. Rap Brown, *Die Nigger Die! A Political Autobiography* (New York: Last Gasp, 1969), 130–31.

80. Ibid., 124.

81. Alejandro de la Fuente, *Una nación para todos: Raza, desigualdad y política en Cuba, 1900–2000* (Madrid: Editorial Colibrí, 2000), 293–355.

82. Brown, *Die Nigger Die!* 128.

83. Ibid., 129.

84. Ibid., 125.

85. Edmundo Desnoes, ed., *Now: El Movimiento Negro en Estados Unidos* (Havana: Instituto del Libro, 1967), 235–41.

86. Ibid., 12–13.

87. Stokely Carmichael, "El poder negro" and "Nosotros y el Tercer Mundo," in Desnoes, *Now*, 285–313.

88. Ibid., 10.

89. Ibid., 14.

90. Passages from Betancourt and Carbonell's essays are featured and commented on in María Poumier, ed., *La cuestión tabú: El pensamiento negro*

cubano de 1840 a 1959 (Las Palmas de Gran Canaria, Spain: Ediciones Idea, 2007), 359–66, 383–93.

7: THE LEAGUE OF MILITANT POETS

1. Committee on Un-American Activities, House of Representatives, "Violations of State Department Regulations and Pro-Castro Propaganda Activities," http://www.archive.org/stream/violationsofstat01unit/violationsofstat01unit_djvu.txt.

2. For a discussion of this intellectual movement and its relation to the Cuban Revolution, see Van Gosse, *Where the Boys Are: Cuba, Cold War, America, and the Making of the New Left* (New York: Verso, 1993), 137–76; Gosse, *Rethinking the New Left*, 53–62; and Todd F. Tietchen, *The Cubalogues: Beat Writers in Revolutionary Havana* (Gainesville: University Press of Florida, 2010), 50–68.

3. Ezra Pound, *Guide to Kulchur* (New York: New Directions, 1952), 136.

4. Ibid., 134 and 183–187.

5. Ibid., 134.

6. Ibid., 44.

7. Ibid., 183–87.

8. Ibid., 7.

9. William S. Burroughs, "The Conspiracy," *Kulchur* 1 (1960): 5–8.

10. Paul Bowles, "Ketama-Taza," *Kulchur* 1 (1960): 31–35.

11. Allen Ginsberg, "Paterson," *Kulchur* 1 (1960): 37.

12. Mason Klein and Catherine Evans, *The Radical Camera: New York's Photo League, 1936–1951* (New York: Jewish Museum, 2012), 30–45.

13. Williams, *Negroes with Guns*, 68 and 104.

14. *Lunes de Revolución*, July 4, 1960. The referenced articles in this issue are the following: Richard Gibson, "El negro americano mira hacia Cuba," 6; Richard Gibson and Robert F. Williams, "La constante lucha de los negros por su libertad," 7–8; James Baldwin, "El ghetto de Harlem," 9–11; Harold Cruse, "El arte negro y el arte occidental," 12–14; and John Henrik Clarke, "Transición en el cuento negro norteamericano," 17–18.

15. Marc Schleifer, "Cuban Notebook," *Monthly Review*, July/August, 1961, 72–83; Todd F. Tietchen, *The Cubalogues*, 113–17.

16. Jones's "Cuba Libre" piece was originally published in *Evergreen Review* (November 1960): 346–53. It was reprinted almost immediately in *Kulchur* 2 (Winter 1960): 54–89, where Jones worked as a contributing editor, and was also released as a pamphlet by the Fair Play for Cuba Committee in 1961. "Cuba Libre" was later included in LeRoi Jones's collection *Home* (New York: William Morrow, 1966). Citations from the essay in this chapter are taken from the reprinted edition of the latter work: LeRoi Jones (Amiri Baraka), *Home: Social Essays* (New York: Akashic Books, 2009).

17. Werner Sollors, *Amiri Baraka/LeRoi Jones: The Quest for a "Populist Modernism"* (New York: Columbia University Press, 1978), 64–72; William J.

Harris, *The Poetry and Poetics of Amiri Baraka: The Jazz Aesthetic* (Columbia: University of Missouri Press, 1985), 7–8, 75–76, and 83–84; Tietchen, *The Cubalogues*, 1–20.

18. Jones, "Cuba Libre," 57.
19. Ibid.
20. Ibid., 61.
21. Ibid., 67.
22. Ibid., 68.
23. Ibid., 78. Note: the final phrase of this citation, "A bland revolt," is included in the early printings of the essay but does not appear in the edition cited in this chapter.
24. Amiri Baraka, *The Autobiography of LeRoi Jones* (New York: Freundlich Books, 1984), 163.
25. Ibid., 166–67 and 202.
26. LeRoi Jones, *The Dead Lecturer* (New York: Grove Press, 1964), 13–14 and 26.
27. Ibid., 61–64, 66, 73–74, and 78.
28. Kimberly W. Benston, *Baraka: The Renegade and the Mask* (New Haven: Yale University Press, 1976), 30–44.
29. LeRoi Jones, *The System of Dante's Hell* (New York: Grove Press, 1965), 35–36 and 61–68.
30. Manning Marable, *Malcolm X: A Life of Reinvention* (New York: Penguin Books, 2011), 158–59, 172–73, and 399.
31. Carson, *Malcolm X*, 63, 93, and 197–99.
32. Amiri Baraka, *Daggers and Javelins: Essays, 1974–1979* (New York: William Morrow, 1984), 88–109; 149–65; 182–200.
33. *Pa'Lante* issue, May 19, 1962, 5.
34. Ibid.
35. Ibid.
36. Ibid., 6–25, 27–35, and 48–52; Juan Marinello, *Conversación con nuestros pintores abstractos* (Santiago, Cuba: Universidad de Oriente, Departamento de Extensión y Relaciones Culturales, 1960), 11–20.
37. *Pa'Lante* issue, 56–57; Ginsberg, *Deliberate Prose*, 416.
38. *Pa'Lante* issue, 91; Ginsberg, *The System of Dante's Hell*, 496–97.
39. Ibid., 61–73 and 135–45.
40. *Pa'Lante*, May 19, 1962, 53.
41. Ibid., 94.
42. Ibid.
43. Ibid., 95.
44. Ibid.
45. Ibid., 96.
46. Ibid., 99.
47. Ibid., 97.
48. Ibid., 96 and 98.
49. Ibid., 97.
50. Ibid., 100.

51. José Yglesias, *The Goodbye Land* (New York: Pantheon Books, 1967), 3–5 and 114–16.

52. José Yglesias, *In the Fist of the Revolution: Life in Castro's Cuba* (New York: Penguin Books, 1968), 67–93.

53. Ibid., 14–15.

54. Ibid., 201–27

55. Ibid., 94–119, 171–200, 208–9, and 246–67.

56. Sutherland [Martínez], *The Youngest Revolution*, 104–14.

57. Ibid., 125–31. Members of the *Caimán Barbudo* editorial board in 1966 included Jesús Díaz, Luis Rogelio Nogueras, and Guillermo Rodríguez Rivera, among others. *Pensamiento Crítico* was directed by philosopher Fernando Martínez Heredia.

58. Ibid., 138–68

59. Ibid., 242–73.

60. Ibid., 275–77.

8: THE SKIN OF SOCIALISM

1. Committee on the Judiciary, United States Senate, "Hearings before the Subcommittee to Investigate the Administration of the Internal Security Act and Other Internal Security Laws," January 10, 1961, http://www.archive.org/stream/fairplayforcubac0102unit/fairplayforcubac0102unit_djvu.txt.

2. Britton, *Carleton Beals: A Radical Journalist*, 30–50; Christopher Neal, "Carleton Beals: Disidente solitario."

3. Carleton Beals, "Rebels without a Cause," *Nation*, June 20, 1957, 560–68.

4. Carleton Beals, "The New Crime of Cuba," *Nation*, September 21, 1957, 140. See also Llerena, *La revolución insospechada*, 86–88.

5. Carleton Beals, *Mexico: An Interpretation* (New York: B. W. Huebsch, 1923), 1.

6. Ibid., 3–27.

7. Ibid., 39–52.

8. Ibid., 89–112 and 131–44.

9. Ibid., 151–78.

10. Ibid., 232–47.

11. Ibid., 200–216.

12. Carleton Beals, *The Crime of Cuba* (Philadelphia: J. B. Lippincott, 1933), 81–94.

13. Carleton Beals, *Mexican Maze* (Philadelphia: J. B. Lippincott, 1931), 9–30.

14. Ibid., 31–54.

15. Ibid., 352–61.

16. Ibid., 361.

17. Ibid.

18. Carleton Beals, *Banana Gold* (Philadelphia: J. B. Lippincott, 1932), 16–33.

19. Ibid., 106–7.
20. Ibid., 116.
21. Ibid., 120–28.
22. Ibid., 264–71.
23. Carleton Beals, *Porfirio Díaz: Dictator of Mexico* (Philadelphia: J. B. Lippincott, 1932), 7–11.
24. John A. Britton, *Carleton Beals: A Radical Journalist in Latin America* (Albuquerque: University of New Mexico Press, 1987), 51–70.
25. Beals, *The Crime of Cuba*, 55–60, 67–80, and 81–94.
26. Ibid., 5–7.
27. Ibid., 445–68.
28. Ibid., 7.
29. Alberto Lamar Schweyer, *Cómo cayó el presidente Machado* (Madrid: Espasa Calpe, 1934), 7–16.
30. Carleton Beals, *The Coming Struggle for Latin America* (Philadelphia: J. B. Lippincott, 1938), 13–44, 45–55, 86–104, and 133–58.
31. Ibid., 156–57.
32. Ibid., 371–80.
33. Carleton Beals, *The Story of Huey P. Long* (Philadelphia: J. B. Lippincott, 1935), 5–11; John Dewey et al., *Preliminary Commission of Inquiry into the Charges Made against Leon Trotsky in Moscow Trails* (New York: Harper, 1937), 12–23.
34. Carleton Beals, *Latin America: World in Revolution* (New York: Abelard-Schuman, 1963), 28.
35. Juan José Arévalo, *Anti-Kommunism in Latin America: An X-Ray of the Process Leading to a New Colonialism* (New York: Lyle Stuart, 1963), 9–16.
36. Carleton Beals, "Terror under Neon Lights," *Nation*, June 29, 1957, http://www.thenation.com/article/terror-under-neon-lights.
37. Beals, *Latin America: World in Revolution*, 259–79.
38. Beals, "Terror under the Neon Lights."
39. Ibid.
40. Carleton Beals, "Cuba: Revolution without Generals," *Nation*, January 17, 1959, 43–45.
41. "La única revolución de donde no había salido, ni saldrá, un solo general," Fidel Castro, "Discurso pronunciado por el Comandante en Jefe Fidel Castro Ruz, a su llegada a La Habana, el 8 de enero de 1959, en Ciudad Libertad," http://www.cuba.cu/gobierno/discursos/1959/esp/f080159e.html.
42. Ibid., 28.
43. Ibid., 29.
44. Carleton Beals, *The Nature of Revolution* (New York: Thomas Y. Crowell, 1970), 1–10, 17–48, and 107–24.
45. Ibid., 187–231.
46. Ibid., 252.
47. Ibid., 255.
48. Fair Play for Cuba Committee, http://www.archive.org/stream/fairplayforcubac0102unit/fairplayforcubac0102unit_djvu.txt.
49. Beals, *The Nature of Revolution*, 257–74.

50. Sutherland [Martínez], *The Youngest Revolution*, 5.
51. Ibid., 275–77.
52. Gilles Mora, ed., *Walker Evans: Havana 1933* (New York: Pantheon Books, 1933), 5.
53. Beals, *The Crime of Cuba*, 471–502.
54. Gilles Mora, *Walker Evans*, 42–43, 85, and 96.
55. Sutherland [Martínez], *The Youngest Revolution*, 275–77.
56. Roland Barthes, *Camera Lucida: Reflections on Photography*, trans. Richard Howard (New York: Hill and Wang, 2000), 26–27.
57. Walter Benjamin, *Sobre la fotografía* (Valencia, Spain: Pretextos, 2004), 13–24; Susan Sontag, *On Photography* (New York: Picador, 1977); Barthes, *Camera Lucida*, 80.
58. Sontag, *On Photography*, 47.
59. Barthes, *Camera Lucida*, 5 and 9.
60. Ibid., 5–6.
61. Ibid., 10–11 and 111.
62. Ibid., 102.
63. Sontag, *On Photography*, 85–100 and 115–30.
64. Barthes, *Camera Lucida*, 115.
65. Sutherland [Martínez], *The Youngest Revolution*, 275–77.
66. Néstor Almendros, "Cine: Pasado Meridiano," and Gerardo Muñoz, "La política del gesto: Néstor Almendros defiende PM." Articles are available at http://archivodeconnie.annaillustration.com/?p=1504.

EPILOGUE

1. Arendt, *On Revolution*, 59–70 and 117–40.
2. Ibid., 12.
3. Susan Buck-Morss, *Hegel, Haiti, and Universal History* (Pittsburgh: University of Pittsburgh Press, 2009), 21–77.
4. Arendt, *On Revolution*, 73, 247–48, 257–58, 267, and 328.
5. Beals, *The Nature of Revolution*, 255.
6. Jeremy Adelman, "Pasajes: Albert O. Hirschman en América Latina," in *Historia de los intelectuales en América Latina*, vol. 2, *Los avatares de la ciudad letrada*, ed. Carlos Altamirano and Jorge Myers (Buenos Aires: Katz, 2010), 652–86. See also Jeremy Adelman, *Worldly Philosopher: The Odyssey of Albert O. Hirschman* (Princeton: Princeton University Press, 2013), 360–73 and 379.
7. Cristina Vives, "Culture and Counterculture in Times of Revolution (Seen from the Perspective of Cuban Photography)," *Arte Cubano* 2 (2013): 18–32.
8. Lomnitz, *The Return of Comrade Ricardo Flores Magón*, xxxv–xlii.

REFERENCES

ARCHIVES

Archivo Histórico del Fondo de Cultura Económica, México D. F., Fuentes, Carlos, file 1, folios 5–6; Orfila Raynal, Arnaldo, file 6, 1959–62, folio 132; Wright Mills, C., 1957–63, box 7, file 367, 78 folios.

The Carleton Beals Collection, Howard Gotlieb Archival Research Center, Boston University.

Charles Wright Mills Papers, Briscoe Center for American History, University of Texas at Austin.

Committee on Un-American Activities. House of Representatives. Violations of State Department Regulations and Pro-Castro Propaganda Activities in the United States (Hearings). https://archive.org/details/violationsofstat02unit.

National Archives and Record Administration (NARA), Washington, DC, USA, Department of State, Lot Files, Record Group 59, Papers of Arturo Morales Carrión, box 9, folder 5.

Socialist International Information, Firestone Library. Princeton University, Vols. 9–12, 1961–63.

Violations of State Department Regulations and Pro-Castro Propaganda Activities in the United States (Hearings). Full text available at http://www.archive.org/stream/violationsofstat01unit/violationsofstat01unit_djvu.txt.

Waldo Frank Papers, Special Collections Department, University of Delaware Library.

Waldo Frank Papers, Rare Books and Manuscript Library, University of Pennsylvania.

PERIODICALS

Dissent (1959–71)
Harper's Magazine (1960–63)
Kulchur (1959–62)
Lunes de Revolución (1959–61)
Monthly Review (1959–71)
New York Times (1959–71)
Pa'Lante (1962)
Pensamiento Crítico (1967–71)
Village Voice (1959–71)

BOOKS AND ARTICLES

Abrahams, Edward. 1986. *The Lyrical Left: Randolph Bourne, Alfred Stieglitz, and the Origins of Cultural Radicalism in America*. Charlottesville: University of Virginia Press.

Adelman, Jeremy. 2010. "Pasajes: Albert O. Hirschman en América Latina." In *Historia de los intelectuales en América Latina*, ed. Carlos Altamirano and Jorge Myers. Vol. 2, *Los avatares de la ciudad letrada*. Buenos Aires: Katz.

———. 2013. *Worldly Philosopher: The Odyssey of Albert O. Hirschman*. Princeton: Princeton University Press.

Allen, Robert L. 1968. "La estrategia del gran capital." *Pensamiento Crítico* 17:98–107.

Almendros, Néstor. 1961. *Cine: Pasado Meridiano*, Gerardo Muñoz, *La política del gesto: Néstor Almendros defiende PM. Cuba: El archivo de Connie*. http://archivodeconnie.annaillustration.com/?p=1504.

Althusser, Louis. 1971. "Ideology and State Ideological Apparatuses (Notes toward an Investigation)." Trans. Ben Brewster. In *Lenin and Philosophy and Other Essays*. New York: Monthly Review Press.

Anderson, Perry. 1969. "Componentes de la cultura nacional." *Pensamiento Crítico* 34/35:53–121.

———. 1968. "Limitaciones y posibilidades de la acción sindical." *Pensamiento Crítico* 13 (February 1968): 113–30.

Arendt, Hannah. 1963. *On Revolution*. New York: Viking Press.

Arévalo, Juan José. 1963. *Anti-Kommunism in Latin America: An X-Ray of the Process Leading to a New Colonialism*. New York: Lyle Stuart.

Aronowitz, Stanley. 2012. *Taking It Big: C. Wright Mills and the Making of Political Intellectuals*. New York: Columbia University Press.

Artaraz, Kepa. 2009. *Cuba and Western Intellectuals since 1959*. New York: Palgrave.

Baldwin, James. 1960. "El ghetto de Harlem." *Lunes de Revolución*, July 4.

Baraka, Amiri. 1984. *The Autobiography of LeRoi Jones*. New York: Freundlich Books.

———. 1984. *Daggers and Javelins: Essays, 1974–1979*. New York: William Morrow.

Baran, Paul A. 1961. "The Commitment of the Intellectual." *Monthly Review* (May).
———. 1959. "Marxism and Psychoanalysis." *Monthly Review* (October).
———. 1956. "On Soviet Themes." *Monthly Review* (July).
———. 1961. "Reflections on the Cuban Revolution." *Monthly Review* (January).
———. 1961. "Reflections on the Cuban Revolution, II." *Monthly Review* (February).
Baran, Paul A., and Paul M. Sweezy. 1966. *Monopoly Capital: An Essay on the American Economic and Social Order.* New York: Monthly Review Press.
Barquet, Jesús J., ed. 2011. *Ediciones El Puente en La Habana de los años 60.* Chihuahua, Mexico: Ediciones del Azar.
Barthes, Roland. 2000. *Camera Lucida: Reflections on Photography.* Trans. Richard Howard. New York: Hill and Wang.
Beals, Carleton. 1932. *Banana Gold.* Philadelphia: J. B. Lippincott.
———. 1938. *The Coming Struggle for Latin America.* Philadelphia: J. B. Lippincott.
———. 1933. *The Crime of Cuba.* Philadelphia: J. B. Lippincott.
———. 1959. "Cuba: Revolution without Generals." *Nation* (January).
———. 1963. *Latin America: World in Revolution.* New York: Abelard-Schuman.
———. 1931. *Mexican Maze.* Philadelphia: J. B. Lippincott.
———. 1923. *Mexico: An Interpretation.* New York: B. W. Huebsch.
———. 1970. *The Nature of Revolution.* New York: Thomas Y. Crowell.
———. 1957. "The New Crime of Cuba." *Nation* (September).
———. 1932. *Porfirio Díaz: Dictator of Mexico.* Philadelphia: J. B. Lippincott.
———. 1957. "Rebels without a Cause." *Nation* (June).
———. 1935. *The Story of Huey P. Long.* Philadelphia: J. B. Lippincott.
———. 1957. "Terror under Neon Lights." *Nation* (June). http://www.thenation.com/article/terror-under-neon-lights.
Bender, Thomas. 1987. *New York Intellect: A History of Intellectual Life in New York, from 1750 to the Beginnings of Our Times.* Baltimore: Johns Hopkins University Press.
Benjamin, Walter. 2004. *Sobre la fotografía.* Valencia: Pretextos.
Benston, Kimberly W. 1976. *Baraka: The Renegade and the Mask.* New Haven: Yale University Press.
Bettelheim, Charles. 1959. "China's Economic Growth." *Monthly Review* (March).
Bittner, William. 1955. *The Novels of Waldo Frank.* Philadelphia: University of Pennsylvania Press.
Blackburn, Robin. 1969. "Introducción a la cultura burguesa." *Pensamiento Crítico* 34/35:3–52.
Blackburn, Robin, and Perry Anderson. 1968. "The Marxism of Régis Debray." In *Régis Debray and the Latin American Revolution*, ed. Huberman and Sweezy.
Blake, Patricia. 1961. "We Don't Breathe Easily." *Harper's Magazine* (May).
Bloom, Alexander. 1986. *Prodigal Sons: The New York Intellectuals and Their World.* Oxford: Oxford University Press.

Bosch, Juan. 1968. "An Anti-Communist Manifesto." In *Régis Debray and the Latin American Revolution*, ed. Huberman and Sweezy.

Bowles, Paul. 1960. "Ketama-Taza." *Kulchur* (Spring).

Brewer, James L. 1955. *The Anticommunist Peril of Waldo Frank*. Halifax: New Christian Books.

Brown, H. Rap. 1969. *Die Nigger Die! A Political Autobiography*. New York: Last Gasp.

———. 1968. "La guerra de guerrillas es la solución que se impone." *Pensamiento Crítico* 17:67–68.

Brick, Howard. 1998. *Age of Contradictions: American Thought and Culture in the 1960s*. Ithaca, NY: Cornell University Press.

Britton, John A. 1987. *Carleton Beals: A Radical Journalist in Latin America*. Albuquerque: University of New Mexico Press.

Brown, Archie. 2009. *The Rise and Fall of Communism*. New York: HarperCollins.

Buchanan, Keith M. 1962. "Algeria, Vietnam and Punta del Este." *Monthly Review* (March).

———. 1959. "The Many Faces of China." *Monthly Review* (May).

———. 1961. "The Sino-Soviet Dispute." *Monthly Review* (December).

———. 1959. "South from China." *Monthly Review* (September).

Buck-Morss, Susan. 2009. *Hegel, Haiti, and Universal History*. Pittsburgh: University of Pittsburgh Press.

Buhle, Paul. 2013. *Marxism in the United States: A History of the American Left*. New York: Verso.

Burroughs, William S. 1960. "The Conspiracy." *Kulchur* (Spring).

———. 2012. *Rub Out the Words*. New York: HarperCollins.

Cabrera Infante, Guillermo. 1960. "Los escritores versus USA." *Lunes de Revolución* (April).

Camacho Navarro, Enrique. 2003. "Fidel Castro en la perspectiva estadounidense: El primer año de la Revolución." In *Desde el Sur: Visiones de Estados Unidos y Canadá desde América Latina*, ed. Paz Consuelo Márquez-Padilla, Germán Pérez Fernández del Castillo, and Remedios Gómez Arrau. Mexico City: UNAM.

Carmichael, Stokely. 1968. "Después de la muerte de Luther King." *Pensamiento Crítico* 17:93–97.

———. 1967. "El poder negro" and "Nosotros y el Tercer Mundo." In Desnoes, *Now*, 285–313.

———. 1971. *Stokely Speaks: From Black Power to Pan-Africanism*. New York: Vintage.

Carmichael, Stokely, and Charles V. Hamilton. 1967. *Black Power: The Politics of Liberation in America*. New York: Random House.

Carson, Clayborne. 2012. *Malcolm X: The FBI File*. New York: Skyhorse.

Carter, Paul J. 1967. *Waldo Frank*. New Haven, CT: United Printing Services.

Castro, Fidel. 1959. "Discurso pronunciado por el Comandante en Jefe Fidel Castro Ruz, a su llegada a La Habana, el 8 de enero de 1959, en Ciudad Libertad." http://www.cuba.cu/gobierno/discursos/1959/esp/f080159e.html.

———. 1960. "A Real Democracy." *Monthly Review* (September).

Catelli, Giampaolo, and Anna Solling. 2005. *Charles Wright Mills: Lupo solitario*. Rome: Bonnano Editore.

Clarke, John Henrik. 1960. "Transición en el cuento negro norteamericano." *Lunes de Revolución* (July).

Cleaver, Eldridge. 1999. *Soul on Ice*. New York: Dell.

Cleeton, Christa. 2012. "Fidel Castro Visits Princeton University." *Mudd Manuscript Library Blog*, Princeton University, October 5. https://blogs.princeton.edu/mudd/2012/10/fidel-castro-visits-princeton-university/.

Clytus, John. 1970. *Black Man in Red Cuba*. Miami: University of Miami Press.

Committee on Un-American Activities, House of Representatives. 1963 (May). "Violations of State Department Regulations and Pro-Castro Propaganda Activities." http://www.archive.org/stream/violationsofstat01unit/violationsofstat01unit_djvu.txt.

Cooney, Terry A. 1986. *The Rise of the New York Intellectuals: Partisan Review and Its Circle: 1934–45*. Madison: University of Wisconsin Press.

Cortázar, Julio. 1986. *Último round*. Vol. 2. Buenos Aires: Siglo XXI.

The Crusader-in-Exile 3, no. 8 (April 1962).

Cruse, Harold. 1960. "El arte negro y el arte occidental." *Lunes de Revolución* (July).

Daly, Christopher B. 2012. *Covering America: A Narrative History of a Nation*. Boston: University of Massachusetts Press.

Debray, Régis. 1965. "The Long March." *New Left Review* (September–October).

———. 1967. "Problems of Revolutionary Strategy in Latin America." *New Left Review* (September–October).

———. 1967. *Revolution in the Revolution? Armed Struggle and Political Struggle in Latin America*. New York: Monthly Review Press.

de la Fuente, Alejandro. *Una nación para todos: Raza, desigualdad y política en Cuba, 1900–2000*. Madrid: Editorial Colibrí, 2000.

De Palma, Anthony. 2006. *The Man Who Invented Fidel: Cuba, Castro, and Herbert Matthews of the "New York Times."* New York: Public Affairs.

Desnoes, Edmundo, ed. 1967. *Now: El Movimiento Negro en Estados Unidos*. Havana: Instituto del Libro.

Dewey, John, et al. 1937. *Preliminary Commission of Inquiry into the Charges Made against Leon Trotsky in Moscow Trails*. New York: Harper.

Dolgoff, Sam. 1976. *The Cuban Revolution: A Critical Perspective*. Montreal: Black Rose Books.

Dolle, Jean Paul. 1967. "Crítica del izquierdismo y el humanismo socialista." *Pensamiento Crítico* 5:49–75.

Draper, Theodore. 1965. *Castroism: Theory and Practice*. New York: Frederik A. Praeger.

———. 1962. *Castro's Revolution: Myths and Realities*. New York: Frederick A. Praeger.

———. 1961. "Cuba." *New Left Review* (September–October).

Drucker, Peter Ferdinand. 1961. "A Plan for Revolution in Latin America." *Harper's Magazine* (July).

Einstein, Albert. 1949. "Why Socialism?" *Monthly Review* (May).

Fair Play for Cuba Committee. 1960–61. Hearings before the Subcommittee to Investigate the Administration of the Internal Security Act and Other Internal Security Laws of the Committee on the Judiciary United States Senate 87th Congress, First Session, April 29, May 5, October 10, 1960, together with Hearing Held January 10, 1961. http://www.archive.org/stream/fairplayforcubac0102unit/fairplayforcubac0102unit_djvu.txt.

Fanon, Frantz. 1964. *Toward the African Revolution*. Trans. Haakon Chevalier. New York: Monthly Review Press.

———. 2004. *The Wretched of the Earth*. Trans. Richard Philcox. New York: Grove Press.

Ferlinghetti, Lawrence. 1967. *Starting from San Francisco*. New York: New Directions.

Fernández Borchardt, Ricardo. 1997. *Waldo Frank: Un puente entre las dos Américas*. La Coruña, Spain: Universidade da Coruña.

Fitzgerald, F. Scott. 2011. *A Short Autobiography*. New York: Scribner.

Foner, Philip Sheldon, ed. 1970. *The Black Panthers Speak*. New York: Da Capo Press.

Frank, Andre Gunder. 1968. "Class, Politics, and Debray." In *Régis Debray and the Latin American Revolution*, ed. Huberman and Sweezy, 12–17.

Frank, Waldo. 1959. "Carta a Fidel Castro" (October 10, 1959). CubaMinRex. http://europa.cubaminrex.cu/ Patrimonio/ Artículos/ 2009/ Waldo.html.

———. 1922. *City Block*. New York: Waldo Frank and Darren Conn.

———. 1961. *Cuba, isla profética*. Trans. Luis Echávarri. Buenos Aires: Editorial Losada.

———. 1961. *Cuba: Prophetic Island*. New York: Marzani and Munsell.

———. 1920. *The Dark Mother*. New York: Boni and Liveright.

———. 1932. *Dawn in Russia: The Record of a Journey*. New York: Charles Scribner's Sons.

———. 1923. *Holiday*. New York: Boni and Liveright.

———. 1917. *The Unwelcome Man*. Boston: Little, Brown.

Gates, Skip [Henry Louis]. 1975. "Cuban Experience: Eldridge Cleaver on Ice." *Transition* 49:39.

Geary, Daniel. 2009. *Radical Ambition: C. Wright Mills, the Left, and American Social Thought*. Berkeley: University of California Press.

Gerthe, H. H., and C. Wright Mills, eds. 1946. *From Max Weber: Essays in Sociology*. New York: Oxford University Press.

Gibson, Richard. 1960. "El negro americano mira hacia Cuba." *Lunes de Revolución* (July).

Gibson, Richard, and Robert F. Williams. 1960. "La constante lucha de los negros por su libertad." *Lunes de Revolución* (July).

Gilly, Adolfo. 1964. *Inside the Cuban Revolution*. New York: Monthly Review Press.

Ginsberg, Allen. 1984. *Collected Poems, 1947–1980*. New York: Harper and Row.

———. 2000. *Deliberate Prose: Selected Essays, 1952–1995*. New York: HarperCollins.

———. 1977. *Journals: Early Fifties, Early Sixties*. New York: Grove Press.

———. 1960. "Paterson." *Kulchur* (Spring).

———. 1963. *Reality Sandwiches, 1953–60*. San Francisco: City Lights Books.
———. 2001. *Spontaneous Mind: Selected Interviews, 1958–1996*. New York: HarperCollins.
Godelier, Maurice. 1968. "La noción de modo de producción asiático y los esquemas marxistas de evolución de las sociedades." *Pensamiento Crítico* 15:169–214.
González, Manuel Pedro. 1960. "Why Cubans Resent the US." *Monthly Review* (May).
Gorz, André. 1967. "Sobre Sartre y Marx." *Pensamiento Crítico* 5:77–108.
Gosse, Van. 2005. *The Movements of the New Left, 1950–1975: A Brief History with Documents*. New York: Palgrave.
———. 2005. *The New Left: An Interpretative History*. New York: Palgrave Macmillan.
———. 1993. *Where the Boys Are: Cuba, Cold War, America, and the Making of the New Left*. New York: Verso.
Granés, Carlos. 2011. *El puño invisible*. Madrid: Taurus.
Gray, Robert. 1990. "History, Marxism, and Theory." In *E. P. Thompson: Critical Perspectives*, ed. Harvey J. Kaye and Keith McVlelland. Oxford: Polity Press.
Guerra, Lillian. 2013. *Visions of Power in Cuba. Revolution, Redemption, and Resistance, 1959–1971*. Chapel Hill: The University of North Carolina Press.
Guerra, Sergio, and Alejandro Maldonado. 2009. *Historia de la revolución cubana*. Navarra, Spain: Editorial Txalaparta.
Guerrero, Gustavo. 2008. *Historia de un encargo: La Catira de Camilo José Cela*. Barcelona: Anagrama.
Guevara, Ernesto Che. 1961. "Cuba, Exceptional Case." *Monthly Review* (July–August).
———. 1970. *Obras*. Vol. 2. Havana: Casa de las Américas.
Guevara, Ernesto Che, et al. 2005. *El gran debate: Sobre la economía en Cuba, 1963–64*. Mexico City: Ocean Sur.
Habermas, Jürgen. 1989. *The Structural Transformation of the Public Sphere: An Inquiry into a Category of Bourgeois Society*. Boston: MIT Press.
Hall, Stuart. 1961. "The Siege of Cuba." *New Left Review* (January–February).
Hamilton, Scott. 2011. *The Crisis of Theory: E. P. Thompson, the New Left and Postwar British Politics*. New York: Manchester University Press.
Harris, William J. 1985. *The Poetry and Poetics of Amiri Baraka: The Jazz Aesthetic*. Columbia: University of Missouri Press.
Hart, Armando. 1961. Letter from Armando Hart, Minister of Education, to Raúl Cepero Bonilla, President of Banco Nacional, July 5, 1961. National Archives and Record Administration (NARA), Washington, DC, Department of State, Lot Files, Record Group 59, Papers of Arturo Morales Carrión, box 9, folder 5.
Heilbroner, Robert L. 1968. "Counter-Revolutionary America." In *A Dissenter's Guide to Foreign Policy*, ed. Irving Howe, 241–59.
Hemingway, Ernest. 1992. *Complete Poems*. Lincoln: University of Nebraska Press.
———. 2009. *A Moveable Feast*. New York: Scribner.

Hobsbawm, Eric. 1969. "Los campesinos, las migraciones y la política." *Pensamiento Crítico* 24:75–107.

Hollander, Paul. 1998. *Political Pilgrims: Western Intellectuals in Search of the Good Society.* New Brunswick: Transaction.

Howe, Irving. 1970. *The Decline of the New.* New York: Harcourt, Brace, and World.

———, ed. 1968. *A Dissenter's Guide to Foreign Policy.* New York: Frederick A. Praeger.

———. 1957. *Politics and the Novel.* New York: Horizon Press Books.

———, ed. 1967. *The Radical Imagination.* New York: New American Library.

———, ed. 1966. *The Radical Papers.* New York: Anchor Books, Doubleday.

Howe, Linda S. 2004. *Transgression and Conformity: Cuban Writers and Artists after the Revolution.* Madison: University of Wisconsin Press.

Huberman, Leo, and Paul Sweezy. "Algeria, Vietnam and Punta del Este." *Monthly Review* (March 1962): 497–504.

———. 1961. *Cuba: Anatomy of a Revolution.* New York: Monthly Review Press.

———, eds. 1968. *Régis Debray and the Latin American Revolution.* New York: Monthly Review Press.

———. 1969. *Socialism in Cuba.* New York: Monthly Review Press.

Hunt, Lynn. 2007. *Inventing Human Rights: A History.* New York: W. W. Norton, 2007.

Hurtado, Oscar. 1960. "¿Una generación derrotada?" *Lunes de Revolución* (April).

Illades, Carlos. 2008. *Breve introducción al pensamiento de E. P. Thompson.* Mexico City: Universidad Autónoma Metropolitana.

Isserman, Maurice. 2000. *America Divided: The Civil War of the 1960s.* Oxford: Oxford University Press.

———. 1987. *If I Had a Hammer: The Death of the Old Left and the Birth of the New Left.* New York: Basic Books.

Jacoby, Russell. 2000. *The Last Intellectuals: American Culture in the Age of Academe.* New York: Basic Books.

Jones, LeRoi (Amiri Baraka). 2009. "Cuba Libre." In *Home: Social Essays.* New York: Akashic Books.

———. 1964. *The Dead Lecturer.* New York: Grove Press.

———. 1965. *The System of Dante's Hell.* New York: Grove Press.

Jumonville, Neil. 1991. *Critical Crossings: The New York Intellectuals in Postwar America.* Berkeley: University of California Press.

Kalugin, Oleg. 1994. *The First Directorate: My 32 Years in Intelligence and Espionage against the West.* New York: St. Martin's Press.

Karol, K. S. 1968. "China: El otro comunismo." *Pensamiento Crítico* 16:144–80.

Kazin, Alfred. 1961. "Among Russia's Jews." *Harper's Magazine* (May).

Keucheyan, Razmig. 2013. *The Left Hemisphere: Mapping Critical Theory Today.* New York: Verso.

Klein, Mason, and Catherine Evans. 2012. *The Radical Camera: New York's Photo League, 1936–1951.* New York: Jewish Museum.

Kohan, Néstor. 2000. *De Ingenieros al Che: Ensayos sobre el marxismo argentino y latinoamericano*. Buenos Aires: Biblos.

Kornbluh, Peter, and LeoGrande William. 2014. *Back Channel to Cuba. The Hidden History of Negotiations between Washington and Havana*. Chapel Hill: The University of North Carolina Press.

Kosambi, D. D. 1959. "China's Communes." *Monthly Review* (March).

Kunitz, Joshua. 1956. "Khrushchev and the Jews." *Monthly Review* (July).

Labini, Paolo Sylos. 1959. "Chinese Economy and Economics." *Monthly Review* (July–August).

Labrador Méndez, Germán. 2009. *Letras arrebatadas: Poesía y química en la transición española*. Madrid: Devenir Ensayo.

Laqueur, Walter. 1968. "Reflections on the Third World." In *A Dissenter's Guide to Foreign Policy*, ed. Irving Howe, 173–94.

Larner, Jeremy, and Irving Howe. 1968. *Poverty: Views from the Left*. New York: William Morrow.

Lasch, Christopher. 1965. *The New Radicalism in America, 1899–1963: The Intellectual as Social Type*. New York: Norton.

Lippmann, Walter. 1922. *Public Opinion*. New York: Harcourt, Brace.

Llerena, Mario. 1981. *La revolución insospechada: Origen y desarrollo del castrismo*. Buenos Aires: Universidad de Buenos Aires.

Lomas, Laura. 2008. *Translating Empire: José Martí, Migrant Latino Subjects, and American Modernities*. Durham, NC: Duke University Press.

Lomnitz, Claudio. 2014. *The Return of Comrade Ricardo Flores Magón*. New York: Zone Books.

Lowenthal, Richard. 1968. "The Prospect for a Maoist International." In *A Dissenter's Guide to Foreign Policy*, ed. Irving Howe, 208–23.

Ludwig, Emil. 1948. *Biografía de una isla*. Mexico City: Editorial Centauro.

Luis, William. 2003. *Lunes de Revolución: Literatura y cultura en los primeros años de la Revolución Cubana*. Madrid: Verbum.

Mackenzie, G. Calvin, and Robert Weisbrot. 2008. *The Liberal Hour: Washington and the Politics of Change in the 1960s*. New York: Penguin Press.

Mailer, Norman. 1959. *Advertisements for Myself*. New York: G. P. Putman's Sons.

———. 1965. *An American Dream*. New York: Dial Press.

———. 1968. *The Armies of the Night: History as a Novel, The Novel as History*. New York: New American Library.

———. 1991. *Harlot's Ghost*. New York: Random House.

———. 1968. *Miami and the Siege of Chicago: An Informal History of the Republican and Democratic Conventions of 1968*. New York: World.

———. 1961. "Open Letter to JFK and Fidel Castro." *Village Voice* (April 27).

———. 1967. *Why Are We in Vietnam?* New York: G. P. Putnam's Sons.

Malcolm X. 1968. "Para el capitalismo es imposible sobrevivir." *Pensamiento Crítico* 17:5–12.

Mañach, Jorge. 1970. *Teoría de la frontera*. San Juan, Puerto Rico: Editorial Universitaria de Puerto Rico.

Marable, Manning. 2011. *Malcolm X: A Life of Reinvention*. New York: Penguin Books.

Marinello, Juan. 1960. *Conversación con nuestros pintores abstractos*. Santiago, Cuba: Universidad de Oriente, Departamento de Extensión y Relaciones Culturales.
Mario, José. 1969. "Allen Ginsberg en La Habana." *Mundo Nuevo* (Paris) (April).
Marqués de Armas, Pedro. 2006. "Psiquiatría para el Nuevo Estado: Algunos documentos." *La Habana Elegante* 36 (Winter). http://www.habanaelegante.com/Winter2006/Panoptico.html.
Marzani, Carl. 1961. "Reflections on American Foreign Policy." *Monthly Review* (January).
Matthews, Herbert L. 1961. *The Cuban Story*. New York: George Braziller.
Matthews, Wade. 2002. "The Poverty of Strategy: E. P. Thompson, Perry Anderson, and the Transition to Socialism." *Labour/Le Travail* 50 (Fall).
McCann, Gerard. 1997. *Theory and History: The Political Thought of E. P. Thompson*. Aldershot, UK: Ashgate.
Merrill, Robert. 1978. *Norman Mailer*. Boston: Twayne.
Mesa Lago, Carmelo. 1994. *Breve historia económica de la Cuba socialista*. Madrid: Alianza Editorial.
Miles, Barry. 1989. *Ginsberg: A Biography*. New York: Viking Press.
Miliband, Ralph. 1959. "The New Capitalism: A View from Abroad." *Monthly Review* (July–August).
Mills, C. Wright. 1958. *The Causes of World War Three*. New York: Simon and Schuster.
———. 1961. *Escucha, Yanqui: La Revolución en Cuba*. Mexico City: Fondo de Cultura Económica.
———. 1960. "Letter to the New Left." *New Left Review* (September–October).
———. 2000. *Letters and Autobiographical Writings*. Berkeley: University of California Press.
———. 1960. "Listen, Yankee: The Cuban Case against the United States." *Harper's Magazine* (December).
———. 1960. *Listen, Yankee: The Revolution in Cuba*. New York: Ballantine Books.
———. 1962. *The Marxists*. New York: Dell.
———. 2008. *The Politics of Truth: Collected Writings*. New York: Oxford University Press.
———. 2000. *The Power Elite*. New York: Oxford University Press.
———. 2000. *The Sociological Imagination*. New York: Oxford University Press.
———. 1951. *White Collar: The American Middle Class*. New York: Oxford University Press.
Mills, C. Wright, Clarence Senior, and Rose Kihn Goldsen. 1950. *The Puerto Rican Journey: New York's Newest Migrants*. New York: Harper & Brothers.
Mills, Hillary. 1982. *Mailer: A Biography*. New York: Empire Books.
Miskulin, Silvia Cezar. 2009. *Os intelectuais cubanos: Política cultural da Revolucao, 1961–75*. Sao Paulo: Alameda Casa Editorial.
Moore, Carlos. 2008. *Pichón: Race and Revolution in Castro's Cuba, a Memoir*. Chicago: Lawrence Hill Books.

Mora, Gilles, ed. 1933. *Walker Evans: Havana, 1933*. New York: Pantheon Books.

Morray, J. P. 1961. "Cuba and Communism." *Monthly Review* (July–August).

———. 1962. "Questions and Answers on Cuba." *Monthly Review* (September).

———. 1962. *The Second Revolution in Cuba*. New York: Monthly Review Press.

Moyn, Samuel. 2012. *The Last Utopia: Human Rights in History*. Cambridge, MA: Harvard University Press.

Moyn, Samuel, and Andrew Sartori. 2013. "Approaches to Global Intellectual History." In *Global Intellectual History*, ed. Samuel Moyn and Andrew Sartori. New York: Columbia University Press.

Neal, Christopher. 2007. "Carleton Beals: Disidente solitario." *Letras Libres* (May).

Nehring, Holger. 2011. "Out of Apathy: Genealogies of the British New Left in a Transnational Context (1956–62)." In *Between Prague Spring and French May: Opposition and Revolt in Europe, 1960–1980*, ed. Martin Klimke, Jacco Pekelder, and Joachim Scharloth. New York: Berghahn Books.

Nelson, Truman. 2009. *The Old Man: John Brown at Harper's Ferry*. Chicago: Haymarket Books.

Newman, Michael. 2002. *Ralph Miliband and the Politics of the New Left*. London: Merlin Press.

Newton, Huey P. 1968. "Para ser un nacionalista revolucionario se debe ser necesariamente un socialista." *Pensamiento Crítico* 17:108–9.

Ninkovich, Frank A. 1981. *The Diplomacy of Ideas: US Foreign Policy and Cultural Relations, 1938–50*. New York: Cambridge University Press.

Ogarzaly, Michael A. 1994. *Waldo Frank: Prophet of Hispanic Regeneration*. London: Associated University Presses.

Ortiz, Fernando. 1947. *Cuban Counterpoint: Tobacco and Sugar*. Trans. Harriet de Onís. New York: Knopf.

Palmer, Brian D. 1994. *E. P. Thompson: Objections and Oppositions*. New York: Verso.

Pérez, Louis, Jr. 2011. *Cuba in the American Imagination: Metaphor and the Imperial Ethos*. Chapel Hill: University of North Carolina Press.

———. 2007. *On Becoming Cuban: Identity, Nationality, and Culture*. Chapel Hill: University of North Carolina Press.

Phillips, Ruby Hart. 1959. *Cuba: Island of Paradox*. New York: McDowell, Obolensky.

———. 1962. *The Cuban Dilemma*. New York: Ivan Obolensky.

———. 1935. *Cuban Sideshow*. Havana: Cuban Press.

Pipes, Richard. 1961. "The Public Mood." *Harper's Magazine* (May).

Portell Vilá, Herminio, Charles O. Porter, Ira B. Joralemon, Charles S. Grant, Stan Weisberger, Rafael Lecuona, and John W. Dalton. 1961. "Letters." *Harper's Magazine* (February).

Poumier, María, ed. 2007. *La cuestión tabú: El pensamiento negro cubano de 1840 a 1959*. Las Palmas de Gran Canaria, Spain: Ediciones Idea.

Pound, Ezra. 1952. *Guide to Kulchur*. New York: New Directions.

Pratt, Mary Louise. 1992. *Imperial Eyes: Travel Writing and Transculturation*. London: Routledge.

Priestland, David. 2009. *The Red Flag: A History of Communism*. New York: Grove Press.

Rasenberger, Jim. 2011. *The Brilliant Disaster: JFK, Castro, and America's Doomed Invasion of Cuba's Bay of Pigs*. New York: Scribner.

Reeves, Nancy. 1960. "Women of the New Cubans." *Monthly Review* (November).

Reitan, Ruth. 1999. *The Rise and Decline of an Alliance: Cuba and African American Leaders in the 1960s*. East Lansing: Michigan State University Press.

Reynolds, Michael. 2012. *Hemingway: The 1930s through the Final Years*. New York: W. W. Norton.

Robinson, Douglas. 2011. *Translation and Empire: Postcolonial Theories Explained*. New York: Routledge, 2011.

Rollyson, Carl. 1991. *The Lives of Norman Mailer: A Biography*. New York: Paragon House.

Rostagno, Irene. 1989. "Waldo Frank's Crusade for Latin American Literature." *Americas* 46.1:41–69.

Roszak, Theodore. 1969. *The Making of a Counter Culture*. New York: Doubleday.

Rutland, Robert A. 1973. *The Newsmongers: Journalism in the Life of the Nation, 1690–72*. New York: Dial Press.

Salvatore, Nick. 2007. *Eugene V. Debs: Citizen and Socialist*. Chicago: University of Illinois Press.

Sanders, Edward. 2000. *The Poetry and Life of Allen Ginsberg*. New York: Overlook Press.

Sartre, Jean Paul. 1961. *Sartre visita Cuba*. Havana: Ediciones R.

Sawyer, Mark Q. 2006. *Racial Politics in Post-Revolutionary Cuba*. New York: Cambridge University Press.

Schafer, William J. 1989. *The Truman Nelson Reader*. Washington, DC: Thompson Shore.

Schleifer, Marc. 1961. "Cuban Notebook." *Monthly Review* (July/August).

Schlesinger, Arthur M., Jr. 2000. *Journals: 1952–2000*. New York: Penguin Books.

———. 1965. *A Thousand Days: John F. Kennedy in the White House*. Boston: Houghton Mifflin.

Schudson, Michael. 1978. *Discovering the News: A Social History of American Newspapers*. New York: Basic Books.

Schumacher, Michael. *Dharma Lion: Biography of Allen Ginsberg*. New York: St. Martin's Press, 1984.

Schweyer, Alberto Lamar. 1934. *Cómo cayó el presidente Machado*. Madrid: Espasa Calpe.

Shepard, Richard F. 1996. *The Paper's Papers*. New York: Random House/Times Books.

"The Siege of Cuba." 1961. *New Left Review* (January–February).

Silva, Cléa. 1968. "The Errors of the Foco Theory." In *Régis Debray and the Latin American Revolution*, ed. Huberman and Sweezy.

Silvers, Robert B. 1961. "The Voice of a Dissenter." *Harper's Magazine* (May).

Skwiot, Christine. 2010. *The Purposes of Paradise: US Tourism and Empire in Cuba and Hawaii*. Philadelphia: University of Pennsylvania Press.

Socialist International Information. 1961. Firestone Library, Princeton University, vol. 11, no. 17, April 29, 256.
Sollors, Werner. 1978. *Amiri Baraka/LeRoi Jones: The Quest for a "Populist Modernism."* New York: Columbia University Press.
Sombart, Werner. 1976. *Why Is There No Socialism in the United States?* New York: M. E. Sharpe.
Sontag, Susan. 1966. *Against Interpretation and Other Essays.* New York: Macmillan.
———. 1977. *On Photography.* New York: Picador.
———. 2009. *Reborn: Journals and Notebooks, 1947–1963.* New York: Picador.
———. 1969. "Some Thoughts on the Right Way (for Us) to Love the Cuban Revolution." *Ramparts* (April).
Soper, Kate. 1990. "Socialist Humanism." In *E. P. Thompson: Critical Perspectives*, ed. Harvey J. Kaye and Keith McClelland.
Sorel, Georges. 2002. *Reflections on Violence.* Cambridge: Cambridge University Press.
Stam, Robert, and Ella Shohat. 2012. *Race in Translation: Culture Wars around the Postcolonial Atlantic.* New York: New York University Press.
Starobin, Joseph, Stanley Moore, and Paul Baran. 1959. "Marxism." *Monthly Review* (September).
Stavans, Ilán, ed. 1999. *Mutual Impressions: Writers from the Americas Reading One Another.* Durham, NC: Duke University Press.
Strong, Anna Louise. 1956. "Critique of Stalin Era." *Monthly Review* (July).
Stonor Saunders, Francis. 2001. *Who Paid the Piper? The CIA and the Cultural Cold War.* London: Granta Books.
Sturm, Hobert P., and Francis D. Wormuth. 1959. "The International Power Elite." *Monthly Review* (December).
Sutherland [Martínez], Elizabeth. 1969. *The Youngest Revolution: A Personal Report on Cuba.* New York: Dial Press.
Swados, Harvey. 1967. "C. Wright Mills: A Personal Memoir." In *The Radical Imagination*, by Irving Howe.
Sweezy, Paul M. 1956. "Marxian Socialism." *Monthly Review* (November).
———. 1972. *Modern Capitalism and Other Essays.* New York: Monthly Review Press.
———. 1953. *The Present as History: Essays and Reviews on Capitalism and Socialism.* New York: Monthly Review Press.
———. 1949. *Socialism.* New York: McGraw-Hill.
———. 1942. *The Theory of Capitalist Development: Principles of Marxian Political Economy.* New York: Oxford University Press.
Sweezy, Paul M., and Leo Huberman, eds. 1950. *F. O. Matthiessen: A Collective Portrait (1902–1950).* New York: Henry Schuman.
Szulc, Tad. 1986. *Fidel: A Critical Portrait.* New York: William Morrow.
Szulc, Tad, and Karl E. Meyer. 1962. *The Cuban Invasion: The Chronicle of a Disaster.* New York: Ballantine Books.
Taber, Robert. 1962. "Playa Girón: Réquien al imperialismo." In *Playa Girón: Derrota del imperialismo*, 1:305–16. Havana: Ediciones R.
———. 2002. *War of Flea: The Classic Study of Guerrilla Warfare.* Washington, DC: Brassey's.

Talese, Gay. 1966. *The Kingdom and the Power.* New York: World.
Temkin, Moshik. 2009. *The Sacco-Vanzetti Affair: America on Trial.* New Haven: Yale University Press.
Thompson, E. P. 1966. *The Making of the English Working Class.* New York: Vintage Books.
———. 1988. *William Morris: Romantic to Revolutionary.* Stanford, CA: Stanford University Press.
Thoreau, Henry David. 1986. *Walden and Civil Disobedience.* New York: Penguin Books.
Tietchen, Todd F. 2010. *The Cubalogues: Beat Writers in Revolutionary Havana.* Gainesville: University Press of Florida.
Torres, Simón, and Julio Aronde. 1968. "Debray and the Cuban Experience." In *Régis Debray and the Latin American Revolution*, ed. Huberman and Sweezy, 44–62.
Trachtenberg, Alan, ed. 1973. *Memoirs of Waldo Frank.* Amherst: University of Massachusetts Press.
Vives, Cristina. 2013. "Culture and Counterculture in Times of Revolution (Seen from the Perspective of Cuban Photography)." *Arte Cubano* 2:18–32.
Wald, Alan M. 1987. *The New York Intellectuals: The Rise and Decline of the Anti-Stalinist Left from the 1930s to the 1980s.* Chapel Hill: University of North Carolina Press.
Walzer, Michael. 1961. *Cuba: The Invasion and the Consequences.* New York: Dissent Publishing Association.
———. 1965. *The Revolution of the Saints: A Study in the Origins of Radical Politics.* Cambridge, MA: Harvard University Press.
Welch, Richard E. 1985. *Response to Revolution: The United States and the Cuban Revolution.* Chapel Hill: University of North Carolina Press.
Williams, Robert F. 1960. "El cielo guarda silencio." *Lunes de Revolución* (July).
———. 1962. *Negroes with Guns.* Ed. Marc Schleifer. New York: Marzani and Munsell.
Williams, William Appleman. 1968. "Black Power and Student Power." In *Régis Debray and the Latin American Revolution*, ed. Huberman and Sweezy, 84–87.
———. 1959. "Empire, New Style." *Monthly Review* (July–August).
Wilson, Robert Anton. 1984. "The Poet as Radar System." In *On the Poetry of Allen Ginsberg*, ed. Lewis Hyde. Ann Arbor: University of Michigan Press.
Worsley, Peter. 1968. "Revolutionary Theory: Che Guevara and Régis Debray." In *Régis Debray and the Latin American Revolution*, ed. Huberman and Sweezy, 119–38.
Yglesias, José. 1967. *The Goodbye Land.* New York: Pantheon Books.
———. 1968. *In the Fist of the Revolution: Life in Castro's Cuba.* New York: Penguin Books.
Zweig, Stefan. 1942. *Brasil: País del Futuro.* Madrid: Espasa Calpe.

INDEX